Bible Stories

Written by Patricia Hunt

Illustrated by Angus McBride

Ward Lock Limited·London

Front endpaper The Passover (page 46)
Back endpaper The Raising of Lazarus (page 187)

First published in 1981 in Great Britain
by Ward Lock Limited, 8 Clifford Street,
London W1X 1RB, an Egmont Company.

Reprinted in 1986

Printed and bound in Czechoslovakia

**British Library Cataloguing in Publication
data**
Hunt, Patricia
  Bible Stories.
  1. Bible stories
  I. Title   II. Angus McBride
    220.9′505   BS551.2

ISBN 0-7063-5805-8

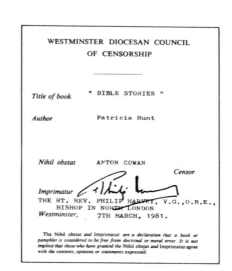

WESTMINSTER DIOCESAN COUNCIL
OF CENSORSHIP

Title of book   " BIBLE STORIES "

Author   Patricia Hunt

Nihil obstat   ANTON COWAN
                                        Censor
Imprimatur
THE RT. REV. PHILIP HARVEY, V.G.,O.B.E.,
      BISHOP IN NORTH LONDON
Westminster,   7TH MARCH, 1981.

The Nihil obstat *and* Imprimatur *are a declaration that a book or
pamphlet is considered to be free from doctrinal or moral error. It is not
implied that those who have granted the Nihil obstat and Imprimatur agree
with the contents, opinions or statements expressed.*

Contents

THE
OLD
TESTAMENT

The Creation of the World

Long, long ago, in the very beginning of time, even before there was history, there was God. The Bible tells us there has never been a time without Him.

There was no shape to the earth then, and total darkness and raging waters covered everything. Everywhere was waste and empty until God set about creating the world. He said 'Let there be light', and the light came. God divided the light from the dark, and He called the light 'Day' and the darkness 'Night'. Evening came and morning, and that was the first day.

Then God made the sky, like a great dome covering everywhere. It separated the water underneath from the water above. Evening and morning came, and that was all done on the second day.

Next God made the earth. He ordered the waters below the sky to come together, and so it happened. He named the waters 'Seas', and the dry land which was left He named 'Earth', and He was pleased with what He saw. Then He ordered all kinds of plants to grow upon the earth—plants which bore grain and plants which bore fruit and plants with flowers. Evening and morning came, and that was the end of the third day.

Then God ordered great shining lights to appear in the sky. They were to give light to the earth, and to mark the years, the seasons and the days. The two largest lights were the 'Sun' and the 'Moon'; the sun was to rule over the day, and the moon was to rule over the night. The smaller lights were the stars, including planets, comets and meteors. Evening and morning came, and so ended the fourth day. God was very pleased with what He saw, for the world He had made was very beautiful.

However, there were as yet no living creatures in it. So the next day God made fish and birds. He filled the waters with all kinds of fish, from enormous sea-monsters and whales down to the tiniest minnows and sticklebacks.

In the air He put all kinds of birds, from great eagles to tiny wrens and linnets; and each feather of each bird was perfectly and wonderfully made. The sea and the skies were full of beautiful creatures. God was pleased with what He saw and He blessed all the living things He had made. He told them to reproduce themselves and have families, so that their numbers would be increased; and when evening and morning had passed, that was the fifth day.

Then God said, 'Let the earth produce all kinds of animals.' He made a wonderful variety of creatures to live in the world; there were enormous beasts, like elephants, giraffes and rhinoceros, and tiny ones like moles and mice, shrews and spiders, caterpillars and kittens, mosquitoes and moths. All were perfectly and beautifully made, and God was pleased.

Then He said, 'I will make human beings, who will be something like Me. They will take care of the fish, the birds and the animals, and all creatures which move in the sea and the sky, and on the earth.

So next He made a man, and breathed life-giving breath into him, and the man became a living soul. He was named Adam. God blessed him and placed him in the east of the world, in the beautiful Garden of Eden.

'You must have many children,' God said, 'so that they will grow and live all over the earth and look after it. You and they will be in charge of the fish, the birds and the animals.'

Out of the ground God made grass and trees grow, and leafy plants for the animals and birds to eat; and He provided all kinds of grain and all kinds of fruit for people to eat—so that none would go hungry.

He looked at everything He had made and was pleased. Evening and morning came, and that was the sixth day.

Now the universe was finished. God had completed His wonderful and flawless work. There was order and there was great variety, and God had made the world to be both beautiful and useful. It was perfect.

So He stopped creating, and on the seventh day He rested. Then He blessed this seventh day and set it apart, and ever since then one day in seven has been a special day for people to rest from their work.

At first this day was always the seventh day of the week, the day which the Jews called their Sabbath (Saturday). But when Jesus came to earth and was killed and rose again three days later, on the first day of the week, Christians decided that their day of worship and rest should be the first day of the week (Sunday) as a constant reminder of the Resurrection.

The Garden of Eden

In the Garden of Eden, where God had placed Adam, there grew all sorts of beautiful trees, which bore good fruit. A stream flowed through the garden to water it and, beyond Eden, this divided into four rivers; they were called the Pishon, the Gihon, the Tigris, and the Euphrates.

There were also two special trees in the middle of the garden. One was the Tree of Life and the other was the Tree of the Knowledge of Good and Evil.

When God put Adam in the Garden of Eden, He wanted him to cultivate it and take care of it, and so be a fellow-worker with Him. He said to Adam, 'You may eat the fruit of any of the trees in the garden, except the fruit from the Tree of the Knowledge of Good and Evil. That fruit you must not eat; if you do then you will surely die.'

Then God brought all the animals and birds in front of Adam, and Adam gave them all their names.

God had decided that it was not good for Adam to be all alone in the garden, so when Adam was asleep, He took one of Adam's ribs and from it He made a woman to share life in the garden with Adam.

Adam named her Eve, and they both began a happy life together looking after the beautiful garden and everything in it.

One of the creatures living in the garden was a snake, and he was very cunning. One day he glided up to Eve and said, 'Did God really say that you must not eat the fruit of any of the trees in the garden?'

'No,' replied Eve, 'we may eat the fruit from any of the trees, except from that tree in the middle—the tree which is called the Tree of the Knowledge of Good and Evil. God said that if we ate any of that fruit, then we would surely die.'

The crafty snake smiled a cunning smile within himself. 'That's not true, you know,' he hissed. 'God said that because He knew that if you ate that fruit, then you would know all about good and evil, and so you would be like God Himself.'

Eve looked at the beautiful tree again and saw how delicious its fruit looked. Perhaps a taste would not matter—and it would be wonderful to be as wise as God, she thought. It would do no harm if she took a bite. She would try it and see what happened. So she plucked one of the tempting fruits and ate it. It tasted nice, so she gave some to Adam and he ate too.

However, as soon as they had eaten, they suddenly realized what they had done and both felt very ashamed that they had disobeyed God. They knew they had chosen their own way and not God's, and that they had spoilt the beauty of that perfect garden by doing wrong. For the first time they became aware that they were naked and in their embarrassment they rushed to make clothing for themselves out of leaves.

That same evening, they heard God walking in the garden, but they felt so guilty that they ran away and tried to hide from Him among the trees.

But God called out, 'Adam, where are you?'

'I heard You coming,' answered Adam, 'and I was afraid, so I hid myself from You.'

'Have you eaten any of the fruit that I commanded you not to eat?' asked God.

'Eve gave the fruit to me and I ate it,' said Adam, who was not feeling very brave and was ready to put the blame on to someone else.

God turned to Eve and said, 'Why did you do this?'

Eve, too, tried to put the blame on to another, and she said, 'The snake tricked me into it.'

God was very sad at what had happened, for he felt that Adam and Eve could no longer be trusted and so were not fit to stay in the lovely garden any more. He knew that their wrong-doing had to be punished.

Then He turned to the snake and said, 'You, of all the animals, must bear the punishment for this. From now on you will have to crawl along the earth and eat dust for as long as you live. You and the woman will always be enemies with one another.'

To Eve God said, 'You will have to suffer pain when your children are born.' And to Adam He said, 'You listened to your wife and you ate the

fruit which I had forbidden you to eat. Because of this you will have to work hard all your life to make the earth produce enough food for you. There will always be weeds and thorns and you will have to toil all the time to make anything grow on the land at all.'

So where before Adam had been looking after a perfect and fertile garden, now he would have to struggle in a wilderness of weeds and thistles.

Then God said, 'Now man has become like Me and has knowledge of good and evil. He cannot be allowed to eat the fruit of the Tree of Life also and thus live forever.'

So God sent Adam and Eve out of the Garden of Eden, and Adam was set to work to cultivate the land outside it.

In order to keep either Adam and Eve, or anyone else, from coming near the Tree of Life, God placed winged creatures as a symbol of His majesty and presence at the east of the garden, and also a flaming sword which turned in all directions to keep out intruders.

Cain and Abel

In due time Adam and Eve had two sons. The one born first they named Cain, and the one who was born next they named Abel. When the boys grew up, Cain became a farmer and Abel became a shepherd.

One day they both went to make their offering to God as was the custom then, just as it is today when people still bring offerings to their church at

Harvest Thanksgiving and other festivals. Cain brought some of the best crops and fruit which he had grown, and Abel brought the first lamb born to one of his sheep and gave the best parts of it as his offering.

Now God was pleased with Abel's gift, because it had been given in the right spirit; but somehow Cain had the wrong attitude to giving his, and so God was not pleased with it.

Cain became very angry that his gift was not acceptable, and he scowled in fury at his brother. 'Why are you so angry?' asked God. 'Why are you frowning like that? If you had offered your gift in the right spirit, you would be smiling now instead of looking as black as thunder. You must be careful, for it is just when you feel as you do that sin is waiting to conquer you and make you do worse things. You must overcome it.'

But Cain didn't listen to this good advice. He just let his angry feelings smoulder inside him and, as God had warned, his thoughts soon turned into deeds.

Not long afterwards Cain said to Abel, 'Let's go out into the open country.' Abel agreed, so off they went, and when they were far out into the fields, Cain turned upon his brother and killed him.

Perhaps he thought that, as they were far away from everyone, no one would ever find out what he had done; but God knew, and He asked Cain, 'Where is your brother Abel?'

Cain was scared and made things worse by replying, 'I don't know. Am I supposed to look after my brother all the time?'

He knew perfectly well that the answer to that was 'Yes', but he tried to hide his wicked deed.

'What have you done?' said God. 'Your brother's blood is crying out to me from the ground like a voice calling for revenge. You must leave here. No longer may you farm the earth which has soaked up your brother's blood. If you try to grow crops, the land will not produce anything. From now on you will remain a homeless wanderer.'

Cain was horrified. He said to God, 'This punishment is much too great for me to bear. You are driving me away from the land and from Your presence.' For Cain thought that God could only be found in his old home. He did not know that God was everywhere.

'I shall be a fugitive,' Cain went on, 'a wanderer, and anyone who finds me will kill me.'

Cain must have shown the beginnings of sorrow, for God put a special mark upon him as a warning to anyone who met him not to kill him.

Sadly Cain went away and lived in a land whose name means 'Wandering' and which lies to the east of Eden.

Later Adam and Eve had another son named Seth, and Eve became less unhappy and said, 'God has given me a son in place of Abel whom Cain killed.'

Noah and the Flood

The sins of Adam and Eve and of Cain, their son, had brought evil into the world, and for a while people became very bad indeed and allowed their wicked thoughts to grow into deeds. God saw all the evil and violence these caused and He was sad. He felt sorry He had made such a beautiful world, filled with wonderful living creatures, if people were going to spoil it all by their wickedness.

However, there was one man with whom God was very pleased. He was a good man and his thoughts and deeds were noble and right. His name was Noah.

One day God said to Noah, 'I have decided that this evil on earth cannot continue. A new start must be made; therefore a great flood will come which will destroy the wicked. Build yourself a boat—an ark—out of good timber; cover it with tar both inside and out, and make rooms inside it and a roof over it. Make three decks and put a door in the side. Then, when the flood comes, you and your wife and your sons and their wives will all be safe in the boat.'

Probably Noah found this news rather startling, but he knew that he must do as God had said. He told his three sons, named Shem, Ham and Japheth, that they would have to help him with the building of his big boat so that it would be ready in time.

God had told him to make it 133 m (146 yd) long, 22 m (24 yd) wide, and 13 m (42 ft) high. Moreover, as well as taking all the Noah family into the ark, God said that Noah was also to take two of every kind of living creature—birds, animals and creeping things—in order to keep them alive, and there was to be a male and a female of each so that they would be able to reproduce again on the earth when the floods had gone, for there would be nothing else left alive.

Lastly God reminded Noah, 'Take all kinds of food with you into the ark, both for you and for all the living creatures, for in seven days' time the rains will start, and it will rain for forty days and forty nights without stopping and you will not be able to leave the ark.'

Noah did everything exactly as God had told him.

With the building of the ark finished, Noah had a thoroughly waterproof new home. Then he and his family began to round up all the animals and birds and insects and reptiles, as God had directed, and together they all went into the ark. Lastly Noah and his wife, and Shem, Ham, Japheth and their wives went into the ark themselves, and the door was firmly closed behind them. Then they settled down to watch the weather and wait for the promised rain. No doubt their actions were viewed with great amusement by those who saw the building of the ark. However, Noah's faith in God was justified.

Seven days later, just as God had said, it began to rain; and it rained in torrents, never stopping, for forty whole days and forty whole nights. The waters rose higher and higher, and the floods covered the whole earth, drowning every living thing. There was nothing left alive in the world except Noah, his family and the animals in his keeping.

Noah looked out upon the world he had known, and could see nothing but water, no matter which way he looked. All the land and the trees and the places where people had lived were covered. Everything was being swamped by the flood

waters. But God had promised Noah that he and his family would be saved, and Noah knew that God could be trusted.

The water was now deep enough for the ark to float, and as it became even deeper, the ark began to drift about on the surface.

Noah could not tell where they were, for the floods had risen so high that they had covered every part of the land. They went on rising so much that soon they were 7 m ($7\frac{1}{2}$ yd) above the tops of the highest mountains. There was nothing to be seen in any direction except water.

And they stayed like that for 150 days and nights. It must have seemed a very long time.

Then a great wind began to blow, and at last the waters started to go down. The rains stopped and gradually, for another 150 days, the waters began to go lower and lower. The ark stopped rocking to

and fro, and at last it came to rest on a mountain called Ararat.

The waters continued to go down and one day, when Noah looked out, he found that he could see the tops of other mountains.

Noah waited for another forty days. Then he opened a window in the ark and let a raven fly out. It flew around for a while and then flew away and did not come back.

Next Noah sent out a dove to see if the flood waters had gone down, but the dove could not find anywhere to land and, after a while, it flew back to

the ark. Noah reached out his hand and lifted it in through the window.

He waited for another week; then he sent the dove out again. On the evening of that day it came back and, in its beak, it held a fresh olive leaf. Now Noah knew that somewhere the waters had gone down far enough for the trees to be appearing again.

He waited one more week before he sent out the dove again. Out it flew, round and round, and out of sight. This time it did not return, and Noah knew that it must have found somewhere to settle among the trees.

A little time later, Noah was able to look out of the ark and to see that the ground was becoming drier. In time it became completely dry and the waters disappeared.

Then God said to Noah, 'You may now leave the boat. Take your wife with you, and your sons and their wives, and all the birds and animals, so that they can settle on the earth and start having families again to replace all those that were drowned in the great flood.'

So out came Noah and his family and all the living creatures whom God had preserved during the great flood. The first thing Noah did was to take some stones and build an altar to God, to offer a sacrifice upon it and thank Him for keeping them safe.

God was pleased and said, 'Never again will I destroy all living creatures as I have done this time. As long as there is a world, there will always be seed-time and harvest, cold and heat, summer and winter, day and night, and they shall not cease,' and as He promised, all these things have gone on ever since.

As a sign of His promise to Noah, God said, 'I shall put a rainbow in the clouds. Whenever the sky is cloudy and a rainbow appears, I will remember my promise to you and to all living creatures, that a flood will never again destroy all that live on the earth.'

The Tower of Babel

Now it was time for Noah and his family to settle the earth and become a nation. Noah's sons scattered out over the land and soon began to raise families who, in turn, had children of their own, so that in no time at all Noah had many grandchildren, great grandchildren and great great grandchildren. The Bible tells us that Noah lived to be a very old man indeed and no doubt he was pleased to see God's work being carried out by his descendants. Pretty soon the families grew so large that they really became tribes, although they all still spoke the same language.

The peoples of these tribes were anxious to stay together as one nation and felt that they ought to have something that would be a constant reminder of what a great and famous people they were. They really had a very good opinion of themselves! It was decided that they would build a great city, and inside this a tower so tall that it would reach up through the clouds to heaven itself. The place they chose for this great work was the Plain of Shinar, which is now part of present-day Iran.

The architects, builders and brickmakers all set to work to plan and carry out this new project. Everywhere there was furious activity as the foundations were laid and the bricks were baked. Soon the building of the tower itself began, mainly of brick, with slime used as cement or mortar. The tower rose higher and higher, so that people marvelled at it and thought themselves more wonderful than before—almost godlike some said!

God watched with increasing concern and at last He decided He must put a stop to all this vanity and folly if this new people were not to become as wicked and silly as those before the flood. His way of doing this was very simple and very clever. He did not use His powers to cause another flood or an earthquake to bring the tower crashing to the ground. He achieved His purpose without causing any harm to a single person.

One morning the people awoke and set off to work on the great tower as usual. However, when the workmen and builders arrived and began to discuss the day's plans, they discovered, to their astonishment and dismay, that not one of them could understand a single word the others were saying. Instead of proper speech, people were uttering peculiar noises and jumbled-up nonsense words. Quite soon everyone was waving his or her arms about and shouting, and no doubt many tempers were lost. Of course work stopped, because no one could give any directions or understand any orders.

Feeling very confused, and probably a little lost, people began to gather in small groups where they found they could understand each other even a little, and eventually these groups started to drift away from the others to settle in some place by themselves. They began to see the other groups as strangers, belonging to different nations with different languages of their own.

The tower became known as the Tower of Babel which means chaos or confusion and never again did any people try to rival the power of God.

Abraham

In the ancient city of Ur in Babylonia there lived a good man named Abram. One day he and his family set out from Ur to go to the land of Canaan, but when they came to the city of Haran, they decided to settle there instead.

When Abram was an old man, God spoke to him and said, 'You must leave your country and your native home and go to a land which I will show to you. You will have many descendants and they will become a great nation. I will bless you and your name will become famous.'

Abram had no idea where this new land was, but he believed and trusted in God, so he set out with his wife Sarai, his nephew Lot, and a great company of slaves and cattle and all their other possessions.

At last they reached a place between Bethel and Ai and there they settled for a time. Abram had become a very rich man, with lots of cattle, sheep and goats, as well as gold and silver. Lot also had sheep, goats and cattle, and his own family and servants.

Because they had so many animals between them, there was not enough pasture land for them both and Abram's herdsmen and Lot's herdsmen began quarrelling.

So Abram said to Lot, 'We should not quarrel like this, for, after all, we are relatives. The whole land is before us, so let us separate. Choose which part of the land you want, and you can go your way and I will go the other way.'

Lot looked around and he thought that the Jordan Valley looked very fertile, so he moved away to the east and camped near Sodom which was a very wicked city, so much so, that both it and the city of Gomorrah were later destroyed.

Abram stayed in the southern part of Canaan, and God said to him, 'Look in all directions. This is the land which I am going to give you and your children and their children, and it will be yours for ever. You will have so many descendants that no one will be able to count them all.'

Although Abram had no children at that time, he believed and trusted in God's word. He set up his camp near the sacred trees of Mamre at Hebron, and there he built an altar to the Lord.

One day the voice of God spoke to him and said, 'I am the Almighty God. Obey me and always do what is right.'

Abram bowed down and his face touched the ground. God repeated His promise that Abram would be the ancestor of many nations, and then He said, 'Your name will no longer be Abram, but Abraham; no longer shall you call your wife Sarai; from now on her name is Sarah. I will bless her, and she will be the mother of many peoples, and there will be kings among her descendants.'

Abraham must have found this news hard to believe, for both he and Sarah were very old.

One hot day Abraham was sitting by the door of his tent when he looked up and saw three strangers coming towards him. People were always very welcoming and polite to travellers in that country, so Abraham ran out, bowed to the men and said, 'Sirs, please do not pass my door without stopping. Let me bring water to wash your feet and some food; it will help you on your journey. You have honoured me by coming here, so now let me serve

you with the best that my house can provide.'

'Thank you,' said the newcomers. 'We accept gladly.'

So Abraham ran into the tent and said to his wife Sarah, 'Quickly, let us prepare a meal for our visitors.'

He took bread, cream, milk and some tender meat and set it before his guests.

Then the visitors asked him, 'Where is your wife?'

'She is in the tent,' answered Abraham.

'In the spring, she will have a son,' said one of the men.

Sarah was just behind the tent entrance, and she heard what the man had said, and she laughed. 'I am much too old to have a baby,' she thought to herself, 'and Abraham is too old to be a father.'

'Why did Sarah laugh?' Abraham was asked. 'Is there anything which is too hard for the Lord to do?'

The strangers left and Abraham walked with them part of the way. By now he had realized that the men were messengers from God. He knew that if God had planned it, then Sarah would certainly have a son.

On the way the men told Abraham that the cities of Sodom and Gomorrah were so full of wickedness that they would have to be destroyed.

Later Abraham remembered that Lot had gone in that direction, so he pleaded with God to spare the cities for the sake of any good people who might be living there. 'Will you spare the cities if there are fifty good men there?' Abraham asked God, and God said He would.

Then Abraham thought that there might not be as many as fifty good men, so he asked God if He would spare the cities for forty-five, and again God said He would.

'For forty?' asked Abraham, and then, 'For thirty?', 'For twenty?', 'For ten?' Each time God promised He would save the cities if He found there were that many good men there.

Sadly, however, there were not even ten good men to be found in the cities of Sodom and Gomorrah—but what about Lot?

After speaking to Abraham, the strangers had gone down to find Lot and to get him out of the cities before they were destroyed.

'Flee for your life,' they urged. 'Take your wife and your daughters and run to the hills! Don't stop to look back or you will be killed!'

Lot and his family ran out, but Lot's wife did look back, and she was turned into a pillar of salt.

The cities of Sodom and Gomorrah were destroyed by fire, but God, remembering Abraham, allowed Lot to escape.

The promise which the strangers had brought to Abraham from God came true, and before long Sarah had a son, just as they had said. Abraham and Sarah were delighted, and they called the boy Isaac, which means 'full of laughter'. Perhaps this was because they laughed with happiness when he was born, or it may have been because they remembered Sarah laughing in the tent when they first heard of their son yet to be born.

'God has brought me great joy and laughter,' said Sarah.

Isaac grew up to be a fine boy and his parents loved him very much.

The Sacrifice of Isaac

When Isaac was still a young man, God put Abraham to the test to see whether he really trusted Him.

He called to him one day, 'Abraham!'

'Yes,' replied Abraham, 'Here I am.'

'Take your son,' said God, 'your only son, Isaac, whom you love so much, and set out for the land of Moriah. I will show you a mountain there, and on it I want you to offer your son as a sacrifice to Me.'

Abraham must have wondered if he had heard God rightly. In those days human sacrifices were not uncommon, and people always offered to God the best that they had, but could God really want Abraham to kill and offer his only son whom God Himself had sent?

However, Abraham's trust in God was very great, and he believed that God's commands must be obeyed, so he did not delay.

Early next morning he called Isaac and told him

they were going off into the mountains. He cut some wood for the sacrifice and loaded it upon his donkey. Then, with Isaac and two of his servants, he set out, walking with a sad and very heavy heart.

After three days' journeying, Abraham saw the mountain ahead. He turned to the servants and said, 'Stay here with the donkey, while Isaac and I go over there to worship; and then we will come back.'

In saying this, he hoped that perhaps in some way God would be able to save his son for him.

Abraham carried the knife and the coals for the fire, while Isaac carried the wood. As they climbed the mountain, Isaac began to look puzzled and at last he said, 'Father, we have the coals and the wood, but where is the lamb which we are going to sacrifice?'

All Abraham could reply was, 'God Himself will provide one.' With that Isaac had to be content, and the two of them walked on together.

When they arrived at the place of which God had told him, Abraham began to build an altar and to arrange the wood on it. Then he took Isaac and bound him and placed him on the altar on top of the wood. He stretched out his hand and took the knife to slay his son.

At that moment the voice of an angel called out to him from heaven, 'Abraham, Abraham!'

'Yes, here I am,' answered Abraham.

'Do not lay your hand on the boy or do anything to hurt him. Now I know that you really trust God, because you have not kept back your only son from Him.'

What a great relief Abraham felt! He looked round and there he saw a ram with its horns caught in a bush. God had sent it for him to sacrifice. He went over and freed it and offered it as a sacrifice in place of his son.

God was pleased with this great proof of Abraham's love and trust in Him.

Then the angel called to Abraham a second time and said, 'God says, because you did this, and did not hold back your only son, He will indeed bless you. You will have as many descendants as there are stars in the sky or grains of sand on the seashore, because you have obeyed His voice without question.'

So God confirmed the promises which He had made to Abraham.

Abraham named the place of sacrifice Jehovah-Jireh, which means 'The Lord will provide'. Even today people say, 'On the Lord's mountain He provides.'

Isaac, Esau and Jacob

Abraham was now very old, and he wished to see his son Isaac married. One day he sent his servant to Mesopotamia, where Abraham had first come from, to look for a wife for Isaac, as was the custom.

The servant set out taking ten camels and many costly gifts, and eventually he came to a well. While he rested by it, a beautiful young woman named Rebecca came to fill her water jar.

'Please give me a drink of water from your jar,' said the servant, and Rebecca gave him water for himself and his animals. Then she took him back to meet her family. Rebecca's parents felt it was a sign that God must want Rebecca to be Isaac's wife, so they said to the servant, 'Take her and let her become the wife of your master's son.'

Isaac was forty years old when he married her, and after some years they had twin sons whom they named Esau and Jacob. They were not at all alike as some twins are. Esau, the first-born, had red hair and a rough, hairy skin; he liked hunting and being out in the fields; but Jacob's skin was smooth, and he was quieter and preferred staying at home. Esau was his father's favourite, and Jacob was Rebecca's.

One day when Jacob was cooking some bean soup, Esau came in, tired and hungry from his hunting. 'Give me some of that,' he said to his brother, 'for I am starving.'

Jacob replied, 'Certainly I will, if you will let me have the rights that go with being the first-born son.' (One of these rights was that the first-born was given a double portion of his father's inheritance.)

Esau answered, 'All right. I think I'm about to die of hunger anyway, and what good will my birthright be to me then? Now give me the soup.'

So he sold his rights to Jacob, which showed how little he cared for them. The incident passed and for a while no one thought any more about it.

Isaac's Blessing

When Isaac grew very old, he became almost blind and could hardly tell the difference between his sons, Esau and Jacob. One day, feeling that he had not much longer to live, he said to Esau, 'Take your bow and arrows and go out and kill an animal for me; then prepare my favourite dish and bring me some to eat. After I have eaten it, I will give you my special blessing before I die.'

Now Rebecca overheard this, and she was anxious that her favourite, Jacob, should receive his father's blessing; so she said to Jacob, 'Go out to the flock and pick two young goats so that I may cook your father the dish which he loves. Then you can take it in to him and he will bless you instead.'

'But, mother,' Jacob objected, 'you know that Esau has a hairy skin and that I have a smooth one. If father were to touch me he would know I was deceiving him, and then he would curse me.'

Rebecca had thought of that too, but she said, 'Just go and get the goats as I asked.'

Then Rebecca took some of Esau's best clothes, which were in the house, and she asked Jacob to put them on. Next she put the skins of some goats over Jacob's neck and arms, and then she sent him in to his father with the food.

'Which of my sons are you?' asked the blind old Isaac as Jacob entered.

'I'm your elder son, Esau,' lied Jacob, 'and I've brought you some meat as you asked.'

'How did you find it so quickly?' asked Isaac.

Jacob replied, 'The Lord God helped me.'

Isaac must have felt a bit doubtful, for he said, 'Come closer, that I may touch you.'

Jacob moved nearer and his father felt his arms and his neck. Then he said, 'Your voice sounds like Jacob, but your arms feel like those of Esau. Are you really my son Esau?'

'Yes, I am,' answered Jacob.

When Isaac had eaten, he said to Jacob, 'Come closer my son and kiss me.'

Jacob did so, and Isaac noticed the smell of the fields which clung to Esau's clothes, and this seemed to convince him that it really was Esau. So he gave Jacob the blessing.

No sooner had Jacob left his father, than Esau returned from his hunting. He cooked the meat he had brought and took it in to Isaac. 'Here, Father,' he said, 'sit up and eat this meat, and then you can give me your blessing.'

'But who are you?' asked the bewildered Isaac.

'Your elder son, Esau,' was the reply.

This greatly distressed Isaac, and he trembled and asked, 'Who was it who came here then, whom I blessed with the blessing which cannot now be taken back?'

When Esau realized that Jacob had tricked him, he cried out bitterly, 'Bless me too, Father!'

'But your brother came deceitfully and has taken away your blessing,' answered Isaac.

'This is the second time he has cheated me,' said Esau. 'First he took my birthright, and now he has taken my blessing!'

Isaac did give Esau a blessing, but it was a poor one compared with the one he had given to Jacob.

Esau was furious with Jacob and even said he would kill him, but when Rebecca heard this, she sent Jacob away to stay with his Uncle Laban in Haran, hoping that his brother's anger would pass.

Jacob set out on foot on the long journey to Haran, which would take him many days. One night as he lay down to sleep, using a stone for a pillow, he had a wonderful dream.

He dreamt he saw a ladder, reaching from earth to heaven, and on it were angels going up and down. At the top he saw God Himself who said, 'The land on which you are resting will belong to you and your descendants. I will be with you to take care of you wherever you go.'

Jacob awoke full of awe.

He took the stone, stood it up on end, and poured oil upon it and dedicated it to God. He named the place 'Bethel', which means 'House of God'.

After many more days, Jacob came to Haran and stopped by a well in a field. There were flocks of sheep around it, and Jacob asked their shepherds if they knew his Uncle Laban.

'Yes,' they replied, 'and look, here comes his daughter Rachel with his sheep.'

Jacob removed the cover from the well and gave water to Rachel's sheep. Then he kissed her and told her that he was her cousin.

When Laban heard the news, he asked Jacob to stay and work for him. Jacob now found that Rachel had an elder sister named Leah.

Laban said to Jacob, 'You shouldn't work for nothing just because you are my relative; what shall I pay you?'

Now Jacob loved Rachel, who was very beautiful, and he replied, 'I will work for you for seven years if you will let me marry Rachel.'

Laban agreed, and Jacob worked his seven years which seemed to pass very quickly because he loved Rachel so much.

At the end of the seven years, Laban planned a great wedding feast, but, instead of giving Rachel to Jacob, the other daughter, Leah, was brought to him. It was dark and the bride was closely veiled, and it was not until afterwards that Jacob found he had been deceived.

Naturally he was angry and asked Laban why he had tricked him so. Laban explained that it was not the custom of the country for a younger daughter to be married before the elder one.

'Let us continue the festivities', said Laban, 'for another week, and then we will give you Rachel in return for serving me another seven years.'

Jacob did so, for it was not unusual in that country for a man to have more than one wife.

The Coat of Many Colours

Jacob was to have a large family, and he already had ten sons when Joseph was born. Joseph became his father's favourite, and this made the other brothers very jealous. When Jacob gave Joseph a beautiful, long, multi-coloured robe, with sleeves, they were even more envious, for this was the kind of coat worn by persons of distinction.

Then the brothers hated Joseph so much that they could hardly speak a friendly word to him.

One night, when Joseph was still in his teens, he had a dream. Later he told his brothers about it.

'I dreamt we were all in the fields, tying up sheaves of wheat,' he said, 'and my sheaf stood upright while yours stood in a circle round mine and bowed down to it.'

In those days people thought that dreams were a sign of what would happen in the future, so Joseph's brothers were naturally very angry at this and said, 'Do you think you are going to be a king and reign over us then?'

Then Joseph had a second dream, which he told to his brothers and also to his father. 'This time I saw the sun and the moon and eleven stars all bowing down to me,' he said.

Jacob was not very pleased when he heard this, and he said, 'Do you mean that your mother, your brothers and I will all bow down to you?' but although he scolded Joseph, Jacob could not help thinking about the dream and wondering what it all meant.

Some time later, Joseph's brothers went to a place called Shechem to look for pasture for their sheep. When they had been gone some time, Jacob said to Joseph, 'Will you go to Shechem and see if your brothers are safe and if the sheep are all right?

Then come back here again and let me know.'

Joseph agreed and off he went. However, when he arrived at Shechem he could not find his brothers, so he asked a man he met if he knew where they were. The man replied, 'Yes, they've left here. I heard them say they were going to Dothan.'

This was some 6 km (4 miles) further on, but Joseph set off to find them nonetheless.

As he drew near to Dothan, his brothers saw him coming in the distance, and they began to plot against him. 'Here comes the dreamer,' they scoffed. 'Let's kill him and throw his body into one of these pits. Then when we're asked, we can say that a wild animal has killed him. We'll see then what will become of his dreams!'

One of the brothers, named Reuben, was not very happy about this plan, and he tried to save Joseph. 'Let us not kill him' he said, 'but just throw him into the pit without hurting him—for after all, he is our brother.' Reuben hoped he might be able to rescue Joseph later on and send him back to their father unhurt.

When Joseph came up, the brothers ripped off his splendid robe and threw him down into the pit. Then they sat down to have their meal.

Suddenly they heard a noise and looked up to see a procession of camels approaching. They belonged to a party of Ishmaelite traders who were journeying to Egypt, and they were laden with all kinds of goods which the traders were taking to sell.

One of the brothers, Judah, had an idea. 'What will we gain if we do kill Joseph and then have to cover up the murder?' he said. 'Let's sell him to

these traders instead; then we won't be hurting our own flesh and blood.'

The brothers thought this a good idea and, when the traders came near, they hauled Joseph out of the pit and sold him to them for twenty pieces of silver.

Reuben hadn't been with them while this was happening; he had perhaps gone to tend the sheep. When he came back and found Joseph gone, he was most upset. 'What shall I do?' he cried. 'The boy has gone!' But it was too late for him to do anything to save his brother.

Next the other brothers killed a goat and dipped Joseph's robe in its blood. Then they took the coat home and showed it to their father. 'We found this,' they exclaimed. 'Does it belong to Joseph?'

'Yes, yes, it does!' cried the old man in horror. 'Some wild animal must have killed him and torn him to pieces!'

Jacob wept and mourned for Joseph for a very long time. Although his family tried in every way to comfort him, he would not be consoled for the death of his favourite son. 'I will still be mourning for Joseph when I die,' he said.

Joseph's New Life
Meanwhile the traders and Joseph had arrived in Egypt, and there he was sold to a man named Potiphar who was one of the officers of the Pharaoh, the King of Egypt, and captain of the palace guard.

So Joseph lived in the house of his new Egyptian master and, because God was with him, he was successful in all that he did.

Potiphar made him his personal servant and put him in charge of his house and all that he owned. He found he could leave everything to Joseph and that Joseph was honest and did his work very well.

Potiphar's wife, however, was not so nice, and she told lies about Joseph to her husband. She said Joseph had behaved very wickedly towards her. This was completely untrue, but unfortunately Potiphar believed his wife and had Joseph thrown into prison.

Here the jailer soon realized that Joseph was indeed a trustworthy man, and so he put him in charge of the other prisoners. He also made him responsible for all the work that was done in the prison, and this relieved the jailer of many of his duties.

Some time later two other officials were put into the prison. One was Pharaoh's butler, or cup-bearer, and the other was his chief baker. Both had offended Pharaoh and they were due to spend a long time in jail.

One morning Joseph went to their cell and found them both looking very miserable. 'What's the matter with you two?' he asked. 'Why are you looking so worried?'

They answered, 'We both had a dream last night and there is no one here who can tell us what the dreams mean.'

'Only God knows the meaning of dreams,' said Joseph. 'But tell them to me and I will ask Him to help us understand them.'

So the butler said, 'In my dream I saw a grape-vine with three branches on it. The leaves came out, then the blossom and then the grapes ripened. I held Pharaoh's cup under the grapes and squeezed the juice into it and gave it to him.'

'The three branches are three days,' said Joseph, 'and it means that in three days Pharaoh will set you free and restore you to your old position. Please remember me when you go out and ask Pharaoh if he will let me out of this prison—for I have done nothing wrong to deserve to be here.'

Then the chief baker told his dream. 'I was carrying three breadbaskets on my head,' he began, 'and in the top one were all kinds of baked food for Pharaoh, and the birds were eating them up.'

Joseph told the baker that his dream had a sad meaning. 'It means that in three days Pharaoh will have you hanged and the birds will eat your flesh.' Three days later it was Pharaoh's birthday and he gave a party for all his officials. He released the butler and the baker, gave the butler his old job back, and had the chief baker hanged—just as Joseph had said.

However, when the butler was set free, he did not give Joseph another thought, and completely forgot to ask Pharaoh to have him set free.

Two years passed, and then something happened to remind the thoughtless butler that Joseph was still in prison.

Pharaoh's Dream
Pharaoh himself had a dream. He dreamt he was standing by the River Nile when seven fat cows came up out of the water and began to eat the grass. Then seven thin bony cows came up and stood by the fat cows on the riverbank; and the thin cows ate up the fat cows. And then Pharaoh woke up.

He soon fell asleep again and this time he had another dream. Now he saw seven fat, full ears of corn all growing on one stalk; then seven more ears grew which were thin and damaged by the east wind. And the thin ears swallowed up the fat ones.

Pharaoh awoke feeling very worried. He knew it had only been a dream, but he was sure the dreams meant something. So he sent for all his magicians and courtiers and all his wise men and asked them, but none of them had any idea what the dreams meant.

Suddenly the butler remembered Joseph. At once he went to Pharaoh and said, 'Two years ago you were angry with me and put me in prison along with the chief baker. While we were there, we both had a dream, and there was a young Hebrew man, also a prisoner, who was able to tell us the meaning of our dreams. And all he told us came true!'

'Send for him,' commanded Pharaoh, and Joseph was quickly brought out of his dungeon. When he had washed and shaved himself and put on clean clothes, he went in to see Pharaoh. 'I have had a dream,' said Pharaoh, 'and no one can explain it, but I have been told that when you hear a dream you can interpret it.'

'No, your Majesty,' said Joseph. 'I can't, but God can. I can only tell you the interpretation which God gives me.'

Then Pharaoh told his dreams to Joseph.

Joseph said, 'The two dreams really mean the same thing, and through them God is telling you what is going to happen. The seven fat cows are seven years, and the seven full ears of corn are seven years; the seven thin cattle and the seven poor, empty ears are also seven years. What it means is that there will be seven years of plenty— good harvests and more than enough food for everyone. These will be followed by seven years of terrible famine and poor harvests—so bad that the seven good years will be entirely forgotten. The fact that you have had the dream twice means that the matter is fixed by God and that it won't be long before it happens.

'I think you should appoint a wise and careful man and put him in charge of the whole country. Then appoint overseers to take a fifth part of all the produce of the land during the seven good years. The officials can then store all of this up. Thus it will be at hand when the famine comes, and so the people will not starve.'

Pharaoh and his servants thought this was a very good idea. The only problem was where could they find a man wise, honest and clever enough to take charge of the whole plan. Then Pharaoh thought, 'Who could be better than Joseph himself? The spirit of this god must be in him.'

He said to Joseph, 'Since your god has shown you all this, I will put you in charge of the country, and everyone must obey your orders. Only as regards the throne will I be greater than you. Your authority will be second only to mine. I will appoint you governor over all Egypt.'

Then Pharaoh took a ring from his finger and put it on to Joseph's finger. He put fine linen robes on him and a gold chain round his neck; and he gave him his second-best chariot to ride in.

Joseph was thirty years old when he began his great task as governor of Egypt, and he travelled all over the country making provision for the famine which was ahead of them.

During the seven good years the land produced huge crops of corn, and Joseph had it collected and stored in the cities. There was so much corn that it was like the sands of the seashore and Joseph soon stopped measuring how much there was. All the storehouses were packed full.

Then the seven years of plenty came to an end, and the seven years of famine started. There was famine in other countries as well, but because of Joseph's wise plan, there was food in Egypt. When the people felt hungry and went to Pharaoh, he told them, 'Go to Joseph and do as he tells you.' And Joseph opened the storehouses and sold the corn which he had stored.

People heard about it in other starving countries and they came from all over the world to buy some of Egypt's corn, because there was such a severe shortage everywhere else.

Joseph in Egypt

In Canaan there was famine too, and when Jacob heard about the corn in Egypt, he said to his sons, 'Why don't you do something about it? Don't just stand there looking at one another; go to Egypt and buy some grain to keep us from starving.'

So the ten brothers set out on the long journey southwards to Egypt. There was now one more brother, who had been born after Joseph, and his name was Benjamin. Benjamin was now Jacob's favourite in place of Joseph, and his father would not allow Benjamin to go to Egypt with the others, because he was afraid that something might happen to the boy. So Benjamin remained at home.

When the ten brothers arrived in Egypt, they had to go first to Joseph like everyone else. He was busy organizing the buying and selling.

The brothers went and bowed low before him, and Joseph knew them immediately, but pretended not to; they did not recognize him in his Egyptian robes. Also he was talking in Egyptian and spoke to them through an interpreter. 'Where do you come from?' he asked roughly.

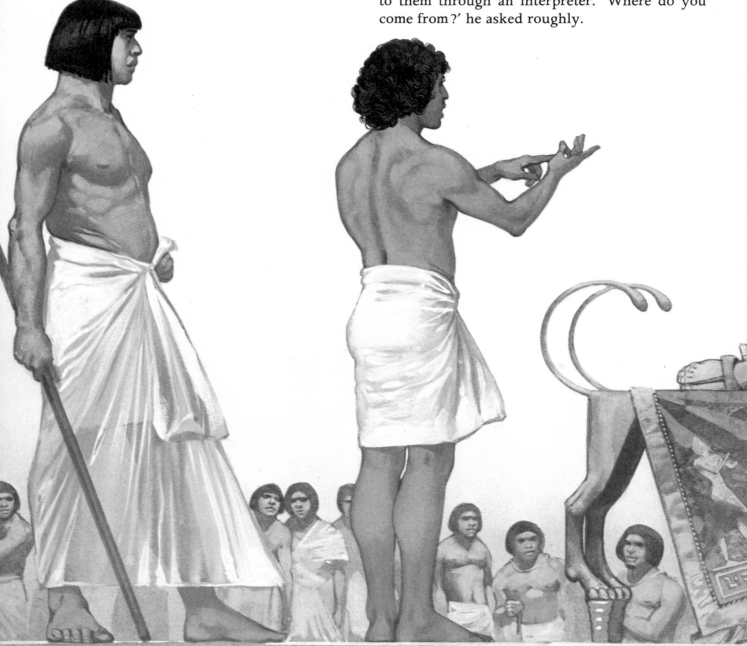

'We've come from the land of Canaan to buy food,' they replied.

'You are spies!' said Joseph. 'You've come to find out where we are weak and open to attack.'

'Oh no, sir,' they said. 'We have only come for food. We are all brothers, honest men—not spies, sir. We were twelve brothers in all, but one brother is dead and the youngest is at home.'

Joseph wondered if they were sorry about the brother whom they thought was dead, and he decided to find out. 'I think you are spies,' he repeated, 'but I will test you to find out. You will not leave here until I have seen this youngest

brother you tell me about. One of you must go back and bring him, while the rest of you remain here under guard. This is how I will discover whether you are telling me the truth.' And he put them all together in prison for three days. On the

third day Joseph came to them and said, 'I am a God-fearing man and I will let you go on one condition. That is that one of you stays here while the rest go back to take corn to your starving families. Then you must return, bringing back that youngest brother to me.'

The brothers began preparing for their journey and talked among themselves as they did so. 'It serves us right for what we did to Joseph,' they said.

Reuben said, 'I told you not to hurt him, didn't I? But you took no notice, and now look at us.'

Joseph was secretly listening to all this, but because they thought he was an Egyptian, they did not know that he understood their words. It upset Joseph very much to hear them talking like this, and he left them because he was so overcome.

When he came back later, he chose Simeon, the second oldest brother, as the one to remain behind.

Then he gave orders for every brother's sack to be filled with grain, and he quietly added, 'Put each man's money back in his sack, and give them all food for the journey home.' The servants obeyed and brought the full sacks in to the brothers. Then the nine set off for Canaan.

When they came to rest for the night, one of them opened his sack to give food to his donkey. He was very surprised to find his money at the top of the bag, and it made all the brothers afraid.

When at last they reached home, they went and told Jacob all that had happened. As they emptied their sacks, each man found his money inside.

Jacob was very sad when they asked about taking Benjamin back. He said, 'Joseph is gone, Simeon is gone, and now you want Benjamin!'

'I'll take care of him,' said Reuben.

But Jacob would not be moved. 'No,' he said. 'His brother Joseph is dead, and something might happen to Benjamin on the way. It would kill me.'

However the famine in Canaan got worse, and the corn which the brothers had brought back was soon eaten. 'You will have to go back and buy us a little more food,' said Jacob to his sons.

'But we can't,' said the fourth brother whose name was Judah. 'The man said very sternly that he would not see us again unless we took Benjamin.'

'Why did you bring about all this trouble by telling the man about Benjamin?' Jacob asked.

'The man asked us about ourselves; he thought we were spies. We had to answer his questions, and how were we to know what he would ask of us.'

Judah said he would pledge his own life for the boy's. 'Please let us go at once, or we shall all starve.'

At last Jacob had to agree that Benjamin could go. 'But take a present to the governor,' he said, 'and double the money, because you must take back the money that was returned before. Perhaps they made a mistake in giving the money back.'

So the brothers and Benjamin set out for Egypt, and when they arrived they went into Joseph's presence. They were surprised when Joseph commanded that they should all go to his own house.

The brothers were afraid and thought they were to be punished because of the money which had been returned in their sacks. So they explained to Joseph's servant just what had happened.

'Don't worry,' said the servant. 'I received the payment all right. Your god must have put the money into your sacks.' Then he brought Simeon to them, and took them all into the house.

When Joseph came in, they gave him their gifts and bowed low before him. 'How are you?' asked Joseph. 'And your father? Is he still alive and well.'

Then he saw Benjamin. 'So this is the youngest brother,' he said. 'God bless you, my son.' Joseph felt as though he was about to break down, and had to leave the room hurriedly so that they would not see his tears. When he had washed his face, he came back and ordered the meal to be served. Joseph sat at a separate table, because Egyptians did not eat with Hebrews. The brothers sat in order of age at their table, from the oldest to the youngest. Food was served from Joseph's table, and the brothers noticed that Benjamin was given five times as much as anyone else.

After the meal, Joseph went to his servant and said, 'Fill the men's sacks with food, as much as they are able to carry, and put their money in the tops of their sacks again. In the youngest boy's sack, put my silver cup as well.' The servant did so.

Early next morning, as soon as it was light, the brothers set off with their donkeys laden. They had not gone far when Joseph's servant, sent by Joseph, caught up with them and demanded, 'Why have you stolen my master's silver cup?'

'We have done no such thing,' protested the brothers in amazement. 'Don't you remember that we brought back the money that we found in our sacks the last time—so why should we now steal from your master? If that cup is found in any of our sacks, that man shall die, and the rest of us will come back and be your master's slaves.'

'All right,' said the servant, 'but only the one who has the cup shall be a slave; the rest of you can go free.'

Feeling sure they had nothing to fear, the men allowed the servant to open their sacks, beginning with the eldest man.

Of course, the cup was found in Benjamin's sack. Shocked and unhappy, the brothers loaded their donkeys and returned to Joseph's house. Here Judah spoke up for them all. 'Sir, what can we say? We must all be your slaves—not just Benjamin.'

'No, no,' said Joseph, 'Only the one with the cup shall be my slave; the rest of you may go home.'

'Please sir,' said Judah, 'let me speak, and don't be angry. We had to plead with our father for a long time before he would let Benjamin come, and now if we go back without him, our father will die of grief. He loves him particularly, because he has lost one son already. I made myself responsible for the boy, so let me stay here in his place.'

Then Joseph could hold back no longer. He sent everyone out of the room except the brothers. Then he said, 'Look, I am Joseph, the brother whom you sold into Egypt. But don't be upset or angry with yourselves because you sold me. You see, God sent me here to save people's lives. This is but the second year of famine, and there will be five more. Now I can rescue you and make sure that you do not starve.'

Joseph went on, 'Now hurry back to my father, and tell him that his son Joseph is alive and is ruler of all Egypt. Bring him back without delay, and you and all your families can come to live in the land of Goshen, where you will be near me. I don't want any of you to starve during the rest of the famine.' Then he threw his arms round Benjamin and wept for joy, and he hugged his brothers too.

When the news reached the palace that the men from Canaan were Joseph's brothers, Pharaoh and his staff were delighted. Pharaoh ordered that when Jacob and the brothers and their families returned, they should be given the best of everything in Egypt. The brothers were to take wagons and food for their journey back to Canaan. Joseph gave them all changes of clothing and sent presents back for Jacob.

'Joseph is alive!' they told Jacob when they got home, 'and he is ruler over all Egypt!'

At first Jacob would not believe them—he was too shocked. But when he saw the wagons that Joseph had sent to take him back to Egypt, he said, 'Joseph is alive! I must see him before I die!'

So Jacob and his sons and their families packed their belongings and set off for the land of Egypt. On the way, at Beersheba, Jacob stopped and offered sacrifices to God; and God said to him, 'Don't be afraid to go to Egypt, for I will make you a great nation there. I will be with you, and I will bring your descendants back to this land.'

When at last they reached the land of Goshen, Joseph came up in his chariot to meet his father. He threw his arms round his father's neck and wept for joy.

Then Joseph went to Pharaoh and told him that his father and brothers had arrived with their flocks and herds, and that they were now in Goshen. He took five of the brothers to Pharaoh.

'What is your occupation?' asked Pharaoh.

'We are shepherds, sir,' replied the brothers.

Pharaoh turned to Joseph and said, 'Let them settle in the land of Goshen, and if any are especially able men, put them in charge of my own cattle.'

Then Joseph took Jacob in to Pharaoh, and Jacob blessed Pharaoh. Jacob and his family settled in Goshen, where they became rich and had many children. Eventually Jacob died there, but his body was taken back to Canaan to be buried.

The Baby in the Bulrushes

Some years later, after Joseph had died, a new Pharaoh came to rule over Egypt. By this time Jacob's descendants, the Israelites, had been living in Egypt for many years, and there were now a great number of them.

The new Pharaoh knew nothing about Joseph and all that he had done to save the people from starvation, and he said, 'These Israelites are getting so many that they are becoming a threat to us. If there was a war they might join up with our enemies. We must find a way to suppress them.'

So the Egyptians put slave-drivers over the Israelites to make them work harder and harder, and they made them build store-cities for Pharaoh. The more cruelly they were treated, however, the more the Israelites seemed to increase in numbers. The Egyptians grew to fear them and made their lives miserable by being cruel and forcing them to work even more.

In the end Pharaoh issued an order that all baby boys born to the Israelites should be killed as soon as they were born. Baby girls, however, should be allowed to live. The nurses to whom this order was given refused to obey it, because they feared God, so finally Pharaoh made an order to all the people saying that every new baby boy born to the Israelites should be drowned in the River Nile, but that they could let the girls live.

Naturally the Hebrews were most unhappy about this law. One family already had two children—a girl named Miriam and a boy named Aaron—and to them another baby boy was born. He was a fine baby, and the mother could not bear to see him drowned, so she managed to keep him hidden for three months.

As he grew bigger, the time came when she could hide him no longer, and so she and the family had to think of another plan. She made him a little basket from the bulrushes or reeds which

grew at the side of the Nile and which were often used to make boats. Then she covered the basket with a tar-like substance to make it watertight. She put the baby into it and carried it down to the river. There she hid the basket among the reeds which were growing at the water's edge.

The baby's sister, Miriam, waited a little distance away to see what would happen to her baby brother.

Presently, Pharaoh's daughter came down to the river to bathe, and as she and her servants walked along the riverbank, she suddenly spotted the basket in the reeds. She sent one of her slave-girls to fetch it. The girl brought it and when the princess opened it she saw the baby boy. He began to cry and the princess felt sorry for him. 'This is a Hebrew baby,' she said.

Then his sister Miriam had an idea. She ran forward from where she had been hiding and said, 'Shall I go and ask one of the Hebrew women to come and look after him for you?'

'Yes, please do so,' answered Pharaoh's daughter, and clever Miriam hurried off and brought back her own mother.

'Take this baby and look after him for me,' said the princess, 'and I will pay you for doing so.'

The baby's mother was delighted to have her own baby back again, although she may have realized that the princess would want to keep him in due course, when he was older. However, in the meantime, the mother gladly took back her own baby to nurse him in safety.

Later, when the boy was older, she took him again to Pharaoh's daughter, and the princess adopted him as her own son. 'I drew him out of the water,' she said, 'and so I will call him "Moses".' (The name 'Moses' sounded rather like the Hebrew word meaning 'to draw out'.)

So Moses grew up as a prince in Pharaoh's court.

Moses Flees from Egypt

One day when Moses was grown up, he went out to see how his own people, the Hebrews, were living under the hard conditions of the Egyptians.

He was horrified when he happened to see an Egyptian kill one of the Hebrews. In his anger, Moses in his turn killed the Egyptian and buried his body in the sand. He thought no one had seen him, but that did not make his wrong-doing any better.

The next day, he went out again, and this time he saw two Hebrew men fighting. He went up to them and asked one of them, 'Why are you fighting with one of your own countrymen?'

The man answered rudely, 'Who made you a judge and ruler over us? Are you now going to kill me like you killed that Egyptian yesterday?'

Then Moses was afraid. 'People know what I did,' he thought to himself.

His wicked deed reached the ears of Pharaoh himself who thought that Moses deserved to be killed for what he had done. Moses was terrified and fled from the country, and went to live in the land of Midian. When he reached there, he sat down by a well, and at the same time the seven daughters of the priest of Midian, a man named Jethro, came down to draw water for their father's sheep and goats. Some shepherds tried to drive them away, but Moses went to their rescue and saw that they got the water for their animals.

When they reached home, their father asked how it was that they were back early that day. 'An Egyptian helped us,' they said. 'He even drew the water for us.'

'Why did you leave the man out there?' asked Jethro. 'Go back and invite him to come and have a meal with us,' he said hospitably.

So the girls went and brought Moses to their home. He agreed to live with them and helped to take care of Jethro's sheep and goats. After a time, he married one of the daughters whose name was Zipporah.

Many years later the Pharaoh of Egypt died, but the people of Israel were still suffering in their slavery, and they asked God to help them. God remembered the promises He had made to Abraham, to Isaac and to Jacob, and He promised He would send someone to deliver them from their bondage.

The Burning Bush

One day, when Moses was looking after the flocks of his father-in-law, Jethro, he led them over the desert towards the west, until he came to the holy mountain named Sinai, or Horeb.

While he was there an angel appeared to him as a flame of fire coming from the middle of a bush. Although it was on fire, the bush itself did not seem to be burning up.

'This is strange,' thought Moses. 'I will go nearer and see why this bush is not burnt.'

When he got closer, the voice of God called out, 'Moses! Moses!'

'Here I am,' answered Moses.

'Do not come any nearer,' said God. 'Take off your shoes, for the place where you are standing is holy ground. I am the God of your ancestors, the God of Abraham, the God of Isaac, and the God of Jacob.'

Moses hid his face, for he was afraid to look at God.

Then God said, 'I know how cruelly My people are suffering in Egypt, and I have heard their prayers to be rescued from the Egyptians. I shall deliver them and bring them out of Egypt to a rich and fertile land. I shall send you to the King of Egypt so that you may rescue the Israelites from his country.'

Moses was appalled at the thought of this tremendous task. He was sure he would not be able to do it, and he thought of one excuse after another, but God had the answer to each of them.

'I am nobody important,' began Moses. 'Who am I to go to Pharaoh? I am not up to such a job.'

God answered, 'But I will be with you.'

'When you have brought the people out,' said God, 'you will worship Me on this mountain.'

'How can I explain who You are?' asked Moses. 'If I say, "The God of your fathers sent me," they will ask, "What is His name?" What shall I say then?'

God replied, 'I am who I am. Tell the people the one who is called "I AM" has sent you, the God of Abraham, Isaac and Jacob. The people will listen to you. But when you ask Pharaoh to let the people go so that they may offer sacrifices to Me, I know he will not do so unless he is forced. I will use My powers and after that he will let you go.'

But Moses still thought of the difficulties of this tremendous task. 'What shall I do if the people don't believe me?' he asked. 'Suppose they say You did not appear before me at all?'

God's answer to this was to give Moses three signs. First He asked Moses to throw the rod he was carrying on to the ground, and when he did so it became a snake. When God told him to pick it up by the tail, it became a staff again. 'Do this to prove to the people that the Lord God has sent you,' said God.

Next He told Moses to put his hand inside his robe, and when Moses did so his hand was suddenly diseased; but when he put it in and took it out a second time, it was normal and healthy again.

'If they are not convinced by that first miracle,' said God, 'then show them this second one. But if they don't believe even these two signs, take some water from the River Nile and pour it on the dry ground, and it will turn to blood.'

Moses was still not happy. 'Don't send me, Lord,' he said. 'I am no good at talking. I'm slow and have never been a good speaker.'

God reminded Moses where all powers came from. 'Who is it who gives a man his mouth? Who gives him sight?' He asked. 'It is I, the Lord, and I will help you and tell you what to say.'

'Lord God,' implored Moses, 'please send someone else.'

God was not pleased that Moses did not trust Him enough to obey, but He replied, 'Your brother Aaron speaks well. In fact, he is on his way to meet you now and will be glad to see you. You can go to Pharaoh together, and you can tell Aaron what to say. I will help you both, and he can be your spokesman. And take your staff with you, for with it you will be able to do great wonders.'

So Moses went back to Jethro, his father-in-law, and said, 'Let me go back to my people in Egypt and see if they are still alive.'

Jethro understood and said, 'Go in peace.'

Before Moses left Midian, God reassured him by saying, 'Go back to Egypt, for those who wanted to kill you are now dead.'

Moses set out, and on the way he met his brother Aaron, as God had said. The brothers kissed one another, and Moses told Aaron all that God had said to him and all the signs and wonders that He had shown him.

Moses and Aaron went off to Egypt, and when they arrived they gathered together all the leaders of the Israelites. Aaron told them all that God had said to Moses, and Moses performed the miracles which God had shown him. The people believed him, and when they heard that God had seen their sufferings under the Egyptians, and that Moses and Aaron had been sent to deliver them, they bowed their heads and worshipped.

The Plagues of Egypt

Together Moses and Aaron went to Pharaoh and said, 'The Lord God of Israel says "Let my people go, so that they can travel for three days into the desert and hold a festival in My honour."' (The Israelites would have to leave Egypt to do this because their sacrifices would offend the Egyptians if they took place on Egyptian soil. The Egyptian religion was quite different to that of the Israelites.)

'Who is the "Lord God"?' demanded Pharaoh haughtily. 'Why should I do as he says? I don't know him and I won't let the Israelites go. You're making them neglect their duties. Get those slaves back to work! They are already more numerous than us Egyptians, and now you want to stop them working. No!'

He ordered the slave-drivers and foremen, 'Stop giving the Israelites straw to make bricks. Make them find the straw themselves—but they must still make the same number of bricks. They can't have enough work to do if they want me to let them go and make sacrifices to their god. If they work harder they won't have time to listen to such lies.'

So the Israelites had to search all over the land for straw; if they failed to make the same number of bricks as before, the slave-drivers beat them. When the Israelites complained to Pharaoh, he said they were lazy and sent them back to work and the overseers beat them again.

The Israelite leaders blamed Moses and Aaron for going to Pharaoh at all. 'You've only made matters worse,' they complained. 'You are not helping us at all!'

Moses prayed to God and said, 'Why did You send me here? Pharaoh is treating the people even more cruelly since I came. It seems I have only made things worse for them.'

'Tell the Israelites that I will rescue them from their slavery,' said God, 'and I will bring them to the land which I promised to their ancestors.' But the people were in such despair that they refused to listen to Moses and continued to grumble about their misfortunes.

Then God told Moses to go again to Pharaoh and to warn him that if he did not let the Israelites go, terrible things would happen in Egypt. 'And if Pharaoh wants you to prove yourself,' said God, 'tell Aaron to throw down his rod and it will become a snake.'

Moses and Aaron did as God had said, and Aaron's rod did become a snake. Pharaoh called together all his magicians and wise men, and by their magic, they too made their sticks into snakes, but then Aaron's rod swallowed theirs up. Still Pharaoh refused to listen to Moses and Aaron and they were sent away.

Then God said to Moses, 'Pharaoh is very stubborn. Go and meet him in the morning when he goes down to the river, and take your rod. Tell him that because he has not listened, he will know that I am the Lord by what he sees you do next. Then strike the surface of the river with your rod, and the water will turn into blood. No one will be able to drink from it. The same will happen to all rivers and pools and canals in Egypt and no one will have any water.'

Moses and Aaron did as God commanded, and the Egyptians had to dig along the riverbanks for enough water to drink. But Pharaoh paid no attention and went back into his palace, saying it was all magic tricks.

A week passed and Moses went again to Pharaoh and said, 'Let my people go. God says that if you do not, your country will be overrun with thousands of frogs.'

Pharaoh refused, and God said to Moses, 'Tell Aaron to hold his stick out over the waters, and frogs will come up and cover the land of Egypt.'

Aaron did so, and frogs appeared, hopping everywhere. They went into the palace, on to Pharaoh's bed, into all the people's houses, and even into the ovens and cooking pots. They jumped all over Pharaoh and his officials and on all the Egyptians. Pharaoh could bear it no longer, and he called Moses and Aaron and said, 'Pray to your god to take these frogs away, and then I will let your people go.' So Moses prayed to God, and the frogs died.

As soon as Pharaoh found that he was no more troubled by frogs, he changed his mind again and would not let the Israelites go and ordered them to get on with their work.

Then God sent a plague of gnats, which flew around and bit every man and animal. But still Pharaoh would not let the people go.

Next there came a plague of swarms of flies. The houses of the Egyptians were full of them, and the ground was covered with them, but there were no flies in the region of Goshen where the Israelites lived.

Pharaoh called for Moses and Aaron to come to him and said, 'All right, you can offer sacrifices to your god, but you must do it here in this country where we can keep an eye on you.'

'No, that wouldn't be right,' said Moses, 'because it would offend the Egyptians. We must travel three days out into the desert.'

'Provided you don't go very far,' Pharaoh said. 'And you must pray for me.'

Moses asked God to take away the flies, and He did so. Once more Pharaoh changed his mind and would not let the people go.

Next there came a plague of cattle disease which killed the animals of the Egyptians, but not those of the Israelites—and still Pharaoh remained obstinate.

Then came a plague of boils, on both people and animals. Even so, Pharaoh would not listen to Moses and Aaron.

God told Moses that He would send a heavy hailstorm next day, such as had never been known before. He said that Pharaoh should order all people and animals to be under shelter, for those left outside, unprotected, would die. Some of Pharaoh's servants, who feared God, obeyed, but others took no notice and left their slaves and animals out in the open.

Then the hailstorm began, and there was thunder and lightning, far worse than Egypt had ever known; but in Goshen there was no storm at all. Any animal or person caught in the storm was killed and the crops damaged everywhere except where the Israelites lived.

Pharaoh was frightened and said to Moses, 'I have sinned. Your god is right and I am wrong. We have had enough hail and thunder. I will let your people go.' Moses went out and prayed to God, and the storm ceased. As soon as Pharaoh saw it, he became his old stubborn self again and refused to let the Israelites go.

Exasperated, Moses and Aaron went to him and asked, 'How much longer will you defy God? If you keep on refusing, He will send a plague of locusts tomorrow, and they will eat up everything that the hail did not destroy.'

'You may go,' said Pharaoh, who had been persuaded by his officials to get rid of Moses or Egypt would be ruined. 'But only the men,' he added, 'I won't let the women and children go. They must stay here.'

Moses would have none of this and, as God had said, down came the clouds of locusts. The ground was black with them, and they ate everything until not a single green thing could be seen on any tree or plant. They ate all the harvest and the fodder for the animals too.

'I was wrong,' cried Pharaoh. 'Forgive me once more, and pray to your god to take away the locusts.' God caused a strong east wind to blow, and soon not one locust was left in Egypt. However the damage they had done was clear to everyone.

Yet again, Pharaoh had failed to learn his lesson, and he did not let the Israelites go. Then God sent a great darkness over Egypt for three days, so that the Egyptians could not see one another—although the Israelites still had light where they lived because God was protecting them.

'Go!' said Pharaoh to Moses. 'And take your women and children too—but leave your animals behind.'

But Moses refused to leave a single animal that belonged to his people and insisted that every donkey, ox, goat and sheep owned by the Children of Israel should be free to leave Egypt with their owners.

The Passover

Pharaoh had suffered nine plagues and yet had not learned to obey God. God told Moses that He would send one final punishment to the Egyptians and that then Pharaoh would certainly let the Israelites go.

So Moses went to Pharaoh with a final message from God and said, 'The Lord says that at about midnight He will go through the land of Egypt, and every first-born son will die, from your own son down to the son of the lowest maidservant, and the first-born of all the cattle will die too. Then,' finished Moses angrily, 'you will beg me to go, and I shall leave.' Even this had no effect on Pharaoh who did not change his mind.

God gave Moses and Aaron detailed instructions for the Israelites for what later became known as the Feast of the Passover.

Each family was to choose a young lamb; it had to be a special animal, without any defect or blemish, and to be a one year old male. If a family was too small in numbers to eat a whole animal, then they were to share one with the next-door neighbours.

They were to keep the animal for fourteen days, to make sure there was no blemish that they had missed. Then they were to kill it and, with a sprig of hyssop dipped in its blood, they were to mark the doorposts and lintels of the house in which the animal was to be eaten. This marking would show the houses where the Israelites lived so that the angel of death, sent by God, would pass those houses by and leave the inhabitants untouched.

The meat was to be roasted and eaten with bitter herbs and bread made without yeast (known as unleavened bread). The bitter herbs would be a reminder of their bitter bondage under Pharaoh, and the unleavened bread indicated the haste in which they were to eat it, for there would not be time to wait for yeast to rise as it does in ordinary bread.

None of the meat was to be kept until the morning, and any that was left over was to be burnt to ashes.

They were to eat this special meal quickly, and were to be dressed for a journey, with sandals on their feet and a stick in their hands. They were all to stay indoors that night and no one was to leave the house until the morning. The doors and windows were to remain closed.

Moses told the people that when they had left Egypt and had been taken to the rich and fertile land which God had promised, they were to continue to celebrate this festival of unleavened bread every year.

'When your children ask what it means,' he said, 'you must tell them that it is the sacrifice of the Passover, because God passed over the houses of the Israelites in Egypt and spared them; but the Egyptians were killed.

As God had said, so it happened. At midnight, the first-born son of every family in Egypt died. Pharaoh and all his servants rose up during the night, and there was loud weeping in Egypt, because there was not one house in which the eldest son had not died. There was great sorrow throughout Egypt. The animals died also, just as Moses had told Pharaoh they would, but not one Israelite died or any animal that belonged to an Israelite.

Pharaoh summoned Moses and Aaron that same

night and said, 'Get out! You and all the people of Israel. Go and worship your god, and take your flocks and herds too. And pray for a blessing for me also.'

The Egyptian people were anxious to see the Israelites go as well. 'Hurry up and leave our country,' they said, 'otherwise we shall all be dead.' And they gave the Israelites gold and silver and clothing and anything else which they asked for.

The Israelites packed up their belongings and hurriedly left the land of Egypt—so quickly that they did not have time to get food ready or prepare leavened bread.

Happily they set out on foot, a great company of them, free at last from the bondage of Pharaoh! There were about 600,000 men, not counting women and children, and all their sheep and goats and cattle went with them. There were also a number of other races and Egyptians with them, who had married Israelites or were slaves to them for the Israelites had slaves of their own.

They had been in the land of Egypt for 430 years, and so none of them knew what it was like to be free.

The Passover

Jewish families still celebrate 'the Passover', a festival for which God had given Moses exact instructions.

No foreigner was to be allowed to eat it, nor any temporary resident or hired worker. The whole meal was to be eaten in the house in which it was prepared, and must not be taken outside. No bones of the animal were to be broken.

God told Moses that every first-born male Israelite and every first-born male animal must be dedicated to Him.

No leavened bread was to be eaten for seven days. When the festival began on the seventh day, the parents were to explain to their children that it was a reminder of what God had done for them when they left Egypt. It would also remind them to continue to study God's laws, and to remember that it was God's power which had delivered them from Egypt.

The Crossing of the Red Sea

The way from Egypt to Canaan was north east, but it is not absolutely certain which route the Israelites took. It is thought that they did not take the coast road, because there they would have met with Philistine forces, and they were not ready for such an encounter. Instead they began in a generally southerly direction, and at some point crossed the Red Sea, or 'sea of reeds', which may then have extended further north than it does now.

The long procession left Egypt to head for the promised land of which God had told their ancestors and God Himself went in front to show them the way. He appeared as a pillar of cloud during the day and as a pillar of fire during the night; thus they had light and so could travel both night and day.

They had not been long on the way when Pharaoh and some of his officials had second thoughts about letting them go. 'Who will now do the work which those slaves did?' they asked. 'Why ever did we let them escape like that?' So Pharaoh decided they must try and bring the Israelites back. He got ready his war chariot and his army and 600 of the best and fastest chariots in the land, and they all chased off after the Israelites.

When the Israelites saw them coming, they were terrified. They were hemmed in by sea and mountains, with the Red Sea in front of them and Pharaoh and his chariots behind them, and they cried out in terror to Moses. 'Did you have to bring us here to die? Aren't there any graves in Egypt? Look what you've done now! We'd have been better staying as slaves to the Egyptians than dying out here in the wilderness.'

'Don't be afraid,' said Moses. 'Just stand firm and you will see what God will do to save you. He will fight for you. There is no need for you to do anything.'

Moses knew that the right thing to do was to trust God, and he wanted the people of Israel to trust Him too.

God said to Moses, 'Why do you cry out to Me? Tell the people to move forward. Then lift up your rod and hold it over the water; the sea will divide and you may all walk through on dry ground.' Moses agreed to do so.

Then the pillar of cloud moved back until it was between the Israelites and the Egyptians, and so the night passed without the two forces coming near to one another.

The next day Moses held out his rod over the water, and God sent a strong east wind which blew all night and drove the waters back so that they were divided. Then the people were able to walk through on dry land, with water on both sides of them.

Pharaoh's army saw their chance and galloped into the water after them, with all their horses, chariots and horsemen. But their chariots were so heavy that they began to sink in the soft ground, and their wheels became clogged with mud so that they found it difficult to move. The Egyptians said to one another, 'Let's go back out of here, for God is fighting on the side of the Israelites and is against us, the Egyptians.'

'Hold out your hand over the sea,' said God to Moses, 'and the waters will come back over the Egyptians and their chariots and horses.' Moses did so, and by next morning the sea was flowing normally and not one of the Egyptians had reached the other side.

From the far shore the Israelites could see how God had saved them yet again from the Egyptians. There was great rejoicing and the people began to sing in praise of God. Miriam, Moses and Aaron's sister, and all the other women took up tambourines and danced and sang in praise of God who had delivered them from their enemies.

The Ten Commandments

Under God's guidance, Moses led the people on, away from the Red Sea, and across a great stretch of desert called the Wilderness of Shur. The land was hot, dry and barren, full of sand dunes, scrubland and rocks, and with hardly any water. When they had been travelling for three days, the Israelites became very thirsty and were delighted when they found water at a place called Marah. When they came to drink it, however, they found it very bitter. 'What are we going to drink?' they grumbled to Moses.

Moses prayed to God, and God showed him a tree whose bark and leaves are able to sweeten bitter water. Moses threw some of this into the water, and the water became fit to drink.

From Marah, the Israelites moved on to Elim, where they found twelve springs of water and seventy palm trees, and here they were able to camp and rest for a while. They could not stay long, however, for they had to continue their journey, and soon they were grumbling again.

'We're hungry,' the people complained. 'At least we had food in Egypt, but now you have brought us out here we shall all starve to death.'

God told Moses, 'I shall send food for you. Each day the people must go out and gather enough for that one day. On the sixth day of the week, they are to gather twice as much as usual.'

That evening a large flock of little brown birds called quail flew into the Israelites' camp; and the people found that their flesh was good to eat.

In the morning, when the dew had gone, the ground was covered with a thin flaky substance, like small white seeds, and as delicate as hoar-frost.

'Manna?' asked the Israelites, which means, 'What is it?', and so 'manna' became its name.

Moses said, 'This is the food which God has provided. You are each to gather as much as you need for the day, but no extra.

The Israelites began gathering, and some gathered more and some less; but it made no difference. Those who had gathered more found that they did not have too much, and those who had gathered little found that there was enough for their needs. Any which was left on the ground melted in the heat of the sun by midday. In spite of Moses's order, some people tried to save some for the next day, but found that it rotted overnight.

Only on the sixth day of the week could they gather twice as much as usual and then it did not go bad; for the seventh day, the Sabbath, was their day of rest, and they were not to gather food on that day. Though some people did go out looking for the manna on the seventh day, there was none to be found. God said to Moses, 'How much longer will the people disobey My commands? Remember that I gave you a day of rest, and that is why I will always provide twice the amount of food on the sixth day. On the seventh day they must stay at home.'

God continued to provide manna for the Israelites for the whole of the next forty years until they reached the land of Canaan.

Food was one thing difficult to find in the desert, but, as the Israelites had already discovered, water was another. As they moved on, they again grumbled to Moses that they were thirsty. 'Why do you keep complaining like this?' asked Moses.

Once again the people said, 'Why did you bring us out of Egypt to this miserable place? Must we all die of thirst?' And they grew very angry. 'What can I do with them?' Moses asked God.

'What can I do with them?' Moses asked God.

'Take some of the leaders and go on ahead of the people,' said God. 'Carry your rod. I will stand before you on a rock on Mount Sinai. Speak to the rock and water will flow out from it.'

Moses went as the Lord had said, but he was so angry with the people that instead of just speaking to the rock, as he had been told, he struck it with his staff. A stream of water flowed out, just the same, and the people and animals were able to quench their thirst. But Moses had not obeyed God and so God told him that he would not be the one to lead the people into the promised land.

Moses Receives the Commandments

By now the Israelites had crossed much desert land and had come to the foot of Mount Sinai. From the mountain God called Moses and said, 'Tell the people that I have said these words, "You saw what happened to the Egyptians and how I have brought you safely to this place. Now if you will obey Me and keep My covenant, you will be My chosen people, dedicated to Me alone."'

When the people heard this they replied, 'We will do all that the Lord has said.'

God then told Moses that the people were to make themselves ready for worship and were to put on clean clothes, for He Himself would come down on Mount Sinai. Moses was to put a boundary round the mountain, and the people were not to cross it, or even go near it until they heard a trumpet sounding a long blast.

The people made themselves ready as instructed. On the third day there was thunder and lightning and thick cloud on the mountain, which indicated God's power and presence, and a loud blast was heard on a trumpet. All the people trembled with fear. Moses led them to the foot of the mountain, which was wrapped in fire and smoke and shook as if there was an earthquake.

Then God called to Moses alone to go to the top of the mountain; and Moses went up and was lost to view in the cloud. He remained up there for forty days.

While Moses was on the mountain, God gave him the laws by which the Israelites were to live. Among these laws were those which are known as the Ten Commandments, which were written on two tablets of stone by God Himself.

These are the Ten Commandments.

1 *You shall have no other gods before me.*
2 *You shall not make for yourself a graven image, or any likeness of anything that is in heaven above, or that is in the earth beneath or that is in the water under the earth; you shall not bow down to it or serve it.*
3 *You shall not take the name of the Lord your God in vain.*
4 *Remember the sabbath day, to keep it holy. Six days you shall labour, and do all your work; but the seventh day is a day dedicated to the Lord your God; on it no one shall do any work. For in six days the Lord made heaven and earth, the sea, and all that is in them, and rested on the seventh day; therefore He blessed the sabbath day and made it holy.*
5 *Honour your father and your mother.*
6 *You shall not kill.*
7 *You shall not commit adultery.*
8 *You shall not steal.*
9 *You shall not bear false witness (tell lies) against your neighbour.*
10 *You shall not covet (long to possess) your neighbour's house or wife, or his manservant, or his maidservant, or his ox, or his ass, or anything that belongs to your neighbour.*

The Golden Calf

Moses was away for such a long time that the people grew tired of waiting. They gathered around his brother Aaron and said, 'We don't know what has become of Moses, and we can't wait any longer. Let us make a god of our own.'

Aaron, on this occasion, was not firm, and he said to the people. 'Take off the gold earrings

which you are wearing, and give them to me.'

They did so, and Aaron took the huge pile of earrings, melted them down, and shaped the gold into a golden calf. Forgetting all about the one true God, the people looked at the golden calf and said, 'This is the god who led us out of Egypt.'

Aaron built an altar before it, and declared that the next day was to be a festival to the Lord. Perhaps he, too, thought it represented the true God, though he should have known better.

Early on the next day, the people brought animals for offerings and they had a great feast.

High up on the mountain God said to Moses, 'You must go down to the people, for they have already forgotten the way I commanded them, and they have made a calf of melted gold and are worshipping that. I am very angry with them.'

So Moses set off back down the mountain, carrying the two stone tablets on which God had written the Ten Commandments. As he was getting near the foot of the mountain, he could hear shouting and noise coming from the people. When he came close enough he saw that they were dancing round the golden calf, and he was so furious that he threw down the tablets and they broke.

He seized the golden calf, melted it and ground what remained to powder. Then he scattered the powder upon the water and made the Israelites drink it as a symbol of their shame and regret.

The next day he went back to God and asked His forgiveness for the sin which the people had committed in worshipping the golden calf. At God's command, he also cut two more tablets of stone, and God gave him the laws again. As a token that they were forgiven, God renewed His promise, or covenant, to the people.

The Tabernacle

As the Israelites were travelling all the time, it was not possible for them to build a permanent place in which to worship God. So God gave Moses instructions for making a Tabernacle or tent-church, and from that time onwards, whenever the Israelites pitched their camps, they erected the Tabernacle in the middle.

The structure of the Tabernacle was like this:

There was the Outer Court, open to the sky, and surrounded by 'walls' made of curtains, supported on pillars. The entrance was at the east end, and, inside, facing the door, was the altar of burnt offering. Behind that was a large bronze basin called a laver, which was used by the priests to wash their hands and feet before they offered a sacrifice or entered the Holy Place.

Towards the west end of the Outer Court was a covered tent which was the central part of the Tabernacle. This was made of fine linen, woven with blue, red and purple wool and embroidered with figures of winged creatures. The tent then had a covering made of goats' hair and two more made of animal skins. The upright frames of the tent were made of acacia wood, covered with gold, and standing on silver bases.

This Tabernacle tent itself was divided into two by a curtain hung from four posts and embroidered like the inner roof covering.

The outer of the two parts was called the Holy Place, while the inner one was the Holy of Holies.

In the Holy Place were three things:

The Altar of Incense, on which was burnt a mixture of substances, such as resins and gums, to make a sweet-smelling smoke.

The Table of Shewbread, a wooden table overlaid with gold, on which twelve cakes of unleavened bread were placed every Sabbath as a sort of thanks offering.

The Lampstand (or seven-branched candlestick) made of pure gold. From its central shaft, three curved arms sprang up on either side, one above the other. Each branch had on it gold flowers, shaped like almond blossoms with buds and petals.

In the Holy of Holies, there was only one object, and that was The Ark of the Covenant, a box of acacia wood, covered with pure gold both inside and out. It stood on four legs and was carried on two poles of acacia wood covered with gold. Its lid was a slab of pure gold, called the Mercy Seat, and at each end was a winged creature, with outstretched wings covering the Ark. Inside the box were the two stone tablets.

The Fall of Jericho

When Moses was very old, God instructed him to go up Mount Nebo in the land of Moab. 'From there,' He said, 'you will see the land of Canaan which I will give to the people of Israel. You will see it only from a distance, for you yourself will not enter it.'

Moses blessed the people and went up the mountain and saw the promised land. Then he died and was buried in the land of Moab. The Israelites mourned him for thirty days, for there had not been a prophet like him before; no other prophet had spoken to God face to face, and no other had performed the wonders which Moses had done through the power of God.

Before Moses died, God had told him who was to be his successor. It was a man named Joshua, the son of Nun, who had been Moses's right-hand man during the wanderings in the desert. He was a skilful commander and a man of great faith and courage.

At the start of his leadership God gave Joshua an important message. 'I will be with you as I was with Moses,' He said. 'Be strong and of good courage, and make sure you obey the laws which Moses gave you. If you study My laws and obey them, then you will succeed. Never fear, and remember I will be with you wherever you go.'

Joshua took over command and found that there were two big obstacles in the way of progress to Canaan. First there was the River Jordan to be crossed, and then there was the city of Jericho to pass. He decided he had better find out how difficult this would be, so he sent two men secretly to spy out the land and especially the city of Jericho. They went and found lodgings in Jericho in the house of a woman named Rahab who was willing to help them. She took them up on to the flat roof of her house, which was built against the city walls, and there she hid them under some flax which she had put out to dry.

The King of Jericho heard there were some Israelites in his city and he sent an urgent message to Rahab saying, 'Bring out those men who are lodging with you, for they have come to spy.'

Rahab looked at the king's messengers and said, 'Some men did come to lodge at my house, but I don't know what country they came from. They left when it got dark, before the city gates closed. I don't know which way they went, but if you hurry after them, you might overtake them.'

So the king's men chased off towards the River Jordan. Then Rahab went up to the roof and said to the spies, 'I know your God has given you this land. We were all terrified when we heard how He had brought you out of Egypt and dried up the sea for you. I believe your God is the God of heaven and Earth. Will you promise to treat my family as kindly as I have treated you?'

The men promised that, provided she kept their spying mission secret, they would see that she and her family were well treated when the Israelites came to take the city of Jericho.

Then Rahab took the two men to a window on the city-wall side of her house to let them down by a rope. 'Go into the hills', she urged, 'until the king's men are safely out of the way. Hide there for three days and then you can go on safely.'

The spies said to her, 'We will keep our promise.

When we come to take this city, tie a red cord to this window. Then gather your family together here in the house, and as long as they stay here they will not be harmed.' Rahab agreed, and the men slid down the rope. When they had gone, she tied a red cord to the window.

The two men hid in the hills for three days, and the king's men eventually gave up looking for them. Then the spies returned to Joshua and gave him their report.

The next morning the Israelites rose early and went to the edge of the River Jordan, where they camped to await Joshua's orders. Three days later they received these instructions: 'When you see the priests carrying the Ark of the Covenant you are to follow them. Do not get too near the Ark, but stay about 1 km ($\frac{1}{2}$ mile) behind.'

Then God said to Joshua, 'This day the people will see that I am with you just as I was with Moses. When the priests carrying the Ark reach the river, they are to step into the water and stand still.'

The priests and people obeyed, and as soon as the priests stepped into the river, it stopped flowing and began to pile up like a great wall. The priests stood there and the people were able to cross on dry ground. When they were all safely over, God said to Joshua, 'Take twelve men, one from each tribe, and order them to take twelve stones out of the River Jordan, and put them down where you camp for the night.'

The men did so, and Joshua said to them, 'When your children ask what these stones mean, you can tell them how the waters of the Jordan stopped flowing while the Ark of the Covenant crossed the river.'

Joshua had taken note of all that his spies had told him and he was now ready to tackle the city of Jericho. It was surrounded by a high wall, and the gates were kept shut, for fear of the Israelites getting in. But Joshua's people were not intending to go through the gates, for God had given Joshua special instructions for taking the city. They were very strange military instructions. All the Israelites were to march round the outside of the city in silence once a day for six days. Seven priests, each carrying a trumpet, were to lead them, and behind them the Ark of the Covenant was to be carried. The only noise, apart from the tramp of feet, was to be that of the priests blowing their trumpets.

Probably the people of Jericho were puzzled at first; then no doubt they laughed. Here was a silly way to take a city, they thought!

On the seventh day God had instructed Joshua to walk round the city seven times, and when the priests sounded one long loud blast, the Israelites were all to give a great shout. The people obeyed, and when the loud blast on the trumpets was heard, Joshua cried, 'Shout! for God has given you the city!'

The people shouted—and the walls of Jericho crashed to the ground, flat.

Joshua had more instructions for his troops. While the city would be destroyed, Rahab, and her family in the house with her, were to be saved, as the spies had promised. Moreover, the Israelites were not to steal from the city for themselves; all silver and gold and vessels of bronze and iron were to be set aside for God's treasury. Had the Israelites taken loot for themselves, they would have been greedy, and Joshua did not wish to encourage that sort of behaviour. His army must be disciplined.

In the end, the city was burnt, but Rahab and her family were saved, and she became honoured among the Israelites.

Joshua's fame spread throughout the land and people knew that God was with him. However, there was one man among the Israelites who defied Joshua's orders. He rebelled against God and took some of the things which he found in the city and kept them for himself. His name was Achan.

At first Joshua was unaware of what Achan had done, and he sent some men on to the next city, called Ai, to spy out the land. They returned with the news that Ai was not a big city, and that about 3,000 men should be sufficient to take it.

Joshua sent 3,000 men, but to his surprise they failed and were forced to retreat. The men of Ai chased them all away from their gates and killed

about thirty-six of them. The Israelites lost their courage and trembled with fear.

Joshua was ashamed and upset, and he threw himself on the ground in the depths of despair and said to God, 'Lord, why did you bring us across the Jordan? Are we going to be destroyed? We would have been better to have stayed on the other side of the river and been content. What can I say now that the Israelite army has turned its back on its enemy—and not a big enemy. Everybody will get to hear of it and we'll be surrounded.

'Get up, Joshua!' God ordered. 'Why have you fallen to the ground like this? The Israelites have broken the covenant which they had with Me and have stolen from the city of Jericho. They have lied about it and have put the stolen goods among their own belongings. This is why they cannot stand up to their enemies, and they will not be able to do so until the stolen things are restored.'

Then God told Joshua how he was to pick out the man who had sinned. Although only one person had sinned, God was teaching the Israelites to be a whole nation. In this way they were all responsible for the sin of one of their number. If the sin went unpunished it would spread to other people who would find it easier to sin themselves.

Achan had kept quiet about his stolen goods, because he thought that no one would find out.

The next morning, under God's instructions, Joshua lined up the Israelites and brought them forward tribe by tribe—and he picked out the tribe of Judah.

Then he brought forward each clan of that tribe,

and out of them he picked the clan of Zerah.

Then he brought forward each family of that clan, and the family of Zabdi was picked out.

Lastly he brought forward Zabdi's household, man by man, and picked out Achan.

'Tell the truth before God and give praise to Him,' said Joshua to Achan. 'What is it that you have done?'

Achan answered, 'I have sinned against the Lord God. Among the things we seized I saw a beautiful cloak, some silver and a bar of gold, and I wanted them so much that I took them and buried them in the earth under my tent.'

He looked miserably at Joshua who sent men to Achan's tent, and there they found the goods, just as he had said. Joshua then took Achan and the goods out to the Valley of Achor. 'Why did you bring all this trouble on us?' he asked.

Then Achan was put to death for his sin.

After the punishment of Achan, Joshua and the Israelites were able to conquer the city of Ai, after which they went on to take other cities in the land of Canaan. The Book of Joshua in the Bible gives full details of their travels and campaigns.

At Shechem, just before Joshua died, he gathered together all the tribes of Israel, and reminded them of all that God had done for them. He warned them to fear God and ended with a very famous command: 'Choose this day whom you will serve. As for me and my house, we will serve the Lord.'

The people promised that they would serve God too, and Joshua warned them not to forsake Him and serve other gods instead.

Gideon

After Joshua's death, many of the Israelites forgot about their promise to serve God, and began to worship heathen gods. Because of this, they often suffered, and were involved in battles. Among their enemies were the Midianites, a wandering tribe of desert-dwellers who were always ready to raid and make off with what they could steal. They even conquered the Israelites and ruled over them for seven years during which they descended in swarms like locusts and took the Israelites' animals and destroyed their crops. The Israelites were powerless against them and were driven to living in caves and dens in the hills.

One day, one of the Israelites, a young and timid man named Gideon, was secretly threshing some wheat in a winepress—a shallow pit in the ground from which the grape juice ran into vats. It was not a good place to thresh wheat, for there was no wind to blow away the husks, but Gideon did not want to be seen by the Midianites in case they came and stole his wheat. He knew they were quite capable of murder to get what they wanted.

It was hot work and Gideon worked as quietly as he could. Suddenly he looked up and there, sitting under a nearby oak tree, was a man. He was an angel, but Gideon did not know this.

The angel said, 'The Lord is with you, mighty man of valour.'

Gideon was amazed. He did not feel at all like a mighty man; so he said to the angel, 'Sir, if the Lord is with us, why are all these terrible things happening to us? I've heard about all the wonderful things He did for our fathers and how He brought them out of Egypt, but now it seems He has left us to the mercy of the men of Midian.'

The angel answered with a message from God. 'Go in your strength. I am sending you to rescue Israel from the Midianites.'

'Me?' said Gideon, hardly able to believe his ears. 'But how can I save Israel? My family is the weakest of the whole tribe, and I am the least important member of the family. How can I do anything?'

God answered through the angel, 'I will be with you, so you will be able to conquer the Midianites as if they had only been one man.'

Gideon began to feel that, with God's strength, he could be strong, but he was still not too sure about it, so he said to the angel, 'If this is really so, will you give me some sign or proof? But first let me bring you some food.'

The angel promised to stay until Gideon returned, and Gideon brought meat, unleavened bread and broth, and placed them on a rock. The angel touched the food with his staff, and immediately a flame of fire sprang up and burnt them. Then the angel disappeared.

Gideon realized that this was indeed a sign from God, and he cried out, 'I have seen the angel of the Lord!'

'Peace be to you. Do not be afraid; you will not die,' said the voice of God. So Gideon built an altar there and named it, 'The Lord is peace'.

That night God told Gideon to tear down the altar of the heathen god Baal and to cut down the wooden idol of the goddess Asherah, which the people had been worshipping. In their place he was to build an altar to Him.

With God's help, Gideon did this and, before long, many people had heard about him and

flocked to join him. He attracted a large number of followers and the day came when he was ready to attack the Midianites, whose camp lay to the north, below them in the valley.

God said to Gideon, 'Your army is too big. The men must not think that they have conquered the Midianites by their own strength. They must know that it is because I am with them. Make an announcement that anyone who feels afraid may go home.'

Gideon did so, and 22,000 men went, leaving Gideon with 10,000 which was still quite a large force.

But God said, 'You still have too many men; take them down to the water's edge to drink, and I will test them there.'

Gideon obeyed and God said, 'Separate those who lap the water from those who get down on their knees to drink.'

About 300 of the men scooped up the water with their hands and lapped it. All the others who got down on their knees to drink were sent home. It may have been that those who lapped the water were quick to return to their ranks, while those who knelt down could not be trusted to be constantly on the look-out. The reason is not given, but God said, 'I will give you the victory over the Midianites with these 300 men.'

That same night God commanded Gideon, 'Arise and attack the camp. If you feel afraid, take your servant along with you and go and listen to what is being said.'

Gideon went along to the edge of the enemy camp and listened. There he heard a man telling a friend about a dream he had had. 'I dreamt a loaf of barley bread rolled into our camp and hit a tent,' he said.

His friend replied, 'It is the sword of Gideon, the Israelite, and it must mean that God has given him the victory over our army!'

Somewhat encouraged, Gideon returned to his own camp and divided his men into three companies. He gave each man a trumpet and a jar, inside which was hidden a torch. Then he told the men, 'Follow me and do as I do. When my company reaches the edge of the camp and we blow our trumpets, you do the same.'

Just before midnight the Israelites crept out, and when they reached the Midianite camp they stood in a ring around it. At a sign from Gideon, they all blew their trumpets and broke the jars they were holding. Each man held up a flaming torch in his left hand, and with his right hand he held and blew loudly on his trumpet. And they shouted, 'The sword of the Lord and of Gideon!'

At this sudden noise and the sight of the flames round them, the men of Midian were thrown into a panic. They fled from their camp, even attacking one another, and the Israelites chased after them.

Finally they were defeated, and the people of Israel were grateful to Gideon.

'Rule over us,' they besought him, 'and after you your son and your grandson, for you have rescued us from the Midianites.'

'No,' replied Gideon. 'I will not rule over you, nor will my son. The one to be your ruler is God.'

Samson and the Philistines

Some time later, the Philistines ruled over Israel, where there lived an Israelite named Manoah and his wife who, after being childless for many years, had had a son. An angel visited the boy's mother before his birth and told her that the child would be a Nazarite.

A Nazarite was one who was specially dedicated to God's service for a certain length of time. Such men did not cut their hair until the period of the vow was over, nor did they drink strong drink nor anything which came from the grapevine.

This boy was named Samson, and he grew up to be one of the strongest men of Israel. So strong was he that one day, when a lion sprang out at him, he tore it to pieces with his bare hands.

Later he passed that same place on his way to Timnah, where he was going to marry a Philistine girl; his parents would have preferred that he married a girl from among their own people, but Samson did not agree.

As he passed the spot where he had killed the lion, he noticed a swarm of bees and some honey in its dried-up carcass. He scraped out some of the honey and ate it as he went along.

The wedding ceremony lasted a week. There were thirty young men there and, during the celebrations, Samson asked them a riddle. He said, 'If you can tell me the answer to this riddle within the seven days of the feast, I will give you each a linen garment and a feast-day garment; if you can't tell me, then you are each to give such garments to me.'

The young men agreed. 'Ask us the riddle, then,' they said.

Samson said, 'Out of the eater came forth something to eat. Out of the strong came something sweet.'

By the third day the men still had no idea what the answer was. So on the fourth day they went to Samson's wife, and asked her to find the answer and tell them. At first Samson wouldn't tell her, but on the seventh day he did, and she told the young men. Before sunset that day, the young men gave him the answer, 'What is sweeter than honey? What is stronger than a lion?'

Samson was not a good loser and he was very angry that the riddle had been solved. He gave the thirty men their garments, and went back in hot fury to his father's house, leaving his wife behind.

After a while, he returned, hoping to see his wife, but her father would not allow him in. So, in a bad temper, Samson burnt up all the corn in the Philistines' cornfields.

Wicked deeds create more wickedness, and when the Philistines found out who had burnt their corn, they set fire to Samson's father-in-law's house and caused the death of both the old man and Samson's wife.

This in turn caused more trouble, and Samson fiercely attacked the Philistines, killing many of them. Then he went off and lived in a cave.

He was such a source of trouble that the men of Judah went to him one day and said, 'We have come to bind you and hand you over to the Philistines.'

Samson said, 'I only did to them what they did to me.'

The men of Judah tied him up with ropes and

took him to where the Philistines were waiting. Suddenly God's power came upon Samson and he broke through the ropes as easily as though they had been made of flax. He picked up the jawbone of an ass and slew many of the Philistines. Then he made his escape.

One day Samson was staying at Gaza, and when the people heard about it, they decided that this was their chance to capture him. 'He is here for the night,' they said, 'so let us wait until morning to seize him.'

But Samson only stayed until midnight; then he crept out of the city—and took the city gates with him! Once again he had escaped capture.

Samson and Delilah

Some time after this, Samson fell in love with a woman named Delilah, and the lords of the Philistines planned how they might capture him through her. 'Find out what it is that makes him so strong,' they said to her, 'and then we shall be able to overpower him. We will pay you for the information.'

Delilah did her best, but Samson merely teased her and showed off his great feats of strength. He let her tie him up in various ways, saying that he would then be as weak as any man, but it was not true, and he broke loose each time very easily.

At last Delilah said, 'How can you say you love me when you keep making a fool of me like this?'

And she continued to ask him about his source of strength, day after day, until he became so tired of her questioning that he told her the truth. 'I am a Nazarite,' he said, 'and my hair has never been cut. If it were, my strength would go and I would be as weak as any man.'

Hastily Delilah sent to the lords of the Philistines and said that she had at last discovered the secret of Samson's strength. The Philistines came, bringing money with which to pay Delilah.

When Samson had gone to sleep, Delilah called a man to come and cut off his hair. When he awoke, she teased him that his strength had gone, but he did not believe her. It was quite true, however, and the Philistines were able to capture him. They blinded him and took him to prison where they made him work in the grinding mill. However, while he was there his hair started to grow again.

Some time later, the Philistines held a festival to honour their god, Dagon, and to celebrate the fact that they had at last caught Samson. During the festivities they brought him out so that they might mock him, and they stood him between the two main pillars which supported the building.

Then Samson prayed to God to give him strength one more time; he put a hand on each of the pillars and pushed. 'Let me die with the Philistines,' he cried, and the whole building crashed down, killing many of the people there, including Samson himself.

Ruth

In Bethlehem there lived a man called Elimelech with his wife Naomi and their two sons. They were not rich or important, but they were happy. Their only serious worry was that there was a famine in the land and it was very difficult to get enough to eat. It grew so bad that at last they decided they would have to leave the country and go and look for food somewhere else.

So they set off on foot for Moab, a distance of about 80 km (54 miles). When they arrived they soon grew to like their new home and thought they would remain there, but it was not long before Elimelech died, leaving Naomi to support her two sons.

In time the sons married two Moabite girls, named Orpah and Ruth, fine girls of good character, who gave Naomi great contentment. For about ten years they all continued to live happily, and then tragedy struck again and both the sons died. Naomi now only had Orpah and Ruth, but both the girls were very fond of her and did all they could for her.

Some time later, Naomi heard that the famine was over in her country and she decided it would be wise to go back. She started out, and Orpah and Ruth went with her. Then Naomi remembered that the girls were Moabites and would be leaving their own country. 'Go back home to your own mothers,' she said, 'and may God deal kindly with you and make it possible for you to marry again.'

She kissed them goodbye, but the girls did not want to leave her. 'No,' they said, 'we will go with you to your people.'

Naomi implored them again that it would be better for them to stay in their own country, and at last Orpah agreed to go back. 'Look,' said Naomi to Ruth, 'your sister-in-law has gone back; why don't you go too?'

Ruth refused and said, 'Don't ask me to leave you; for where you go I will go, and where you lodge I will lodge; your people shall be my people and your God my God; only death will part me from you.'

When Naomi saw that Ruth was so determined to stay with her, she said no more, and the two of them went on to Bethlehem. The people in Bethlehem were very pleased to see Naomi again, but very sad when they heard of all that had happened to her, and how she had lost not only her husband, but both her sons also.

The barley harvest was just beginning in Bethlehem and Ruth decided she must go out and work in the fields in order to keep both of them. So she went into one of the fields. It was the kindly custom of the reapers to leave some grain round the edges of the field so that the poor might come and gather it. This was called 'gleaning' and this is what Ruth did.

It so happened that the field in which she was gleaning belonged to a man named Boaz. When Boaz noticed Ruth, he asked some of his workers who she was. When they had told him her story, he called her over and said, 'I've heard about your kindness in not leaving your mother-in-law. Don't go and glean in another field; you can stay here with my maidens, and I will see that no harm comes to you. When you feel thirsty, you may drink from these water jars here.'

'You are very kind, sir,' said Ruth gratefully.

Boaz then asked her to share the meal with his workers; and when work started again, he told the workers to let her glean among the sheaves and to pull out and drop some extra barley from their bundles for Ruth to pick up.

Ruth worked on until evening and found that she had nearly 10 kg (22 lb) of barley. Joyfully she took it back to Naomi.

'How did you get all this?' asked Naomi. 'Where have you been working?'

'In a field belonging to a man named Boaz,' said Ruth.

'Boaz!' exclaimed Naomi, 'but he is one of our close relatives!'

'He said I could work there until they have finished the harvest' said Ruth, and Naomi was pleased to hear it.

So every day Ruth went to work in Boaz's fields until all the barley and wheat had been gathered in. She got to know Boaz very well.

Now it was the custom in those days that if a man died leaving no children, his brother or next-of-kin had to marry the widow in order that there should be an heir; he had also to buy the dead man's land in order to keep it in the family.

Boaz was a close relative and therefore he felt some responsibility for Ruth; but he was not her closest relative. So he said to her, 'Tomorrow we will find out whether your closest relative will take on responsibility for you. If he will, then well and good; but if not, then I will do so myself and marry you.'

The next day Boaz went up to the city gate, where people gathered, and where he knew he would catch Ruth's closest relative. At the gate legal business was carried on and there were plenty of people about to act as witnesses to any deals or agreements that were made.

When the man came by, Boaz called him over and asked him to sit down. He also asked ten of the city leaders to come and sit with him too. Then he said to Ruth's relative, 'You know that our relative Naomi has come back from Moab, having lost her husband and sons? As you are the nearest relative, you can buy the piece of land which belonged to Elimelech. If you do not want it, say so, and I will buy it.'

'I will buy it,' said the man.

'Then, according to the law, you must also take Ruth, the widow of Naomi's eldest son, so that the field will stay in the family of the dead man,' said Boaz.

The man thought about it and then he said, 'In that case I will not buy, because the arrangement would interfere with the rights of my own children. You may buy it.'

In those days, a sale or exchange of property was settled by the man who was selling taking off his sandal and handing it to the man who was buying. This was a sign that possession was taken. So the closest relative took off his sandal and handed it to Boaz.

Boaz looked at the city leaders and at the other people who had gathered round, and said, 'You are witnesses that today I have bought from Naomi the land which belonged to Elimelech and his sons, and that Ruth becomes my wife.'

So Boaz married Ruth, and in due time they had a son. The child was named Obed and, years later, he too had a grandson who was to become the great King David.

Samuel

In Ramah, not far from Jerusalem, there lived a man named Elkanah. He had two wives, which was not uncommon in those days; one, named Peninnah, had children, but the other, named Hannah, had none.

Each year the whole family went up to Shiloh, where the Tabernacle was placed, to offer sacrifices; and each year Hannah felt sadder and sadder because she had no children to take with her. Peninnah was not kind about it and used to tease her, so much so that Hannah often wept.

One year Hannah went unhappily into the house of the Lord at Shiloh, and prayed to God that He would send her a son. 'I will dedicate him to You for his whole life,' she said.

Eli, the old priest there, saw her distress and her lips moving, and thought at first that she must be drunk. But when he went up to her, Hannah told him of her trouble. 'Go in peace,' said Eli, 'and may God answer your prayer.'

God did. In due course Hannah had a fine baby boy, whom she named Samuel. As soon as he was old enough, Hannah fulfilled her promise and took him to the house of the Lord at Shiloh. 'Do you remember me?' she asked Eli. 'This is the child whom God sent to me in answer to my prayer. I have brought him here to dedicate him to the Lord.'

So Samuel became a helper to old Eli, and Eli was very glad of his aid. He did have two sons of his own, but they were worthless and dishonest men who had no respect for God or His house.

Every year Hannah came and saw Samuel, and brought him a new robe; and God blessed her further by sending her three more sons and two daughters.

Time passed and Eli grew old and was almost blind. He slept in his own room in the Lord's house, while Samuel slept near the Covenant Box in the sanctuary.

One night, after Samuel had fallen asleep, he was suddenly awakened by a voice calling, 'Samuel! Samuel!'

Thinking it was Eli, Samuel got up and ran to the old man. 'Here I am,' he said. 'You called me.'

'No,' said Eli, 'I did not call. Go back to bed.'

Samuel obeyed, but before long he heard the voice again, 'Samuel!'

Again he got up and ran to Eli, but Eli said, 'I did not call, my son; go and lie down again.'

Samuel did so, and the voice called him a third time, and Samuel, feeling puzzled, went again to Eli. By now, Eli had begun to understand that it was the voice of God who was calling Samuel. So he said to the boy, 'Go back, and if you hear the voice again, say, "Speak, Lord, for your servant is listening."'

Samuel returned to bed, and sure enough, the voice called again, 'Samuel! Samuel!', and Samuel replied as Eli had told him. Then God gave Samuel a sad message. He told him that Eli's family would have to suffer punishment because of the wickedness of Eli's sons.

Samuel stayed in bed until morning, when he got up and opened the doors of the house of the Lord. At first he was afraid to tell Eli of God's message, but Eli asked him, and Samuel told him everything.

Eli looked sad, but said, 'He is the Lord, He will do what He knows is best.'

Samuel the Prophet

Samuel grew up to be a prophet, a fine man who preached God's word. Not everyone listened, however; there were still many who worshipped idols and refused to obey God's laws.

Then the Philistines went to war with the Israelites and thousands of Israelite men were killed, including Eli's two wicked sons. Worse still, in many people's eyes, the Philistines captured the Covenant Box and took it away. The people were shocked, and when Eli heard about it, he was so stunned that he fell backwards and broke his neck and died.

The Philistines put the Covenant Box beside their god Dagon, but Dagon fell forward and was smashed to pieces. Then plagues came upon them, and after seven months they wished they had never taken the Covenant Box and decided they had better return it. Together with some gifts, they put it in a cart, to which they yoked two cows, and sent it on its way back to the Israelites.

How delighted the Israelites were to see the Covenant Box come back! They chopped up the cart on which it came and made firewood, and had a great sacrifice with much rejoicing.

Samuel knew that Israel would not prosper while they worshipped idols and had no faith in the true God. One day he called the people together and said, 'If you will return to the Lord with all your heart, and serve Him only, then He will rescue you from the Philistines.' Then Samuel led the people to fast and to confess that they had sinned against God.

Meanwhile, the Philistines were preparing for another battle and, just as Samuel was offering a sacrifice, they came to attack. But God thundered from heaven against them, and they were thrown into a panic. The men of Israel pursued them, and the Philistines were beaten.

Samuel and Saul

One day, when Samuel was an old man, the people went to him and said, 'You are old, and your two sons are not good leaders; therefore will you appoint a king for us.'

Samuel told them all that a king would mean, and how difficult life would be under him. He would take the men for his armies, they and the women would be forced to work and to pay taxes, and they would not have nearly so much freedom as they had now. He would take their best land, and their servants and their best animals too. But the people insisted that they wanted a king. Samuel felt that their only king should be God, and he asked His help.

Now, there lived a rich man named Kish, who was of the tribe of Benjamin, and he had a handsome son named Saul. Saul was a head taller than most other people, and so he was easily noticed in a crowd. It so happened that Kish's donkeys had wandered away and were lost; so Kish said to Saul, 'Take one of the servants and go and look for those donkeys.'

Saul and the servant set off, and walked for about three days, but still they did not find the animals. Finally Saul said, 'Let's go back, or my father will start worrying about us, as well as the donkeys.'

'Just a moment,' said the servant. 'There is a holy man living in this area; let us just see if he can help us.' So they set off for the town in which the holy man lived.

The holy man was none other than Samuel and, on the day before, God had told him that he would send a man whom Samuel was to anoint king of Israel. When Samuel saw Saul coming towards him, God said to him, 'This is the man.'

Saul went up to Samuel and asked where the holy man lived. 'I am he,' said Samuel. 'Come and eat with me; and don't worry about the donkeys, for they have been found. The man the people of Israel have wanted so much is you.'

'But I belong to the smallest tribe in Israel—the tribe of Benjamin,' said Saul, 'and my family is not very important.'

Samuel took Saul and his servant inside, where there were about thirty people, and they all sat

down to a meal. After this Saul was given a bed for the night—up on the roof, where it was cooler. He felt very puzzled.

Next morning, Saul and his servant were up early, ready to be on their way; Samuel went to the edge of the town with them. There he said, 'Tell your servant to go on ahead.'

When the servant had gone, Samuel took a jar of oil and poured it on Saul's head saying, 'The Lord has anointed you to be ruler of his people Israel.' And he gave him certain signs to prove that it was true.

King Saul began his reign well, and although there were some people who did not at first respect him, when they found he was a good leader, they began to obey him. Later on, however, he became self-willed and arrogant, and did not live up to the high hopes which people had of him.

Before long, the Philistines were again assembling to fight the Israelites. They mustered a huge army of war chariots and horsemen and countless soldiers, and many of the Israelites were terrified and deserted Saul.

Samuel had told Saul to wait seven days for him to come, but Saul thought he knew better and when he saw the people scattering from him, he began to offer a sacrifice without waiting for Samuel. As soon as he had finished, Samuel arrived. He was displeased and told Saul that this disobedience would cost him his kingship, and that God would find another man to become ruler in his place.

The battles against the Philistines went on, but Saul did not continue to be a strong king, for he had disobeyed God's commands.

Then God said to Samuel, 'Take some oil and go to Bethlehem, to a man whose name is Jesse, for I have chosen one of his sons to be the next king.'

Samuel was rather worried about this. 'How can I go?' he asked. 'If Saul hears about it he will kill me.'

'Take a calf with you,' said God, 'and go there to offer sacrifice. Then I will show you what to do.'

Samuel did as God had instructed, and when the elders of the town came out to meet him, he invited them to join in the sacrifice.

When he saw Jesse and his family, he particularly noticed his son Eliab, and thought to himself, 'Surely this is the man whom the Lord has chosen.'

But God said to Samuel, 'Do not just look at his appearance or his height, because he is not the man. I, the Lord, do not see as men see. Men look at the outward appearance, but I look at a man's heart.'

Then Jesse brought out his son Abinadab, but Samuel knew that he was not the chosen one either.

Seven of Jesse's sons came out to Samuel, but the Lord did not choose any of them. 'Are all your sons here?' asked Samuel. 'Are there no more?'

'There is only the youngest,' said Jesse, 'but he is out looking after the sheep.'

'Send and fetch him,' said Samuel, 'for we won't start the sacrifice until he comes.'

So Jesse's youngest son, David, was brought in. He was a handsome youth, with beautiful eyes; and God said to Samuel, 'This is the one I have chosen; anoint him.'

Samuel took the horn of oil and anointed David in front of his brothers who may have thought that this meant David would become Samuel's follower, and in time become a prophet like himself. God's spirit came to David on that day, and Samuel then returned to Ramah.

Meanwhile, evil forces had taken charge of Saul, who often became depressed and even violent. His servants thought it might help if he could be soothed with music, so they said, 'Give us the order, sir, and we will find someone who can play the harp. Then when the evil spirit torments you, the musician can play his harp and you will be all right again.' Saul agreed, and asked for a musician to be brought to court.

One of the servants had an idea. 'There is a man named Jesse in Bethlehem,' he said, 'and he has a son who is a good musician. He is also brave and handsome.'

'Go and bring him,' Saul ordered.

Messengers went to Jesse, and Jesse sent David to the king's court, with gifts of a young goat, a donkey laden with bread, and a leather skin full of wine.

Saul liked David, and sent a message to Jesse to say how pleased he was with his son. From then on, whenever Saul felt tormented by the evil feelings, David was sent for and would bring his harp and play it; and Saul would soon feel better again.

David and Goliath

The fierce battles with the Philistines continued, and at last the Israelite and Philistine armies found themselves facing one another across the mountains with the Valley of Elah between them.

One morning there came out from the Philistine camp two men. The first was a soldier carrying a shield, but it was the man behind him who made the Israelites gasp with horror. He was an enormous giant of a man, nearly 3 m (10 ft) tall, and dressed in a bronze helmet and heavy bronze armour. He wore a bronze coat of mail, bronze armour on his legs, and he carried a huge bronze javelin. His great thick spear had a wicked-looking head of iron on it. The name of this giant was Goliath, and the Israelites trembled at the sight of him.

He stood and glared across at the ranks of the Israelites; then he roared across to them in a terrible voice, 'What do you think you are all doing there lining up for battle? I am a Philistine and you are Saul's slaves. Choose one of your number and send him to fight me! If he can kill me, then we will be your slaves; but if I win, then you shall be our slaves and serve us. I dare you to send somebody to do battle with me!'

The Israelites were terrified and did not dare to send anybody. They were pretty sure who would win when they looked at Goliath! No one in their army could have a hope of beating him; so no one went.

Goliath continued to roar his challenge at them. Every morning and every evening for the next forty days he bellowed across at the Israelites. Saul and his army were dismayed and felt more and more discouraged.

Now Jesse was too old to go and fight in Saul's army, but his three eldest sons had gone—Eliab, Abinadab and the third son whose name was Shammah. David was still taking care of his father's sheep.

One day Jesse said to David, 'Go to your brothers in the army, and take them some food—some roasted grain and loaves of bread. See how they are getting on, and bring back something to prove to me that they are well. Take ten cheeses for their commanding officer also.'

Early next morning David got up, ready for his journey. He left someone else in charge of the sheep and set off with the food which his father had given him.

When he reached the camp, both armies were just preparing for battle. David handed the food to the officer in charge of supplies, and ran in among the soldiers to find his brothers. As he was chatting to them, Goliath came out for his twice-daily challenge to the Israelites, clanking his armour and roaring defiance. The Israelite soldiers were becoming worn down by this performance, and they ran away, trembling.

David asked the soldiers near him what it was all about and they said, 'King Saul has promised a big reward to anyone who kills this giant, and he will also give him his daughter to marry and free him of taxes.'

'Who is this heathen Philistine to dare to defy the army of the living God?' said David scornfully.

Some of the soldiers told Saul what David had said, and the king sent for him. 'Your majesty,' said David, 'I'll volunteer to go and fight this giant. No one should feel afraid of him.'

'No, no,' said King Saul. 'You are only a boy. He's been a fighting soldier all his life.'

'But sir,' said David, 'I look after my father's sheep, and if a bear or a lion comes to seize a lamb, I rescue the lamb, and kill the bear or lion. I've killed many such, and I'll kill this Philistine. The Lord has saved me from lions and bears, and He will save me from this Philistine.'

Saul was impressed. 'All right,' he said, 'you can go and try. No one else has offered. You may wear my helmet and my armour. And God be with you.'

When David was dressed in Saul's armour, he found he could not walk in it; it was so heavy, and he was not used to wearing armour. So he took it all off and went to meet Goliath with only his stick and his sling. On the way he picked up five smooth stones from the stream and put them in his shepherd's bag.

As soon as Goliath saw who was coming to fight him, he laughed with scorn. 'What's the stick for, boy?' he shouted. 'Do you think that I am a dog?'

David replied, 'You are coming to me with might—your sword and spear and javelin. But I come to you in the name of the living God, the God

of Israel whom you have defied. I will defeat you, and the whole world will know that Israel has the true God.'

With that, he ran towards Goliath, taking one of the stones from his bag. He aimed it straight at Goliath's forehead, and it struck the giant who fell on his face on the ground. David ran over and, taking Goliath's own sword from its sheath, he killed the giant.

When the Philistines saw what had happened to their champion, they turned and fled, hotly pursued by the Israelites who won a great victory.

David and Jonathan

After his great victory over mighty Goliath David was taken into the presence of King Saul. While there, he met Saul's son, Jonathan, and came to like him very much. A firm bond grew up between them and they swore eternal friendship. Saul treated David almost like another son, and David did so well in all the missions that he was given that Saul made him a commander in the army, and everyone was delighted with the news as David was very popular.

When the army returned home after their victory over the Philistines, the people danced and sang for joy. 'Saul has slain his thousands, but David his tens of thousands,' they cried. Now Saul did not like to hear this and he began to grow jealous of David. He even began to be afraid of his success. But the people all loved David because he was such a great leader.

In due time, David married Saul's daughter, Michal; but Saul grew more and more moody and had many attacks of bitter jealousy against David for no reason at all.

One day, Jonathan found out that Saul was actually plotting to kill David, so he warned David to go and hide. 'I will talk to my father, and if I find out anything, I will tell you,' he said to David. Then he went to his father, and reminded him of all the great things David had done. Saul listened and understood, and decided that David should not be killed. So David came out of hiding and served the king once more as faithfully as he had always done.

It was not for long, however; another time, Saul's jealous mood returned, and he hurled a spear at David as he was playing the harp. David managed to dodge it and so was not hurt. That night Saul sent some men to David's house to kill him; but David's wife, Michal, heard of it, and let David down from a window so that he escaped. Then she took the figure of an idol from the house and put it in the bed, so that when the soldiers came looking for David, they were tricked and David was able to make his escape in the midst of the confusion.

Naturally, David grew very worried about these attempts on his life, and he asked Jonathan one day, 'What have I done? What crime have I committed that makes your father want to kill me? I have always been his loyal servant.'

Jonathan wanted to do all he could to help his friend and thought that his father would tell him what he was about to do; but David thought that as Saul knew he and Jonathan were friends, he would not tell Jonathan anything about this plots against David.

The next day was the Feast of the New Moon, and David was supposed to dine with the king. He decided not to go, but to hide in the fields instead. He said to Jonathan, 'If your father notices that I am not there, tell him that I have gone to Bethlehem to attend the yearly sacrifice there for all the family. If he says "All right", then I'll be safe. If, however, he is angry, then you will know that he plans some evil against me.'

Jonathan agreed to let David know what happened. Saul did notice David's absence and asked Jonathan about it. When Jonathan said David had gone home to Bethlehem, Saul flew into a rage and said, 'Go and bring him here immediately, for he must die!'

'But why?' asked Jonathan reasonably. 'What wrong has he done?'

For an answer Saul angrily threw his spear at Jonathan, but did not hurt him.

Jonathan was upset and ashamed of his father's evil mood, and the next day he went out into the fields and let David know that he must flee to escape Saul's anger. 'God be with you,' said Jonathan to David. 'The Lord God will be with us and our descendants for ever.'

For a long time there was war between Saul and his men and David and his followers. Yet on two occasions when he had a chance to kill Saul, David would not do so; no doubt he remembered that Saul had once treated him like a son, and, moreover, had he not been anointed king by Samuel, acting on God's instructions?

In the end, King Saul was killed in a battle against the Philistines. Three of his sons were killed in the same battle, and one of them was Jonathan, David's beloved friend.

After this, David was made King of Judah, and later King of the United Kingdoms of Israel and Judah, and he reigned for forty years as a good and wise king.

Mephibosheth

In his later years, David wondered if there were any members of Saul's family still alive. One of Saul's servants, named Ziba, told him that a son of Jonathan's, named Mephibosheth, was still living, but that he was crippled. He had been only five years old when his father was killed in the battle and when his nurse had heard the news, she had picked Mephibosheth up and fled. In her haste, she dropped the child, injuring his feet, so that Mephibosheth had been lame ever since and could not get about very easily.

David remembered his old friend, Jonathan, and felt he would like to show kindness to his son. So he sent for him. Mephibosheth felt a little afraid when he heard that the king wanted to see him, but he went to the palace and bowed low before David. 'I am your servant, sir,' he said a little nervously.

'Don't be afraid,' said David. 'I want to be kind to you for the sake of your father Jonathan, who was my great friend. I am going to give you back the lands which belonged to your grandfather, Saul; and you will always be welcome to eat at my table.'

Mephibosheth was overawed. 'But I am useless,' he said. 'Why should you be so good to me when I cannot repay you?'

David remembered that Mephibosheth was lame and therefore would find it hard to work, so he said to Ziba, 'You and your sons and your servants will farm the land for Mephibosheth, and bring him the produce from it.'

Ziba replied, 'I will do all that my lord the king commands.'

So, because of David's kindness, Mephibosheth ate at the king's table, and became like one of the king's sons.

David was a wise king and a brave soldier, but because he was human, he also did many things which were wrong, as well as many which were right.

The Wisdom of Solomon

King David was now a very old man and people were wondering who would succeed him. His son Absolom was dead, and his eldest surviving son was Adonijah, and some thought that he should be the next king. He even tried to take the throne and get himself crowned king. He was very ambitious and did not think to wait for God to choose someone as He had done with Saul and David.

But two leading men in the kingdom were not on Adonijah's side; they were Zadok the priest and Nathan the prophet, and Nathan spoke to David's wife, Bathsheba, in order to try and find out whom David wished to be the next king. Bathsheba was able to remind David that he had already promised the throne to his son Solomon. So David gave orders that Solomon was to ride on the king's own mule to Gihon, just outside Jerusalem, and that there Zadok and Nathan were to anoint him king. They did as they had been told and, with a loud blow on the trumpet, all the people shouted, 'Long live King Solomon!' Then they played on their pipes and flutes and shouted for joy, making enough noise to shake the earth. There was great excitement.

Adonijah and his followers trembled when they heard the noise, but Solomon said that if Adonijah proved to be a worthy man, not one of the hairs of his head would be touched and that both he and his supporters would be safe.

When David was about to die, he called Solomon to him and gave him much advice. He told him to be strong and to obey God's laws, and that if he did so, then he would prosper in all that he did. Solomon loved God and followed the advice of his father David, but he still offered sacrifices in various places which was against the laws set down in the Ten Commandments.

One day he was at Gibeon, where the Tabernacle was then kept, and he offered many burnt offerings on the altar. That night he had a dream in which the Lord God appeared to him and asked, 'What would you like Me to give you now that you are king?'

Now Solomon was still only a very young man and he had not been king for long. It was not easy to be king after such a great man as David, and he knew there would be a lot to learn. 'I do not know a great deal yet,' said Solomon, 'and there are more people in this kingdom than can be counted. So give me the wisdom I shall need to rule well, so that I shall be able to tell the difference between good and evil and shall be a fair and just ruler over my people.'

God was pleased that Solomon had asked for this, and had not demanded a long life, or riches, or the death of his enemies. He said to Solomon, 'I will give you a wise and an understanding mind, such as no one has had before. Also I will give you gifts for which you have not asked, both riches and honour, so that there will be no other king who can compare with you all your life. If you keep My laws, as your father David did, then I will also give you a long life.'

Not long after this, Solomon's new gift of wisdom was put to the test when two women were brought before him seeking his judgment in a dispute.

One of the women began, 'Your majesty, we are

two women both living in the same house. One day, I gave birth to a baby boy while the other woman was in the house. Then three days later she also gave birth to a baby boy. There was no one else in the house with us; we were on our own during this time.

'Then one night this woman accidentally lay on her baby as she slept and he was smothered and died. She got up, while I was still asleep, and took my baby and put her dead baby in my bed. When I got up in the morning to feed my baby, I saw it was dead; but when I looked more closely, I found that it was not my baby at all but the child of this other woman.'

'No, no,' cried the second woman. 'The living baby is mine and the dead one is yours. You are mistaken.'

'No,' said the first woman, 'the dead child is yours and the living one is mine. I know my own child.'

And they began to argue in front of the king, for they were both very upset. It was a case of one woman's word against another's, and the king was going to need all his wisdom to discover the true facts.

Solomon said, 'Each of you claims that the living baby is hers and that the dead one belongs to the other woman. Bring me a sword.' A sword was brought to the king and he said, 'Cut the living baby in two and let each mother have half. Then each will have a fair share.'

'No, no!' cried the real mother, who loved her baby far too dearly to let such a thing happen to him. 'Let her have the living child, but please don't kill it.'

The other mother, however, was quite agreeable to the king's judgment. 'All right,' she said, 'don't give it to either of us. Cut it in two pieces as you said.'

Then the king knew which was the real mother —the one who would rather someone else brought up her baby than that it should die. 'Give the living child to the first woman,' he said. 'Don't kill it, for it is obvious that she is its mother and that she loves it.'

The news of this judgment spread through the land, and all the people heard of Solomon's wise dealing of such a difficult case. They were full of respect for him and saw that God had given him great wisdom, so that he would rule justly over them all. It seemed that Solomon would indeed prove a worthy successor to his father.

The Wisdom of Solomon

The Building of the Temple

Ever since the Israelites had left Egypt, nearly 500 years earlier, they had had no permanent place of worship. Their Tabernacle, or 'tent-church', had had to be erected wherever they went, and then taken down when they moved on.

King David had always wanted to build a permanent place for God's worship, but because of constant wars and conflict with enemy countries, he was not able to do so. In fact God had told him that it would be built by his son.

Now that the land was more settled and peaceful, King Solomon felt that the time was right to start building. At last the Ark of the Covenant would have a permanent home in Jerusalem.

Everything in the temple, as well as the building itself, was to be of the very best; and if Solomon could not get the best materials from his own country, then he was prepared to import them from other countries. He began by sending a message to his father's old friend Hiram, the King of Tyre, telling him that he was about to begin building a temple for worship. 'Would you, therefore, send your men to cut down some cedars of Lebanon for me,' he asked, 'for none of us here knows how to prepare timber as your men do.'

Solomon knew he would get the best, for cedar of Lebanon was the finest wood available, and there was plenty of it.

King Hiram readily agreed, and sent word that his men would bring the timbers down to the sea, and there they would tie the logs together in great rafts and float them to wherever Solomon directed. He only asked for food for his men in payment.

Then Solomon organized 30,000 men from Israel to start the work, and divided them into three groups of 10,000 men each. Every group was to spend one month in Lebanon and two months back at home in Israel, in turn, so that the work could go on continuously.

There were also 80,000 men in the hillsides quarrying stone for the temple, and another 70,000 whose job it was to haul the prepared stone to Jerusalem. The stones had to be cut and shaped and made quite ready while they were still in the quarry, because there was to be no sound of hammers or axes or any other iron tools on the temple site itself. The temple was a holy place.

It was not to be a huge building, however, for it was intended as a house for God, and not as a place to which large gatherings of people would come. It was to be built, in general, in the style of the Tabernacle, and was to contain two main rooms— the Holy Place and the Holy of Holies.

Inside it was to be 27 m (29 yd) long, 9 m (10 yd) wide and 13.5 m (42 ft) high. In the Holy of Holies there was to be the Ark of the Covenant, containing the two tablets of stone with the Ten Commandments written on them. The cover of the Ark was regarded as the throne of God who was thought of as seated above the two winged creatures whose wings overshadowed it.

In the Holy Place (the outer of the two rooms) there was to be the Altar of Incense and the Table of Shewbread, and ten candlesticks.

Outside in the court, there was to be the Altar of Burnt Offerings, and various vessels used by the priests, including the huge bronze laver resting on the figures of twelve bulls.

Along the sides of the temple there were to be storerooms in which robes and various equipment used for worship would be kept.

The stone walls of the temple were to be covered

inside with carved cedar wood, from floor to ceiling, and the floor was to be of pine. The whole of the inside was to be covered with pure gold. The walls of the main room and the inner room were to be decorated with carvings of winged creatures, trees and flowers, and the doors were to be similarly decorated and covered with gold.

King Solomon enlisted the help of a very clever and skilled worker in bronze. His name was also Hiram and he was put in charge of all the bronze work. Amongst other things, he made two bronze columns which were to be placed in front of the entrance to the temple. At the top each had a capital 2.2 m ($7\frac{1}{4}$ ft) tall, decorated with a design of chains and pomegranates.

The column on the south side of the temple entrance was named Jachin (which sounds like the Hebrew for 'He [God] establishes'); and that on the north side was named Boaz, (which sounds like the Hebrew for 'by His [God's] strength.') Thus they were intended to be symbolic of Israel's faith in God.

Solomon also had furnishings for the temple made in gold—the altar, the ten candlesticks, which stood five on each side of the Holy Place, flowers, lamps, tongs, cups, basins, dishes for incense, and even the hinges for the doors—all were made of pure gold.

It took seven years to build this temple, and it must have looked very beautiful when it was finished. Inside the gold shone gloriously, but no one, except the priests and other ministers ever went inside to see. To Solomon and his builders that did not matter, for the temple was built not merely for men's eyes, but for the glory of God. There the priests would meet Him when they came to worship. When they cast incense upon the coals on the altar, a cloud of sweet-smelling smoke would arise, and the people outside would see it as a sign that God dwelt among them and that they were His people.

When at last the temple was finished, King Solomon ordered all the leaders of the tribes and clans to come before him in Jerusalem. Then, after a ceremony of burnt sacrifices had been offered, the Ark of the Covenant, containing the Ten Commandments, was taken into the temple.

The priests lifted the Ark on its two poles and carried it into the Holy of Holies, while everyone watched. Anyone who stood in the outer room, the Holy Place, could just see the ends of the poles when the priests had set it down. Nothing else could be seen from outside.

As the priests came out of the temple, a great cloud suddenly filled it, so that the priests could not go back inside to carry out their duties. It was said that God's presence had filled the temple.

Then the king addressed the people and asked God's blessing upon them. He told them how his father, David, had planned to build a temple, but that God had said David's son would build it.

Then they had a great festival, lasting seven days, to dedicate the temple, and, on the eighth day, Solomon sent the people home full of joy.

The Queen of Sheba

Now the Queen of Sheba heard reports of Solomon's fame and of his splendid building, and she decided to visit Jerusalem for herself to find out whether or not all that she had heard was true. She was also prepared to test Solomon's wisdom.

Sheba was in south Arabia, and the queen set out for Jerusalem on what was to be a very long journey. She took with her a great number of servants, as well as camels laden with spices, gold and precious stones.

Solomon was no doubt impressed with all this gorgeous procession; but when the queen had asked him all the hard questions she could think of, and he had answered them all, then it was her turn to be impressed. She heard his wise sayings, she saw his buildings, his palace, the food he ate, his officials and servants, their robes, and the sacrifices that were offered in the temple—and she felt quite overcome.

She said to Solomon, 'The reports which I heard of your wisdom and your affairs are quite true, but I did not believe them until I came and saw for myself. I had not heard the half of it! Your wisdom and wealth are far greater than I was told. Praise

be to God who made you the King of Israel, so that you can maintain law and justice.'

King Solomon had a great amount of gold and vast riches, including an ivory throne overlaid with gold. He also had 1,400 chariots and 12,000 horsemen, whom he stationed in other cities besides Jerusalem, and a great fleet of ships which came in every three years bringing him more gold, silver, ivory, apes and peacocks. However, despite his great wealth, it is more usual today to hear of the wisdom of Solomon rather than of his riches.

Elijah

After Solomon's death, the country was again divided into two kingdoms—the tribes of Judah and Benjamin forming the Kingdom of Judah in the south, and the remaining ten tribes forming the Kingdom of Israel in the north. The latter had a succession of kings, but none was very good; these included one of the worst kings ever—Ahab of Israel. He had a wife named Jezebel who was, if anything, worse than he was; they both worshipped idols and put up heathen temples and images, including Baal who was worshipped as a weather-god.

Now, as often happened, God chose someone to pass on His message. This was a prophet called Elijah, who was not afraid of speaking out for God against all the idol-worshippers.

He went straight to Ahab and said there would be no more rain until God (not Baal) said so. This would be a serious matter in any country, but even more so in one with a hot dry climate; God had decided to teach Ahab and his followers that only He had power over sun and rain.

Then God told Elijah to go to the brook called Cherith, where ravens would bring him food each day and he would be able to drink from the stream. This Elijah did, but because there was no rain, after a while the brook dried up.

However, God had a plan for Elijah, and next he told him to go to a place named Zarephath, where there was a widow who would feed him. Elijah obeyed and, when he came to the gates of that city, he saw a woman gathering sticks. In some way he knew that this was the woman to whom God had sent him on his long journey northwards from Cherith. 'Would you please bring me a drink of water and a little bread,' he said to her.

'I haven't any bread,' she replied. 'All I have is a handful of flour in a jar, and a little oil, and I am gathering these sticks so that I may go and prepare a last meal for my son and myself. We have nothing else, and after we have eaten that I fear we shall starve to death.'

'Don't worry,' said Elijah to her. 'Go and prepare the meal for yourself and your son, but bring me a little cake made of the flour; for the Lord God of Israel says that your supply of flour and oil will not run out until He sends rain again on the land.'

She did as Elijah had told her, and found she had enough food for many days. Whenever she thought she had used up the last of the flour or the oil, she always found that there was more in the jar and in the oil jug. Elijah went to lodge at her house and she let him have one of the upstairs rooms for himself.

One day the widow's son became very ill and died. The widow was most upset and decided it was because Elijah was in the house; she thought he may have found out about some sin in her past, and that the death of her son was judgment upon her. 'What have you against me, O man of God?' she said to Elijah.

'Give the boy to me,' said the prophet, and he carried him upstairs and laid him upon his own bed. Then he prayed to God to revive the boy, because he did not want the woman to think she was being punished, for she had been kind to Elijah.

Elijah stretched his arms over the boy three

times and prayed, 'O, Lord God, make this child come back to life.' Then the child started to breathe again, and Elijah took him down to his mother and said, 'See, your son is alive!'

'Now I know that you are a man of God,' said the widow joyfully, 'and that He really speaks through you.'

Elijah and the Prophets of Baal

No rain fell upon the land for three years, and the drought and the famine grew very severe. In the third year God said to Elijah, 'Go to Ahab, and I will send rain.'

About this time Ahab was talking to a man named Obadiah, who was in charge of the palace household. Obadiah was a good man who believed in God, and had even rescued some of God's prophets from the wicked Queen Jezebel when she was about to kill them. He must have found it very difficult working for a man like Ahab.

Ahab said to Obadiah, 'Go out and look at all the springs and riverbeds and see if you can find enough grass anywhere to keep the animals alive.'

Obadiah set off, and on his way whom should he meet but the prophet Elijah coming to see Ahab. 'Go and tell your master that I am here,' said Elijah.

Obadiah was rather fearful. 'The king has been looking for you in every country,' he said, 'and if I tell him you are here, and you have moved on by the time he gets to you, then he will surely kill me.'

'Go and tell him,' said Elijah. 'I promise you I will see him today.'

So Obadiah went and told Ahab, and Ahab set off to meet Elijah. When he saw the prophet he said, 'There you are—the man who is causing all this trouble in Israel!'

'I'm not causing any trouble,' said Elijah; 'it is you and your people who have disobeyed God's commands and are worshipping idols.'

Ahab could not deny this and he did not attempt to.

Elijah went on, 'Order all the people of Israel to come and meet me on Mount Carmel. Bring along the 450 prophets of Baal and the 400 prophets of Asherah whom Queen Jezebel supports.'

Ahab had very little choice. He thought it might be just possible that Elijah's God would send rain, so he gathered the people together.

Elijah looked around at the crowd gathered upon Mount Carmel. 'How long are you going to dither between two ways?' he thundered. 'If the Lord is God, follow Him, but if Baal is god, follow him.'

There was complete silence. The people did not know what to say.

'I am the only prophet of the Lord here,' said Elijah, 'but there are 450 prophets of Baal. Now, bring two bulls for a sacrifice. Let us each take one and put it on the wood, but do not light the fire. Then we shall each pray to our god to send fire, and the one who answers, then he is god.'

The people agreed, and Elijah let the prophets of Baal go first as there were so many of them. They took the bull and prepared it and put it on the wood. Then they cried to Baal from morning until noon, calling, 'O Baal, answer us!' They shouted and danced around, but there was no reply.

'Shout a bit louder,' teased Elijah. 'Perhaps your god has gone on a journey, or perhaps he is asleep. You must waken him.' So the prophets of Baal cried louder and danced about in a frenzy, cutting themselves with their knives and daggers, which was one of their heathen customs. But still there was no answering voice, and no fire.

When they had all worn themselves out, Elijah said, 'Now it is my turn.' The people gathered round him and watched while he repaired the altar which had been torn down. He took twelve stones, one for each of the twelve tribes of Israel, and built it up, and then he dug a trench around it. He put the wood on the altar, and the bull upon the wood. Then he ordered water to be poured over the whole thing, not once, but three times, until the whole trench was full of water, and the wood was soaking wet.

Then he prayed, 'O Lord God, show that You are the true God, so that these people will know You want to bring them back to the true faith.'

Immediately fire came down from heaven, and

burnt up the bull and the wood and the stones and the dust; it even dried up the water that was in the trench. When the people saw this, they were over-awed and fell down on their faces, crying, 'The Lord, He is God; the Lord, He is God.'

Sieze the prophets of Baal,' commanded Elijah. 'Let none of them escape! They have led you wrongly.' The prophets were seized and put to death, by which act the people really proved that they knew they had a new god.

Then Elijah turned to Ahab and said, 'Go and eat, for I hear that rain is coming.' While Ahab was going, Elijah and his servant climbed up to the top of Mount Carmel. 'Go and look towards the sea,' said Elijah, and the servant went.

'I see nothing,' he said.

'Go again', said Elijah, 'seven times.'

At the seventh time, the servant returned and said, 'I saw a little cloud, no bigger than a man's hand, rising up out of the sea.'

'Then go and tell King Ahab to get into his chariot and go home before the rain stops him,' said Elijah.

Soon the sky was covered with dark clouds and the wind began to blow, and great heavy raindrops started to fall. Elijah fastened his robes about him, and ran ahead of Ahab's chariot, all the way back to Jezreel where Ahab's palace was.

When Ahab told his wife all that had happened, she was furious and determined that Elijah must be killed. Elijah had to flee for his life, and he went out in to the wilderness and sat down under a juniper tree. He was hungry and depressed, and tired from his efforts on Mount Carmel, so that he soon fell asleep.

Suddenly an angel touched him and said, 'Arise and eat.' Elijah looked round and found a loaf of bread and a jar of water near his head. So he ate, drank and lay down again, feeling somewhat refreshed.

Some time later the angel woke him a second time. 'Eat,' he said, 'or the journey will be too much for you.' Elijah did so, and found that the food had given him enough strength for the next forty days; he walked to Mount Sinai, the mount of God, and went into a cave there.

Suddenly he heard the voice of God. 'What are you doing here, Elijah?' Elijah, who was still feeling depressed, told God that he had done his best to show the people who was the true God, but that now they were after his life. 'I am the only one left,' he said, 'and now they are searching for me to kill me.'

'Go and stand on the mountain,' said God.

Elijah did so, and there God showed him some of the wondrous works of nature. First there was a

great strong wind which shattered the rocks; after that there was an earthquake, and after that there was a fire. God was not in any of these things, but then there came a still, small voice, and when Elijah heard it, he knew it to be the voice of God. He covered his face and went and stood in the entrance to the cave.

God told him of His plans for the future, and said that there would soon be another prophet named Elisha, whom Elijah was to anoint and who would eventually take his place. God's work would go on. Elijah no longer felt himself alone; he was now certain that God was with him.

Meanwhile Ahab and Jezebel continued with their wicked ways.

Naboth's Vineyard

Near Ahab's palace in Jezreel was a vineyard owned by a man named Naboth. One day Ahab went to Naboth and said, 'Give me your vineyard, because it is near my house. I will give you a better one in exchange for it, or if you prefer, I will give you its value in money.'

But Naboth replied, 'It belonged to my ancestors; I could not let you have it.' It was the law that a man's heritage must be handed on to the next generation, and Naboth felt that it would be unlawful to sell his vineyard. So quite properly he refused.

Ahab, who liked his own way, went off and sulked. He took to his bed, turned his face to the wall, and refused to eat, behaving just like a spoilt child.

The queen went to him and asked, 'What is the matter? Why are you not eating?'

'Because Naboth will not give me his vineyard,' answered the king.

'Are you the king or are you not?' said Jezebel, somewhat disgusted. 'Get up and have a meal, and cheer up. I will get Naboth's vineyard for you.'

So she wrote some letters in the king's name, and signed them with his seal, and she sent them out to some of the leading men in Jezreel. In them she wrote, 'Proclaim a day of fasting; get everyone together, and give Naboth a place of honour. Bring in two wicked men to say that Naboth has cursed God and the king. Then stone him.'

It all happened just as she had planned. The evil men brought in their false charge against Naboth, and he was taken out and stoned to death.

As soon as Jezebel heard that Naboth was dead, she said to Ahab, 'Now you can go and take that vineyard.' And Ahab went straightaway to take possession of it.

Meanwhile God had given Elijah a message. 'Go to Naboth's vineyard, where you will find Ahab, and challenge him about taking possession of it. He shall die where Naboth died.'

Off went Elijah and came face to face with Ahab. 'Have you found me, O my enemy?' said Ahab, knowing full well that he had done wrong.

'Yes, I have,' said Elijah. 'Because you have done evil both you and Jezebel will die. You have led Israel into sin.'

Ahab was terrified. He tore his clothes and put on sackcloth and refused food, and was very unhappy. When God saw he was truly sorry, he spared Ahab's life for a time.

Later, when Ahab was at war with Syria, he decided to go into battle in disguise. But it did not help him, for one of the enemy bowmen shot an arrow by chance, and it pierced Ahab between the joints of his armour. 'I am wounded,' cried Ahab to his chariot driver. 'Turn round and carry me out of the battle.' His servants did so and then propped him up in his chariot facing the Syrians, but by evening Ahab died.

Jezebel died a violent death too, by being thrown from one of the palace windows during another period of trouble in the land.

Elisha

When Elijah first met Elisha, who was to be his successor, Elisha was ploughing with twelve yoke of oxen, for he was a ploughman. Elijah put his cloak over Elisha's shoulders, as a symbol that Elisha was to take over his work, and Elisha went to bid his family goodbye and then went with Elijah.

One day, when Elijah knew his work was coming to an end, they both went down to the River Jordan. Fifty prophets followed them to see what would happen. Elijah took off his cloak, rolled it up and struck the water with it, so that the water divided and the two of them were able to walk over on dry ground.

When they had crossed, Elijah asked Elisha a question. 'What would you like me to do for you before I am taken from you?'

Elisha replied, 'I would like to have a double portion of your spiritual power.'

'That is not an easy thing to ask,' said Elijah, 'but if you see me as I am being taken away from you, it shall be so; if you do not see me, then it shall not be so.'

They continued to talk together for some time. Then suddenly a chariot drawn by horses, all of fire, seemed to drive between them, and a great whirlwind came and took Elijah up to heaven. 'My father, my father! The chariots of Israel and the horsemen!' cried Elisha. He picked up Elijah's cloak and struck the river with it, and the waters parted and Elisha went over to the other side. When the prophets saw him, they bowed low and said, 'The power of Elijah is now come upon Elisha.'

This new prophet Elisha was to carry on God's work for more than fifty years.

Naaman the Leper

Naaman was a commander in the Syrian army who lived during the time of Elisha. The King of Syria greatly respected him because he was a great soldier and had won many victories for the Syrian forces.

Syria was often at war with Israel, and many border raids took place between them. In one of these raids, the Syrians had carried off a little Israelite girl who became a maidservant to Naaman's wife.

Although she was in a rich and important household, the maid noticed that there was an air of sadness about it. The reason was that the great Naaman was suffering from the dread disease of leprosy. It was an illness which would only get worse as time went on, and for which no one knew any cure.

One day the little maid said to her mistress, 'I wish my master could go and see the prophet who lives in Samaria. I am sure he could cure him of his disease.'

When Naaman heard what the little girl had said, he felt that any hope of a cure would be at least worth trying, and he told the king about it. 'Go at once,' said the king. 'I will give you a letter to the King of Israel.'

So Naaman set off, taking with him gifts of silver and gold and ten changes of fine clothing. He had also the king's letter which introduced Naaman and asked that he be cured of his leprosy. But when the King of Israel read the letter, he got into a dreadful state. 'How does the King of Syria expect me to cure leprosy?' he cried. 'Does he think I am God? I think he is just trying to start a quarrel with me.'

Elisha heard about the king's outburst and he immediately sent a message to the palace. 'Why are you getting so upset?' Elisha's message asked. 'Send Naaman to me and he will know that there is a prophet in Israel.'

So off went Naaman with his chariots and horses, and they stopped outside the door of Elisha's house. There Naaman expected Elisha would come out and greet him. But all that happened was that Elisha sent a message to Naaman saying, 'Go and wash in the River Jordan seven times, and your leprosy will be cured.'

When Naaman heard this, he felt that he had been insulted and he was extremely angry. He turned away and said, 'I thought at least he would have come out to meet me, and waved his hand over me, calling upon his God to heal me. Why should I wash in the River Jordan? We've got better rivers in Syria than any in Israel. Could I not have washed in those, if that is all that was needed?' And he stormed off in a rage.

Some of his servants came up and tried to calm him. 'Sir,' they said, 'why not try what the prophet has said? If he had told you to do something difficult, you would have done it. So why not wash in the Jordan?'

Naaman realized that there was some sense in what they said, and he went down to the river and dipped himself in it seven times. After the seventh time, his skin was as clear and healthy as a child's, and no trace of the disease could be seen. Naaman was delighted. With all his company he returned to Elisha and said, 'Now I know that there is no god on earth but the God of Israel. Please let me give you a present.'

'No,' replied Elisha. 'By the living God whom I serve, I will not accept anything.'

He knew that he could not accept a gift for himself for imparting God's blessing and healing on Naaman. Although Naaman continued to try and make Elisha take some reward, he still refused.

Then Naaman said, 'If you will not accept a gift, will you let me take two mule-loads of earth home with me, for from now on, I will not offer sacrifice or worship to any god but the God of Israel.' In those days people believed that a god belonged to his own country and could not be worshipped anywhere else. So that if Naaman was to worship the God of Israel, he thought he must have some of the land of Israel upon which to do it.

'Go in peace,' said Elisha, and Naaman returned to Syria.

Gehazi

Elisha had a servant whose name was Gehazi, and who could be greedy when he chose. Gehazi noticed that his master had refused Naaman's gifts, and he thought he would like some of them for himself. So when Naaman had gone a little way, Gehazi ran after him and caught him up. Naaman saw him coming and asked, 'Is everything all right?'

'Yes,' answered Gehazi. 'My master has sent me to say that he would like some of your gifts after all. Two prophets have just called on him and he would like to give them some silver and fine clothes.'

'Certainly,' said Naaman, and he sent two of his own servants ahead of Gehazi to carry back more gifts than Gehazi had asked for. When he reached Elisha's house, Gehazi took the gifts and put them inside.

'Where have you been, Gehazi?' asked Elisha.

'Nowhere,' lied Gehazi.

But Elisha knew what had happened. 'This is no time to steal and lie,' he said. 'You should be rejoicing over God's power over disease. You have taken Naaman's goods, so now his leprosy will come upon you too.'

Gehazi left Elisha at once, but he found he had the disease already and his skin turned as white as snow.

The Fiery Furnace

Long after Elisha died, the Assyrians conquered Israel, and later still the Babylonians conquered the Assyrians. They destroyed Jerusalem and carried off the Jews into captivity in Babylon. Among these captives were four young men who, because of their noble birth, were taken to be trained for service in the king's own household at the palace.

The king at that time was Nebuchadnezzar who wanted the young men, as part of their training, to eat the rich food which he, the king, ate and to drink some of the wine which he drank and to serve him at table.

The four men were named Daniel, Shadrach, Meshach and Abednego; and Daniel resolved not to obey the king's command, because to eat and drink as the king wished would be against the laws of Israel. Daniel believed in standing up for what he felt was right, even if it was a king who had told him to do otherwise. He knew quite well what God's laws said.

Some time later Daniel achieved fame through being the only person able to interpret one of the king's dreams. The dream was a warning to the king that, in time, all the kingdoms of the earth would pass away, and only God's Kingdom of Heaven would remain. Nebuchadnezzar was so pleased that Daniel had been able to interpret the dream that he made him ruler of the province of Babylon. Shadrach, Meshach and Abednego were also put in charge of affairs in the province and they all proved themselves to be intelligent and hard-working.

It was not long before King Nebuchadnezzar forgot about the dream and its warning and began to think of himself as the most important man in the world. He had a colossal golden statue made, 27 m (87 ft) high and nearly 3 m (3 yd) wide. Then he ordered all the princes and governors, the judges, magistrates, and all the leading officials to come to a great ceremony in order to dedicate the statue.

When they were all gathered, a herald proclaimed in a loud voice, 'You are commanded that whenever you hear the sound of the trumpet, pipes, lyre, harp, bagpipes and all kinds of music, you are to fall down and worship the golden statue which the king has set up. Anyone who does not do so will immediately be thrown into a burning fiery furnace.' It would be a most terrible way to die.

Now Daniel's three friends decided that they were not going to do any such thing. They knew whom they worshipped—the one true God—and no amount of threats would make them worship a golden statue. Some of the Babylonians found out about this, and they reported the disobedience of the three young Jews to the king. 'Those Jewish captives don't take any notice of you,' they told him; 'they don't serve your gods or worship the golden statue. Instead they all worship their own god, the God of Israel.'

In a furious rage Nebuchadnezzar sent for Shadrach, Meshach and Abednego. 'Is this true?' he fumed. 'Now I'll give you one more chance. If you are ready to fall down and worship the statue when you hear the music, well and good. But if you do not, you will be cast into the burning fiery furnace. And where is the god who could save you from that?'

Shadrach, Meshach and Abednego answered the king calmly, 'We have no need to defend our action. Our God is able to save us from the burning fiery furnace if He so wills; but even if He does not, we will still refuse to worship your gods or to bow down to the golden statue which you have set up. It would be quite wrong.'

King Nebuchadnezzar completely lost his temper when he heard this, for he was quite unable to cope with the calm strong will of the three young men, and he did not like being defied. 'Make the furnace seven times hotter than usual,' he ordered his servants. Then he commanded strong men from his army to tie up the three young men and to throw them, fully clothed, into the burning fiery furnace. This they did, and because the flames of the furnace were so hot, they even burnt the men who came near to throw the three young Israelites into the fire.

The furnace was rather like a kiln with an open top and a door at the side through which the prisoners could be seen. The king watched the proceedings from a safe distance, but suddenly he got up looking very worried. 'Did we not bind and throw three men into the fire?' he asked his officials.

'True, O king,' they replied.

'But I can see four men, walking about and not bound up at all,' said the king. 'They show no signs of being burnt, and the fourth looks like a son of the gods.'

Nebuchadnezzar went nearer to the door of the furnace. 'Shadrach, Meshach and Abednego,' he called. 'You servants of the Most High God, come out here to me.'

The three young men came out of the furnace straightaway. The king and his officials gathered round them and were amazed to find that the furnace had not touched them at all. Not a hair of their heads was singed, and their clothes did not even smell of smoke. They were completely unharmed and unmarked.

The king knew he was beaten, and he made a speech blessing the God of Shadrach, Meshach and Abednego. 'These young men,' he said, 'disobeyed me and risked death rather than worship any god but their own. I therefore command that if anyone, of whatever nation or language, speaks anything against the God of Shadrach, Meshach and Abednego, he shall be completely destroyed, and his house laid in ruins. There is no other god who is able to deliver his servants like this. This god is the most powerful of all.

Then he promoted Shadrach, Meshach and Abednego to higher and more important positions in the province of Babylon.

Some time after this, King Nebuchadnezzar had another dream which he asked Daniel to interpret. Daniel was able to say, sadly, that the dream meant that the king would be struck with a rare disease through which he would believe himself to be an animal and eat grass, crawling around on his hands and knees.

Daniel advised the king to show a little more mercy and to live a more righteous life, so that perhaps the dream might not come true after all and the king might be spared.

But a year later, when the king was surveying Babylon from the palace roof, and proudly saying that he had built it by his mighty power for his own glory, he suddenly became ill and behaved just like a strange animal. It was not until he had ceased being proud and had learnt to be humble, that his reason returned to him. In this way Daniel's prophecy came true just as he had predicted it would.

Belshazzar's Feast

Some years after King Nebuchadnezzar's death, a new king, Belshazzar, laid on a great feast in his palace for a thousand people. The party went with a swing and all the guests were eating and drinking and enjoying themselves. In the midst of it King Belshazzar decided to do something spectacular. He ordered that beautiful cups and bowls, made of silver and gold, should be brought in for the king and his guests to drink from. These were no ordinary cups; they were the ones which had been carried off by Nebuchadnezzar from the temple at Jerusalem. They were, therefore, sacred vessels and should not have been used for feasting and merriment.

This did not worry Belshazzar. They were brought in and everyone drank from them, and, as they did so, they praised their own heathen gods—gods made from gold, silver, bronze, iron, wood and stone to which the people gave offerings and said prayers.

Suddenly something strange began to happen. A mysterious hand appeared out of the air and began to write on the wall of the banqueting room, near the lampstand where the light shone brightly. It wrote some very strange words— MENE, MENE, TEKEL and PARSIN.

As the king watched it, he grew very frightened. He went very pale, and his knees began to knock together. Not knowing what else to do, he called for all his magicians, wizards and astrologers to come into his presence. 'If anyone can read this writing,' he said to his wise men, 'and also tell me its meaning, I shall dress him in robes of royal purple, put a gold chain around his neck, and

make him the third ruler in the kingdom. He will become rich and powerful.'

The wise men looked at one another and muttered together, but in the end, they had to say that they could not understand the mysterious writing and so could not tell the king what it meant. Belshazzar was even more perplexed and alarmed and vowed he would not rest until he found out what the strange words said.

Then the queen mother came in with an idea. She had remembered something from the days of King Nebuchadnezzar. 'O king, live for ever,' she began. 'Don't be so alarmed, for there is a man in the kingdom who might help. In the days of King Nebuchadnezzar he proved himself to be very wise and understanding, and Nebuchadnezzar gave him a very high position. He interpreted dreams and explained riddles, and solved all sorts of problems. His name was Daniel. Why don't you call for him and see if he can interpret the writing for you?'

Belshazzar thought this might be a good idea; so he sent for Daniel and explained the problem to him. He also told him about the rewards he had promised to anyone who could interpret the writing.

'I don't want your gifts and rewards,' began Daniel, 'but I will read the writing and tell you what it means. King Nebuchadnezzar was given great glory and majesty, and the people trembled before him and feared him. But he became so proud that all power was taken from him, and he became like a beast and ate grass. At last he learned that the Most High God, and not Nebuchadnezzar himself, was the ruler of men. He gave up his proud and vain opinion of himself. Then he became humble and was cured.'

Belshazzar must have wondered what all this was leading up to. He was not accustomed to being told off by anyone.

Daniel went on, 'You, O king, although you knew all this, have not learnt from it to be humble. You took the sacred vessels from the house of the Lord, and used them for your banquet; as you did so, you praised not the true God, but worthless gods of gold and silver, bronze and iron, wood and stone who cannot see anything or know anything. That is why God sent the hand to write and show you these things, so that you should realize your wrongdoing.'

Then Daniel explained the mysterious words, MENE, MENE, TEKEL and PARSIN.

'"Mene" is number,' he said. 'God has numbered the days of your kingdom and it will be brought to an end. "Tekel" is weight, and it means that you have been weighed in the balance and found wanting. "Parsin" is divisions, and means that your kingdom will be divided up and given to the Medes and Persians.'

Belshazzar was impressed and, despite Daniel's earlier protests, he had the robe of royal purple laid on him, and the golden chain put around his neck, and made a proclamation that Daniel should be the third ruler in the kingdom and hold great power.

However, Daniel's interpretation of the dream was to come true quickly. That very night Belshazzar was killed, and Darius the Mede took over the kingdom and received the royal power and ruled in Belshazzar's place.

Belshazzar's Feast

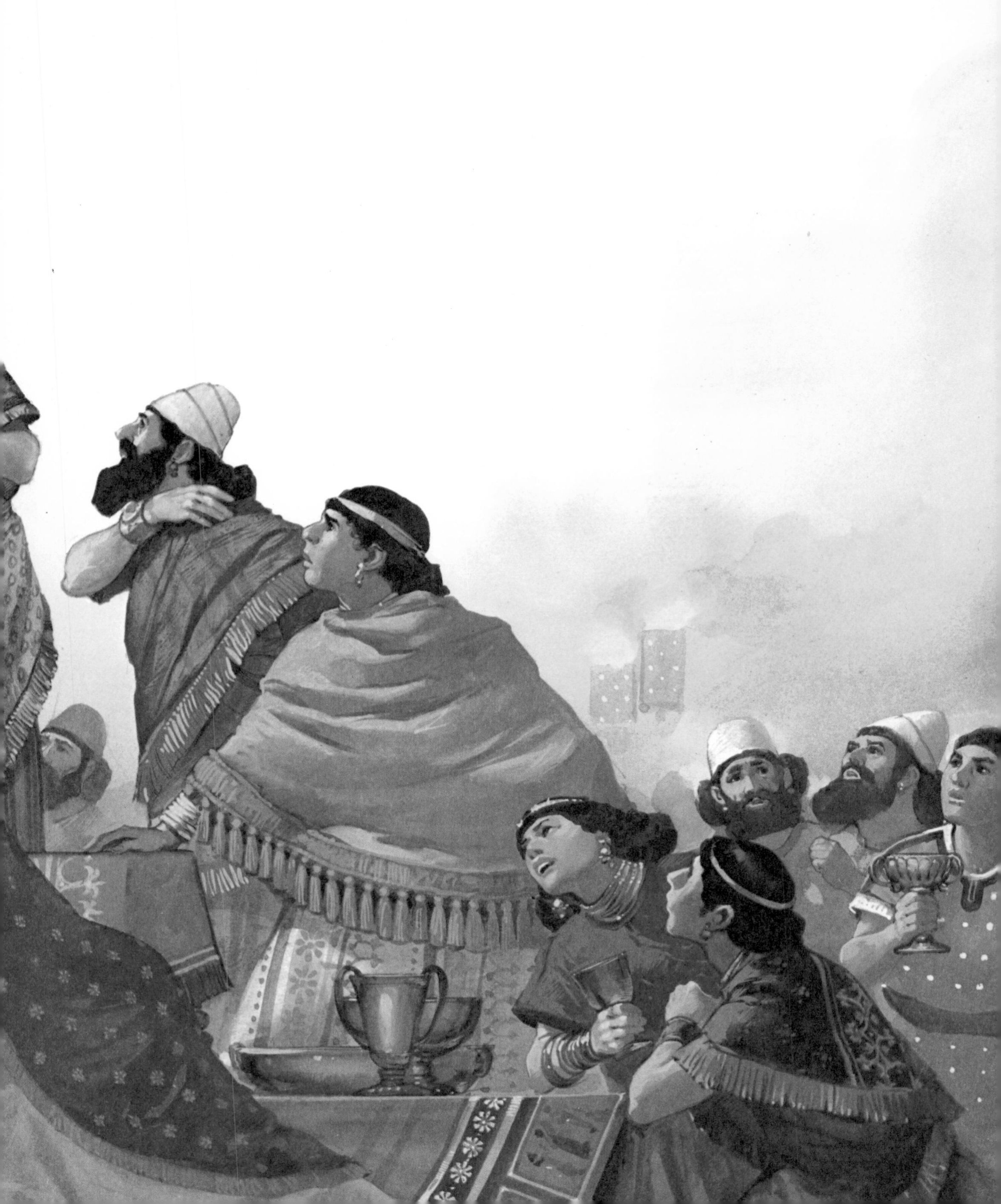

Daniel in the Lions' Den

King Darius divided up the kingdom into 120 districts, over which he set 120 governors. Then he set Daniel and two other men to be supervisors over the governors.

Daniel was now an old man, but he soon showed that his work was better than that of the other supervisors and governors. Indeed it was so outstanding that the king planned to put him in charge of the whole kingdom—perhaps in the same way that Pharaoh had given Joseph a high post over a thousand years earlier.

The other supervisors and governors grew very jealous of Daniel, but he had been a man of God throughout his whole life, and they could never catch him out in anything dishonest or disloyal. They did their best to try and find something wrong with the way he did his work so that they could report him to the king, but they did not succeed.

Then they held a consultation together and said, 'We shall never be able to find anything wrong with Daniel's work; our only hope is to try and catch him out in something connected with the law of his god or with his religion.'

They were well aware that Daniel was in the habit of praying to God three times every day, and they also knew that he had no time for heathen idols and images. So they considered these facts and thought up a crafty plan; then they went to the king with it.

'O king, live for ever,' they said. 'All we governors and officials have agreed that your majesty should issue a new order, and enforce it strictly. It is this: any man who makes any petition to any

god or man for the next thirty days, except of course to you, O king, shall be thrown into a den of lions. Let your majesty make this order and sign it, and so it will become a law of the Medes and Persians which cannot be altered.'

Any command written in the king's name and sealed with his ring was held to be unchangeable.

The king was rather flattered at this request from his officials, and he signed the order right away without giving it very much thought. When Daniel heard about the new law, he knew what he must do. Never in his life had he been prepared to give up worshipping God, no matter what the cost; now, although he was an old man, he was still prepared to do what he knew to be right, and to face any risk rather than deny God.

He could have given up praying to God for the next thirty days while the law was in force, or he could have gone on praying in secret. But such compromises were not for a man of stern courage such as Daniel, so he ignored the order. He went to his house, where the upstairs windows faced towards Jerusalem and were open, and just as he had always done, he knelt down three times a day and prayed and gave thanks to God.

Now his enemies had him where they wanted him. This was just what they were hoping would happen. They hurried off to the king. 'Your majesty,' they said, 'did you not sign a new order which said that anyone who made any petition to any god or man, other than yourself, for the next thirty days, would be thrown into a den of lions?'

'I did,' said the king, 'and the law stands, a law of the Medes and Persians, and so cannot be altered.' Again, just what the officials hoped he would say.

'But that man Daniel', they went on, 'has disobeyed you. He prays to his god three times every day, just as he always did before you made the law.'

The king was very upset when he heard this, for he had a high respect for Daniel, and he realized how he himself had been trapped by his cunning officials. How he wished he had never signed the new order! The problem continued to worry him all day. He tried very hard to see if there was a way in which Daniel might be rescued from certain death, but always he came up against the problem that the laws of the Medes and Persians could not be altered once the king had signed them.

The officials wanted to make sure he did not forget this fact, and they came back to the palace to remind him that the law could not be altered now that it had the royal signature.

At last, the king concluded that there was no possible way out, and he had to give the order for Daniel to be thrown into the den of lions.

Just before Daniel was taken, the king said to him, 'May your god, whom you serve so faithfully, rescue you.'

Then Daniel was cast into the pit, and a huge stone was brought and placed over the entrance. The king sealed it with the royal seal and with the seal of his noblemen, so that no one could come and rescue Daniel without the deed being discovered.

Sadly the king returned to the palace where he spent a sleepless night and ate no food. Immediately it became light next morning, he got up and hurried over to the den of lions. He was hoping it might be possible that Daniel was alive—perhaps his god had saved him? But the king thought it far more likely that Daniel would by now have been torn to pieces. It was an agonizing thought.

As soon as he reached the den, he called out anxiously, 'Daniel, servant of the living god, was your god able to save you from the lions?'

To his joy Daniel's voice called back, 'O king, live for ever! My God sent His angel to stop the mouths of the lions, and they have not harmed me

at all. God knew that I had not wronged Him or you, your majesty.'

The king was delighted and gave orders that Daniel should immediately be brought up out of the den of lions. When he came out, everyone saw that he was completely unhurt.

King Darius then commanded that the men who had accused Daniel should themselves be thrown into the lions' den, and this was done.

In order to show that he believed Daniel's God to be the true God, King Darius sent out a proclamation saying just this to all peoples, nations and races.

Daniel's Visions

Daniel was a man who had visions himself, as well as interpreting the dreams of others. In one vision he saw four beasts rising out of the sea. The first was like a lion with eagle's wings; the second was like a bear; the third was like a leopard; and the fourth was a strange and ferocious-looking creature with ten horns and great iron teeth. One of the horns, a small one, appeared to have human eyes.

Then God appeared on His throne of judgement, and the fourth beast was slain.

Daniel asked for an explanation of this vision and he was told that the four beasts were four empires which would arise on the earth and which would be followed by the Kingdom of God.

The fourth beast was a conquering kingdom and its horns represented kings; the little horn was a king who would put down three of the others, but it would lose its dominion on judgement day, and the everlasting kingdom of saints would follow.

In another vision he saw a two-horned ram which was attacked by a goat; one of the goat's horns was broken and four others came up in its place. The ram represented the Persian empire and the goat the Greek empire; the horn was the first Greek king (Alexander the Great) and the four horns which succeeded it were the rulers of the four divisions of his empire.

Daniel and his dreams and visions seem often to have been a pictorial representation of events which took place in history.

Jonah

Jonah was a prophet, but a different sort of prophet from people like Elijah and Elisha. He lived somewhere about the middle of the eighth century BC.

One day God spoke to Jonah and said, 'Go to the city of Nineveh and speak out against it, for the people there are very wicked.'

Nineveh was the famous capital of the Assyrian empire, and the Assyrians were Israel's enemies. Jonah did not want to go to Nineveh to give the people God's message; he thought that if they then changed their ways through hearing that message, God would forgive them and the city would not be destroyed for its wickedness. Jonah wanted this enemy destroyed, and he also wanted his warnings to come true.

So he disobeyed God's command. Instead of going to Nineveh, he went down to the seaport of Joppa, and there he found a ship going to Tarshish which was in Spain, and in the opposite direction to Nineveh. In Tarshish, he thought, he would get away from the presence of God.

He paid his fare and went aboard, thinking he would now not have to deliver God's message. He went down into the ship's hold, and there he fell asleep.

The ship set sail, and it had not been at sea for long when a great hurricane blew up. The fierce wind tossed the ship about on the seas and it almost seemed as though the vessel would break up. The sailors were terrified and each cried out to his own god for help. Then they began to throw the cargo overboard to lighten the ship and so lessen the danger.

Now the captain happened to go down into the hold of the ship, and there he found Jonah still asleep. 'Get up! Get up!' he ordered. 'There is a terrible storm! What do you mean by sleeping here? Pray to your god for help as everyone else is doing. Perhaps he will spare a thought for us so that we do not perish.'

Now Jonah had an idea that God had sent this storm because of his disobedience. So he told the sailors that he was on their ship because he was fleeing from God's presence.

'Are you to blame for all this then?' they asked. 'What is your job, and where do you come from?'

'I am a Hebrew,' replied Jonah. 'I worship the Lord God who made the sea and the dry land.'

Then the men grew very much afraid. 'What shall we do to you so that the sea will calm down?'

'You had better throw me overboard,' said Jonah miserably. 'I know it is all my fault.'

But the men did not like the thought of doing that, so they rowed all the harder to try and get the ship safely to land. However, it proved to be quite impossible, with the waves getting higher and the sea more tempestuous every moment. They began to pray hard, 'Lord, do not let all our lives be lost for the sake of this man's life.'

Then they saw that they would have to get rid of Jonah, and they picked him up and threw him overboard.

Immediately the sea calmed down and the storm ceased. This made the men so fearful of God that they offered a sacrifice and made vows to serve Him.

Meanwhile Jonah began to float away from the ship and face what he thought would be certain death from drowning. The water seemed to be choking him, and his head got all tangled up in seaweed. He began to sink, and felt that he was leaving the earth and all living things for ever. The waters were all around him and the waves rolled over him, and he knew his life was slipping away.

Then, at God's command, a great fish swam up and swallowed Jonah whole, and Jonah was inside the fish for three days and three nights. During that time, he felt very miserable and began to think. He realized how stupid he had been to disobey God and to try and run away from His presence. He also realized that, although he had been thrown overboard, God had not let him drown. He really felt very grateful.

God ordered the fish to put Jonah out on to the dry land and the fish did so. The voice of the Lord then came to Jonah a second time. 'Go to Nineveh,' said God, 'and proclaim to the people of that great city the message I have given you.' Jonah did not need telling again. He knew better than to disobey this time and he set off straight-away for Nineveh.

Now Nineveh was a huge city—so big that it took three days to walk through it. Jonah started walking and, after he had walked for a whole day, he decided that now was the time to give God's message to the people.

'Nineveh will be destroyed in forty days!' he cried; and the message had an immediate effect for the people believed him and, realizing that they had been wicked, they began to fast and dress themselves in sackcloth to show that they had repented.

The news reached the ears of the King of Nineveh, and he arose from his throne, took off his royal robes, and dressed himself in sackcloth too. He then sent out an official proclamation to all the people of Nineveh: 'By the decree of the king and his nobles, no one shall eat or drink anything, not any man, beast or sheep; but they shall all be covered with sackcloth and pray to God; let every-one turn away from his wickedness, and if we are truly sorry, God may not destroy our city.'

When God saw that the people had repented, He was prepared to forgive them and to save their city, but one person was not at all happy about this, and that was Jonah.

He was very angry when he knew that the people of Nineveh were to be saved. He prayed to God and said, 'Isn't this just what I said would happen while I was still in my own country? This is exactly why I ran away to Tarshish. I knew you were a merciful God, loving, kind and patient, and always ready to forgive people when they are truly sorry. Now let me die, for I am sure I would be better off dead than alive.'

It was a hard lesson that God was trying to teach the prophet. Not only was Jonah's own pride wounded at the thought that his warnings would not now come to pass; it was also that he did not think that the God of Israel should be merciful to the people of Nineveh. God should be loving and merciful only towards Israel, Jonah thought.

'Do you think it is right for you to be angry like this?' asked God, who wanted to arouse Jonah's better feelings, but Jonah did not answer. He simply took himself off outside the city, and made himself a little shelter and sat down in such shade as it gave him. He felt miserable and frustrated and he wanted to see what would become of the city. He thought perhaps God would destroy it after all.

God made a leafy kind of plant grow up beside him to give shade for Jonah's head and save him from the discomfort of the hot sun. Jonah was grateful for the shadow it cast. When the next morning dawned, however, a worm attacked the plant at God's command, and it withered and died, and Jonah felt sorry for it.

When the sun had risen, a hot east wind began to blow; the heat of the sun came down fiercely upon Jonah's head until he began to feel quite faint. 'Let me die, Lord,' he said again. 'It is better for me to die than live.'

When he recovered, he felt angry about the plant that had withered and would not now give him shade. He felt sorry that somehow the plant had been ill-treated, and in a way he was sorry for

it; a withered plant is always a sad sight. 'Are you right to feel angry about that plant?' asked God.

'I have every right to be angry,' said Jonah. 'I'm angry enough to die.'

'This plant grew up in the night,' said God, 'and it disappeared just as quickly the next day, and you pity it. Yet you did no work for it, and you did nothing to make it grow.'

Jonah understood that, but God had more to say. 'How much more then,' He said, 'should I, the Lord, not take pity on the great city of Nineveh, where there are 120,000 people, and their animals, all of whom I have made and over whom I have taken much trouble. They are helpless and ignorant, but they have asked for forgiveness. Should I not take pity on them?'

THE
NEW
TESTAMENT

The Birth of Jesus

In the little town of Nazareth in Galilee there lived a good and gentle young woman named Mary. She was engaged to a local carpenter named Joseph, a fine, kindly man whose family was descended from King David.

One day, as Mary went about her household duties, she had a surprising visitor. An angel named Gabriel suddenly appeared before her. 'Hail, Mary,' he said, 'the Lord is with you.'

Mary was puzzled, for she did not understand what the angel's visit could mean.

'Do not be afraid, Mary,' said the angel, 'for you are to have a son, and His name will be Jesus. He will be the son of the Most High God, and He will be a king whose kingdom will never end.'

'How can this be?' asked Mary, greatly worried. 'I have no husband.'

'The Holy Spirit will come to you,' answered the angel, 'so that God's power will be with you, for the child will be the Son of God.'

This was amazing news, but the angel had more to say. 'Your relation, Elizabeth, is also going to have a son,' he went on, 'although she is thought to be too old to have any children now. With God nothing is impossible.'

'I am God's servant,' said Mary quietly. 'May it happen as you have said.'

And then the angel left her.

Shortly afterwards, Mary went to visit her cousin Elizabeth, and when she told her the news,

Elizabeth said, 'You are the most blessed of women! Why should such a wonderful thing happen that the mother of the Lord should visit me?'

Joseph, however, was troubled at Mary's news and wondered whether he should still marry her. Then an angel appeared to him in a dream and reassured him, 'Do not be afraid to take Mary for your wife. God's Holy Spirit has come to her, and she will have a son who is to be called Jesus—for He will save people from their sins.'

(The name 'Jesus' is in fact the Greek form of the Hebrew name 'Joshua' and means 'saviour').

Bethlehem

Now Palestine in those days was part of the Roman Empire, and some time after the appearance of the angel to Mary and Joseph, the Roman Emperor, Caesar Augustus, issued an order. He commanded that everyone should be 'enrolled', which meant that there would be a sort of census or numbering of the people. To do this, each person was to return to his home town or city to register himself.

For Joseph this meant a long journey of about 115 km (72 miles), from Nazareth in Galilee southwards to Bethlehem in Judea. Bethlehem had been the home of Ruth and Boaz, and also the birthplace of King David.

The journey would be a long and tiring walk, for, apart from a donkey, there was no other means of transport. Joseph had to make careful preparations for the journey, especially as Mary was going with him and would soon be having her baby.

They were both very tired by the time they reached Bethlehem. What a busy town it was! Everywhere was hustle and bustle, for crowds of people had come for the enrolment. There seemed to be no room anywhere for the weary travellers from Bethlehem to stay the night. Joseph was anxious about Mary, and became worried when the last innkeeper they asked told him that he had not a single room left vacant in the inn; he was completely full with visitors.

Then, no doubt, he looked again at Mary and saw how tired she was, and he took pity on her. 'There is the stable where the animals are kept,' he suggested. 'You could shelter there for the night if you wish.'

Joseph was ready to take anything, for he could see that Mary was not fit to travel much further, and he readily agreed. At least the stable would provide shelter, and they could find a warm corner and lie down on some of the animals' straw.

Thankfully, they went into the stable, and during the night, with no one looking on except the animals, Mary's baby was born. She wrapped Him up in strips of cloth, called swaddling clothes, which was the usual custom in that part of the world. There was no cradle where she might lay her baby, so she put Him gently in a manger where hay was kept to feed the animals.

It was a strange arrival for the Son of God. Kings are not normally born in stables; they are born in palaces amid rich pomp and splendour, but when God allowed Jesus to be born in this humble way in the stable, He was showing that He was sympathetic to the poor and was the king of *all* people, not only of the rich and important. By living as the poorest, Jesus would show how He really understood them and took their part.

In the countryside, outside Bethlehem, a group of shepherds were looking after their sheep on the night when Jesus was born.

The work of shepherds was important and dangerous, since not only had they to lead their flocks to pasture, they had also to protect them from any wild animals that came prowling around. To this end, they stayed with their sheep both day and night, and when the flock was herded into the fold, often the shepherd himself would lie across the opening of the doorway, so that nothing could get into the pen without his knowledge.

On this clear night, the Bethlehem shepherds wrapped their cloaks around them against the cold and talked among themselves. Perhaps they remembered that King David had once been a shepherd boy himself. They gazed up at the night sky and saw many bright stars, but they were used to that.

Suddenly there seemed to be much more light than usual. The whole field was lit up with a brilliant radiance, and in the midst of it the shepherds saw the figure of an angel. They were terrified and covered their faces.

'Do not be afraid' said the angel, 'for I have brought you good news; news which will bring great joy to all the people. This very day in Bethlehem, the city of David, the Saviour of the world has been born. He is Christ the Lord.'

The shepherds were amazed; they could hardly take in such an important announcement and naturally they wondered why the angel had come to them with this great news.

The angel continued, 'As a sign to prove it to you, you will find the baby wrapped in swaddling clothes and lying in a manger.'

Hardly had the angel's words died away, than the whole sky surrounding the spot was filled with a multitude of angels. 'Glory to God in the highest,' they sang, 'and on earth peace to men with whom He is pleased.'

Then the angels went away, and the earth grew quiet and still. Only the stars were left in the sky.

The shepherds looked at one another in wonder. Was it true? Could they be dreaming? The Messiah, the Saviour of the world, here in Bethlehem? and in a *stable*? It did not seem possible.

Then one of the shepherds said, 'Come on, let's go and see this wonderful thing which the Lord has told us about through His angel.'

They hurried off, over the hills, and into Bethlehem. Almost certainly they left one of their number behind to take care of the sheep.

But where in Bethlehem should they look? From what the angel had said, the shepherds knew that it would be useless to look in any rich or important house, for the baby would be lying in a manger. Any rich house would provide a proper cot. Mangers were found only in stables, so they must look for a stable if they wanted to find the new-born king.

When at last they looked in at the stable belonging to the inn, there they found the new baby, and they knelt down and worshipped Him in wonder.

Mary, His mother, and Joseph, her husband, were gazing fondly down at Him. The shepherds told them all that the angel had said, but Mary already knew something about her wonderful baby, for the angel Gabriel had told her whom He was to be. So she kept silent, but thought a great deal about the wonderful happening.

The shepherds, however, were greatly excited about the event, and they could not keep quiet about it. They returned to their sheep, singing praises to God. They had heard the angel with their own ears, they had seen the baby with their own eyes; however much other people might find it hard to believe that God's Son had been born in a stable, they knew that it was true.

Forty days after Jesus was born, Mary and Joseph, according to the law, took Him to the temple in Jerusalem to be presented to God. On these occasions, it was necessary to present an offering, which would normally be a lamb. Poor people, however, such as Mary and Joseph, were allowed to offer two turtle-doves or two young pigeons instead.

In Jerusalem at that time, there lived a good man whose name was Simeon. He was a God-fearing man, and it had been revealed to him that he would not die until he had seen the true Christ. ('Christ' comes from a Greek word meaning 'anointed'; and 'Messiah' from a Hebrew word meaning the same thing.) It happened that he was in the temple when Mary and Joseph came in to present Jesus. As soon as Simeon saw Jesus he knew who He was and came forward at once.

Simeon took the baby in his arms and said, 'Lord, now let your servant go in peace, for I have seen the Saviour with my own eyes.'

Mary and Joseph were amazed at the things which Simeon said, for they were only slowly realizing the wonderful truth about their baby. Simeon blessed them too, and then he told Mary that Jesus would be the salvation of many in Israel, but that many people would speak against Him, and that she would suffer much sorrow.

The Visit of the Wise Men

Some time after the birth of Jesus, a group of rather important-looking men arrived in Jerusalem and began asking questions. They were men who studied the stars and their meanings, and were known as astrologers, or sometimes as 'magi', or just 'wise men'.

They had come on a long journey from the east, from where, before they had begun their travels, they had seen a very bright new star in the sky. From their knowledge, they believed that this star meant the birth of the long-promised new King of the Jews. So, wanting to find out more, they had set off on their camels to follow the star. (The Bible does not say that there were three of them, but it has always been generally thought that this was so because they brought three gifts.)

When the star had led them as far as Jerusalem, the wise men began to ask people if this was the place to which they should come to find the new king. Surely Jerusalem was a suitable place for a king to be born, they thought. 'Where is He who is born King of the Jews?' they asked. 'We have seen His star in the east, and have travelled here to worship Him.'

But no one in Jerusalem knew anything about a king being born there. So far as they knew, the only king in the area was Herod.

The news about the wise men's questionings reached the ears of King Herod, and he did not like the sound of it at all. He was a very jealous character, and he wanted no rivals to his throne or his power.

'A new king?' he thought, and became full of mistrust and suspicion. Not only was he troubled, but all the people of Jerusalem were troubled too, for when Herod was upset one never knew what he might do. He had killed many of the leading men of the city not long before, while suffering from a fit of fear and jealousy. He really could not be trusted an inch.

Herod summoned together all the chief priests and teachers of the law and asked them what they knew about it. 'Where will this Messiah, this King of the Jews, be born?' he asked in a pleasant, interested way.

They knew the answer to that one. It had been foretold by the prophet Micah hundreds of years earlier. He had written, 'And you, Bethlehem, in the land of Judah, are not the least of the cities of Judah, for from you there will come a ruler who will guide the people of Israel.' That could only mean the Messiah.

'Bethlehem,' thought Herod. 'Something must be done about this without delay.' So he summoned the wise men from the east to a secret conference. He found out from them at what time the star had appeared, and then he sent them off to Bethlehem to look for the new king whose birth seemed such a threat to him.

'Go and search very carefully for the young child,' he told them, 'and as soon as you have found him, come back here and let me know; for I would like to go and worship him too.' Of course, Herod had no intention of going to worship a rival king. All he wanted was to find out where the child was so that he could have him removed as a rival to the throne and make sure that he, Herod, was the only king the Jews recognized.

The wise men left Jerusalem. They were pleased to see the star again and to follow it until it came to

rest over Bethlehem, and over a certain house there. Now that the enrolling and the census was over, Bethlehem was no longer full of visitors, and Mary and Joseph would have had no difficulty in finding somewhere better than a stable to live in and to bring up the new baby.

Joyfully the wise men went into the house where they saw the young child Jesus and His mother, and they knelt down and worshipped Him, happy that their long search was over.

Then, as it was the custom not to approach a monarch without bringing a gift, they presented their gifts to the new King of the Jews. They were royal gifts—of gold, frankincense and myrrh— costly products of the countries from which the men had come. Frankincense was the resin from the bark of the terebinth tree; it had a pleasant smell and was used by priests in temple worship to make fragrant smoke at the altar. Myrrh was a sweet-smelling gum and was used as a perfume, in medicine and in anointing oils. They were all most suitable gifts for a king.

While in Bethlehem the wise men had a dream, which through their learning they were able to interpret, and in it God warned them not to go back to King Herod, as he had requested; so they went back home another way, slipping quietly across the borders of Israel.

When the wise men did not return to Jerusalem, Herod realized that he had been tricked, and he flew into a furious rage. He gave orders that all baby boys in Bethlehem, who were two years old and under, were to be killed at once. That way, he thought, he would be sure to kill the new king among them.

Meanwhile, after the wise men had departed, Joseph also had a dream in which an angel appeared to him and said, 'Get up quickly, and take the young child, and Mary His mother, and escape into Egypt, for King Herod is looking for the child in order to kill Him.'

So that night, under cover of darkness, Joseph did as the angel had bidden him, and with Mary and Jesus he fled into Egypt, out of the range of Herod's power. So Herod's wicked plot was foiled, and there they remained until the day that Herod died.

Then the angel appeared to Joseph in another dream and said, 'It is quite safe for you to take the child and His mother back to Israel now, for those who were searching for Him, to kill Him, are themselves now dead.'

At first Joseph thought of returning to Judah, perhaps to Bethlehem, but when he heard that Archelaus was now king there, in place of his father Herod, he was afraid, for Archelaus was nearly as suspicious and cruel as his father had been. So Joseph went instead to Galilee and there he, Mary and Jesus settled in Nazareth which lay in lower Galilee on the slopes of the Lebanon mountain range. Like Bethlehem it too was a quite unimportant town that was never to be forgotten because of its links with Jesus. And so it was in Nazareth that Jesus spent His boyhood.

Jesus as a Boy

Jesus was to live in Nazareth until He was about thirty years old, and this is why, although He was born in Bethlehem, He is often known as Jesus of Nazareth. The Bible tells us that He 'increased in wisdom and stature, and in favour with God and man.' In other words, He grew, not only in height, but also in wisdom, knowledge and learning, and with God's blessing, and people loved Him and respected Him.

As a boy, He would help Mary in the everyday tasks of their humble home and also work with Joseph in making articles of wood in their carpenter's shop. There He would become a skilled worker in wood, learning to make roofs, doors, beds, chests, tables and chairs. Carpenters also made agricultural implements, such as ploughs, yokes and threshing instruments, so there would be plenty to keep the boy Jesus busy in the small farming community.

He would also be taught in the local synagogue by the rabbi or scribes, where He would learn about the Jewish law. There would be no books, and education consisted chiefly of repeating words and so learning the facts by heart. Every Sabbath He would attend the synagogue for worship, and when He grew up, He would read aloud the scriptures there as would Joseph and all the other boys and their fathers.

In His free time, He probably wandered about the countryside, where many of the things He saw, He remembered and used later in His teaching when He grew up and told people stories, or parables, about the familiar things of life—cornfields, sowers, vineyards, sheep and shepherds. His own knowledge made the stories very real and appealing to His listeners and helped them to see how the stories made sense in their own lives and dealt with their common problems.

Every year Mary and Joseph used to journey to Jerusalem to join with hundreds of other pilgrims who flocked there from all over Palestine to celebrate the Passover.

When a Jewish boy was twelve years of age, he had to undergo preparation to become an adult in the religious community and to take his full part in the religious life of the village. He would then become what was known as a 'son of the law' and be expected to obey its rules. From that time onward, he would no longer be looked upon as a child, but would be considered as a full member of the Jewish church.

So, when Jesus was twelve, Mary and Joseph decided that the time had come for Him to go with them on their visit to the festival at Jerusalem. Because of all that it meant, it would be a very special visit for Jesus.

People from the same town or village would often make the journey together, walking along the rough highways and sleeping out at nights on the way. They travelled in groups for safety, for there were robbers and other possible dangers. It was a long journey, and they would be on the road for several days. The young boys would find it a very exciting adventure, and would be thrilled when they saw Jerusalem for the first time. They would then take part in ceremonies which they would remember all their lives.

When the festival was over the people started to walk back home again, but on this particular occasion, Jesus stayed behind in Jerusalem, and

did not set off back with His parents, although they did not realize this. No doubt they thought He was somewhere in the great company of people walking back—perhaps with relatives or friends, or with other boys of His own age, racing on ahead, or stopping to explore.

After they had been walking for a day, they made an evening halt, and it was then that Mary and Joseph found that Jesus was nowhere to be seen in the company. Where could He be? Anxiously they asked around among the other travellers, but no one could recall seeing Him that day. Mary and Joseph became very worried and decided that the best thing to do was to retrace their steps to Jerusalem, in the hope that they would find him on the way.

The next day, they set off back to the city, asking everyone they met whether they had seen

Jesus, but no one could help them. At last they reached Jerusalem itself and began looking in the city. It was now three days since they had started out on the homeward journey. After much worried searching, they finally found Jesus in the temple itself. He was sitting with a group of Jewish teachers, listening to them and asking them questions. The teachers were amazed at Jesus's understanding and at His intelligent questions and answers.

Mary and Joseph, too, were astonished when they discovered where Jesus was and what He was doing. Mary said to Him, 'My son, why did you stay behind like this? Why have you treated us so? We have been most worried trying to find you.'

Jesus was surprised—not that they had come back for Him, but at their not knowing where He would be. He had thought they would have known He would be in the temple. 'Why did you need to look for me?' He asked. 'Did you not know that I had to be in My Father's house and about My Father's business?'

By His 'Father', He meant God; for even at that early age, He understood His special relationship with God the Father.

Mary and Joseph did not fully understand His answer, but Jesus then went back to Nazareth with them, and was obedient to them, thus showing His love and respect for them both.

Mary thought deeply about what had happened. She remembered the words of the angel Gabriel before Jesus was born, that her child was to be the Son of God; and also how the aged Simeon in the temple had called Jesus 'the Saviour'. She must have wondered what the future had in store.

John the Baptist

Some little time before Jesus was born, there lived an old priest of the temple named Zechariah (sometimes written Zacharia). His wife was named Elizabeth and she was related to Mary, Jesus's mother. Both were good people, obeying God's laws, but they did not have any children and would have liked one very much. They had prayed for a child, but felt they were now too old.

Once a year Zechariah had to go to the temple at Jerusalem for two weeks to carry out his special duties as a priest. In this particular year, he received an honour which only occurred once in a lifetime. He was chosen to offer the incense in the temple, the most solemn part of the day's service. It was done every morning and evening on the golden altar of incense which stood before the veil of the Holy of Holies inside the temple.

The priest, whose duty and privilege it was, went alone within the temple to offer the incense, and the other priests and people worshipped outside in the temple courts during the hour when the incense was burnt.

As Zechariah was doing his turn of duty, he suddenly looked up and saw an angel at the right-hand side of the altar. He was alarmed and afraid at this strange sight.

'Don't be afraid, Zechariah,' said the angel, 'God has heard your prayers and you and Elizabeth will have a son. You will name him John and he will be a great man in God's sight, filled with the Holy Spirit. How happy you and many others will be when he is born! He will go before the Lord, full of power, like the mighty prophet Elijah. He will prepare the way for the coming of the Lord.'

'But I am an old man,' said Zechariah, 'and my wife is old too. How can I know that what you say is so?'

'I am Gabriel,' the angel answered, 'I stand in God's presence, and it is He who has sent me to bring you this good news. However, since you have not believed me you will remain dumb, unable to speak, until the day when these things which God has promised come true.'

Meanwhile, the people were waiting outside for Zechariah to come out of the temple, and they were wondering why he took so long.

When at last he did come out, he was unable to speak and to give the people his priestly blessing; he could only make signs to them, and so they realized that something had happened to him in the temple.

In due time, Elizabeth had a baby boy, just as God had promised through the angel. All her relatives and friends were delighted that God had been so good to her and had sent her a son in her old age, and they all rejoiced with her.

The time came for the baby to be given his name. Everyone thought he would be called Zechariah after his father, and they were very surprised when Elizabeth shook her head and said, 'No, he is going to be named John.'

'John?' queried the relatives and friends. 'But why? There is no one in your family called by that name.' Then they made signs to Zechariah, who was still dumb, asking him what he would like the baby to be called. Zechariah signalled back, asking for a writing tablet and, when it was brought to him, he wrote on it, 'His name is John.'

Immediately he found he was dumb no longer and could speak again.

This made a great impression on the people, and they were full of fear at what had happened. They all talked about it to everyone they met, and the news soon spread through all the hill country of Judea. People said to one another, 'What is this child going to be? It is plain that the power of God is with him.'

As the boy John grew up he lived in the desert until the time came for him to begin his special work as a prophet among the people of Israel; the work for which God had sent him.

He was a strange, rugged-looking man, dressed in a garment made of cloth woven from camel's hair, with a leather belt round his waist. His food was strange too, for he ate locusts and wild honey. In that land the poorer people often ate locusts, after the wings and legs had been removed and the remaining parts either boiled or roasted. Honey was plentiful in the desert, being found in honey-combs in the crevices of rocks.

Out of the desert came John, a stern, fiery prophet, calling upon the people to repent, to turn away from their sins and to begin a new way of life, because the Kingdom of God was near. News of him travelled fast, and crowds flocked to hear this strange new preacher. They came from Jerusalem and from all the surrounding country of Judea.

'Prepare the way of the Lord,' cried John. 'Make a straight path for Him; fill up the valleys and level off the hill-tops; make the crooked places straight and the rough places smooth. Then every-one will see God's salvation.'

This was a colourful way of saying, 'Get rid of unbelief and the things you have neglected to do (valleys); fill the spaces with new grace; get rid of pride and haughtiness (hills), cast them down and become humble; straighten out all deceit and

untruthfulness (crooked places), and get rid of anger, hatred and malice (rough places).'

'Confess your sins, be truly sorry and come and be baptized,' called John, and hundreds of people came out to be baptized in the River Jordan. Being baptized meant being 'washed' and was a symbol of the cleaning up of the previous life— a sign that all earlier wrongs were washed away and that a new and better life could be started. Because of this baptizing work, John came to be known as John the Baptist.

Many of the people thought that, because they were Jews, they were better than other people, but John would have none of this. He told the Jews that they needed to repent and to confess their sins, just like everyone else. 'You must do the things which will show that you have turned away from your sins and intend to lead a new life,' John told them.

'What shall we do, then?' the people asked.

'Show your intentions by your deeds,' said John. 'If you have two coats, give one to someone who has none. If you have food, see that you share it.'

'What about us?' asked some tax-collectors.

'Do not take any more money from people than the legal amount which you are supposed to take,' said John.

'And what shall we do?' asked some soldiers.

'Do not rob anyone by force,' said John, 'and do not accuse anyone of something which you know is not true. Be content with your wages.'

Not surprisingly, people began to wonder about this new prophet. Was he perhaps the expected Messiah? The Jewish authorities in Jerusalem sent some priests and Levites to ask John who he was.

But John answered, 'No, I am not the Messiah. I baptize with water, but there is One coming who is much greater than I am. I am not even good enough to untie His sandals. He will baptize you with the Holy Spirit and with fire.' By 'fire' John meant 'holy fervour and zeal in God's service'.

The next day John saw Jesus coming towards him. John pointed Him out to the people and said, 'Look, there He is! That is the One who will take away the sins of the world. It was He whom I was talking about when I said there was One coming who was much greater than me. I did not know who He was, but I came to baptize you with water, so that He might be known to the people of Israel.'

John called Jesus 'the Lamb of God'. This is a phrase which comes from Old Testament sacrifices. Sin meant that people were separated from God and therefore under a death-sentence. In Old Testament days it was customary to offer, as a sacrifice, the death of an animal in place of the death of a person, and often this was a lamb. But when Jesus came, He came to save the world. He was to die, giving His life once and for all, on behalf of sinners, just like a lamb being sacrificed for human sin.

John was very surprised when Jesus came forward to the river to be baptized and felt that this was something which he could not do. Surely Jesus should be baptizing him instead, he thought. So he tried to prevent Jesus from being baptized, but Jesus told him it was God's will.

John agreed, and went into the river with Jesus to baptize Him. People went right into the water to be baptized in those days, and this is still done today in many places with warm climates.

As soon as Jesus came up out of the river, it seemed that the heavens opened, and John saw the Holy Spirit in the form of a dove, come down and alight on Jesus. At the same time a voice from heaven was heard saying, 'This is My beloved Son, with whom I am well pleased.'

These words showed that the baptism of Jesus did not mean that Jesus was a sinner who needed baptizing to wash away former sins like everyone else. God's words showed that Jesus was without sin but that He was now ready to identify Himself with all men and to take on the responsibility for their sin.

Temptation in the Wilderness

After Jesus's baptism by John, God led Him into the desert where He was tempted by the Devil. Jesus was in the desert for forty days and nights, during which time He did not eat any food. He was preparing for, and thinking much about the work which He was to do. How should He use His God-given powers? To satisfy His own needs? To compel people to follow Him? No, this was not the way. He knew that His power must serve men, who must only come to follow Him through their own free will. No one can be forced into the Kingdom of Heaven.

In the first temptation which came to Him from the Devil, the Devil asked Jesus, 'If you are really God's Son, command these stones to be turned into bread.' He knew that Jesus had not eaten for a long time and must be hungry, and that therefore it would be a temptation to use His powers to aid Himself.

Jesus replied, 'The scripture says, "Man shall not live by bread alone, but by every word which God speaks".' He meant that 'Since I am here by God's command, He will keep me alive without bread. I trust Him.'

Then the Devil tried a second temptation. He took Jesus to the highest point of the temple in Jerusalem and said, 'If you are God's Son, throw yourself down from the top here; you will be quite safe for the scriptures say that the angels will take care of you so that you won't be hurt on the stones.'

This was a temptation to take a short, easy and spectacular way to being recognized as the Messiah, by falling, unharmed, to the ground from a great height. Again the Devil craftily quoted scripture to support this temptation.

But Jesus firmly rejected this idea saying, 'The scripture also says, "Do not put God to the test."'

He did not want people to follow Him just because they were astounded at His miracles, but rather because they were truly attracted to His life and teaching, and by the love of God which was shown in all that He said and did. He knew that was the only way in which their faith would become deep and lasting.

Then the Devil had a third try. He took Jesus to the top of a very high mountain, from where he showed Him all the kingdoms of the world. 'All these', he said, 'I will give to you, if only you will worship me.'

The Devil wanted Jesus to acknowledge him and to do evil for the sake of becoming rich and powerful.

Jesus gave him a plain, straightforward answer 'Go away. The scripture says, "Worship the Lord your God, and serve Him only."'

After this, the Devil gave up his hopeless task and left Jesus alone.

The Twelve Disciples

Now Jesus was ready to begin His work, and to do this He chose a band of twelve men to help Him. They were quite ordinary people, whom He knew would be capable of great things.

One day, at about four o'clock in the afternoon, John the Baptist was with two of his followers when he saw Jesus walking by. 'There He is!' John pointed out. 'That is the Lamb of God.'

One of the two men was named Andrew. When he and the other man heard what John said, they went after Jesus, and Jesus turned and saw them.

'What are you looking for?' He asked.

'Where do you live, teacher?' they asked Him.

'Come and see,' said Jesus; so they went with Him, saw where He was living, and spent the rest of the day with Him.

Andrew was so impressed with Jesus that he immediately went and found his own brother,

Simon. 'Simon, we have found the Messiah,' he said, and he took Simon to Jesus.

Jesus looked at Simon and saw what was in him. He knew what a great leader this man could be, and He said, 'From now on you will be called Cephas' (which means 'a rock' and is the same word as 'Peter'. This is why Simon is often referred to as 'Simon Peter' or simply as 'Peter'). Because Andrew brought his brother to Jesus, he was really the first Christian missionary.

Both Andrew and Simon Peter were simple fishermen. They worked in their fishing business with two other brothers whose names were James and John, and whose father was named Zebedee. James and John became disciples too, and three of these first four (Peter, James and John) were to become specially close to Jesus.

After this first call, these four attached themselves to Jesus as disciples, or learners, and when they realized that He was the Messiah, they were ready to leave their homes, their business and everything, and to follow Him completely.

It happened that Jesus was walking along the shores of the Sea of Galilee one day when He again saw the fishermen at their work. (The Lake or Sea of Galilee was also called the Sea of Tiberias because the town of Tiberias lay on its western shore. It is a low, freshwater lake, measuring some 21 km [13 miles] long by about 11 km [$6\frac{1}{2}$ miles] wide. Much of Jesus's ministry was to take place in the towns and countryside around the lake, in places like Capernaum and Bethsaida.)

The people were crowding around Jesus, wanting to hear what He had to say about God and His

Kingdom. Jesus saw two boats pulled up to the shore, one of which belonged to Simon Peter. He got into it and asked Simon to push it out a little way so that He could sit in it and teach the people on the shore. They could all see and hear Him more easily that way.

When He had finished speaking, He said to Simon Peter, 'Push your boat out further into the deep water and then let down your nets for a catch.'

'But master,' said Simon, 'we have been out all night and have caught nothing. Still, if You say so, we will obey.'

When the fishermen let down their nets they caught such a great number of fish that the nets were almost broken with the weight. They had to signal to their partners in the other boat to come and help them. Both boats were soon so full of fish that they were about to sink.

Simon Peter was so impressed that he felt himself much too unworthy to remain in the presence of such a powerful person as Jesus. He said to Jesus, 'Depart from me, for I am a sinful man.'

'Don't be afraid,' said Jesus, 'for from now on, all your life you will be catching people not fish.'

On another day, when Jesus was in Galilee, He called a man named Philip to follow Him. Philip came from Bethsaida, the place where Andrew and Simon Peter lived, and he brought another future disciple, Nathanael, also sometimes called Bartholomew, to Jesus.

'We have found the one whom Moses and the prophets wrote about,' Philip told Nathanael. 'He is Jesus, the son of Joseph, from Nazareth.'

Nathanael was doubtful. 'Can anything good come from Nazareth?' he asked.

To which Philip replied simply, 'Come and see.'

When Jesus saw Nathanael coming towards Him, He said that here was an honest and true Israelite.

'How do you know me?' asked Nathanael, and Jesus replied that He had seen Nathanael under a fig-tree before Philip had even called him. Nathanael was quite astonished.

Another time Jesus saw a man who was a tax-collector sitting in his tax office, and said to him, 'Follow me,' and the man followed Him. He was Matthew, also called Levi. Tax-collectors, or publicans, who collected taxes on behalf of the Romans were much despised as they often took more money than they were entitled to. But Jesus did not despise anyone, and He always had a special care for those who were despised and outcast by others.

The full list of the inner band of twelve is— Simon Peter, Andrew, James, John, Philip, Nathanael, Matthew, Thomas, another James (son of Alphaeus), Thaddaeus, another Simon (the Zealot), and Judas Iscariot.

A Wedding at Cana

This is the story, from St John's Gospel, of the first miracle which Jesus performed.

One day there was to be a wedding in the little town of Cana in Galilee, a few kilometres north-east of Nazareth. Jesus, His mother, Mary, and His disciples had all been invited to the feast to celebrate the happy occasion and to offer their best wishes to their friends.

The bride's friends and the female members of her house had to get the bride ready for the ceremony, and to see that she appeared at her very best before the bridegroom. During the evening of the day of the marriage, the bridegroom and his friends would go to the bride's house; then he would take her back to his or his parents' house for the wedding supper. The marriage feast itself was usually held at the bridegroom's house, and all the relatives and friends were invited. It was considered an insult to refuse such an invitation. The wedding was a joyful occasion which lasted several days, and there was plenty of music, laughter and fun.

At the wedding in Cana, where Jesus and His mother were present, an embarrassing thing happened. The supply of wine ran out long before the guests had had enough!

Jesus's mother saw what had happened, and she did as she must have done many a time; she went and told Jesus about it. 'They have no wine left,' she said.

No one knew much about Jesus as yet, for so far He had not performed any miracles, but Mary must have thought that if anyone could do anything to help, then her son could.

Jesus replied gently and respectfully to His mother, 'I am not concerned as you are. My time has not yet come.'

Mary may not have fully understood what Jesus meant by this, but she went over to the servants and said, 'Do whatever Jesus tells you to do.'

Now the Jews had special rules and customs about washing, particularly about washing their hands before eating, and the water for this was put into large stone waterpots. At the wedding at Cana there were six of these large pots, each of which could hold about 100 litres (22 gal). They stood in a corner, out of the way.

Jesus went to the servants and said, 'Fill the jars with water.' This must have sounded a strange thing to do when the feast was short of wine, but the servants remembered Mary's instructions, and so they obeyed and filled the jars right up to the brim.

Then Jesus said to them, 'Now draw some of the water out and take it over to the steward of the feast.'

The steward was usually a friend of the bridegroom and was in charge of the running of the feast—a sort of master of ceremonies. He must have been very worried at what had occurred, and was no doubt wondering whatever he could do to help the bridegroom out of such an embarrassing situation.

He had not seen what had happened with the water jars, but he took what he thought was the water which the servants brought him, tasted it, and found that it was the very best wine. He had no idea where this very superior wine could have come from. The servants knew, and Mary knew,

but probably very few of the other people there were aware of what had happened because they were so busy having a good time.

The steward called the bridegroom over to him and said, 'Everyone else serves the best wine first, and then, if any more is needed, the more ordinary wine is served. But you have kept the best wine until now!'

After the wedding was over, Jesus and His mother, His brothers and His disciples went to Capernaum for a few days.

In this way Jesus performed His first miracle. It was not connected to serious illness or a great disaster, but was a simple act of kindness, done so that people's happiness should not be spoiled.

The Wise and Foolish Maidens

Later Jesus was to use the idea of a wedding in one of the stories He told to explain His second coming and the Day of Judgment.

One of these was about ten young girls, friends of a bride, who went out to meet the bridegroom and bring him in to the wedding feast.

Night was falling and each of the girls took a small lamp with her to light the way. Five of the girls were prudent enough to take extra oil along as fuel for their lamps, but the other five did not think of this.

The girls had to wait a long time for the bridegroom and one by one the lamps of the five thoughtless girls ran out of oil. At last they were forced to leave the group and go to find more oil for their lamps.

In their absence the bridegroom arrived and went to the feast with the five girls who were still waiting for him.

When the others eventually came back they were too late and were unable to join the feast.

Jesus said that He was like the bridegroom for whose arrival mankind should always be prepared.

The Death of John the Baptist

One day Jesus and His disciples were in the country districts of Judea. Further north, at about the same time, John the Baptist was baptizing people at a place named Aenon near Salim—a place where there was plenty of water for John to carry out his work.

People were coming from far and near to John and to Jesus, and it so happened that more people went to Jesus than went to John. This made some of John's disciples jealous and they went to John and said, 'You remember the man whom you pointed out when you were beyond Jordan? Now He is baptizing too and everyone is going to Him instead of coming here.'

Many leaders would have been angry or jealous to hear news like this, but John did not show any bitterness or resentment. He was not surprised to hear of the success of Jesus, and he said to his disciples, 'No one can have anything unless it has been given to him by God. You remember that I told you I was not the Messiah, but had been sent ahead to prepare the way for Him? It is rather like a wedding; the bridegroom has won the bride, and the bridegroom's friend stands by and rejoices in his success. That is what has happened here. Jesus must become greater, while I shall become less important.'

John continued to preach and to teach and to speak out fearlessly against anything which he knew to be wrong. After his period in the region of Aenon, he returned to the territory of Herod Antipas. This Herod was one of the sons of Herod the Great who had tried to kill Jesus, by ordering the death of all baby boys up to two years old, at the time of the visit of the wise men all those years

ago in Bethlehem when that new star had appeared.

Now Herod Antipas had divorced his own wife and had married Herodias who was the wife of his brother Philip, and John the Baptist told him that this was an unlawful thing to do. 'It is wrong for you to be married to your brother's wife,' he said sternly.

For this Herodias bore a grudge against John and wanted to have him killed. Herod would not do that, however; for one thing, he feared the great influence John had over many of the Jewish people who considered him to be a great prophet; and for another, in his heart, Herod knew that John was a just and holy man and he liked to listen to him—even though John's truthful and hard-hitting words often upset him. So he compromised and had John chained and put in prison, instead, hoping to keep him quiet.

Meanwhile, Jesus continued teaching, preaching and healing, with His specially chosen twelve disciples to help Him in His work as he travelled around the country.

All this came to the ears of John the Baptist as he languished in prison feeling very depressed and miserable. Some of John's disciples were still a little jealous of Jesus and doubtful as to who He really was. So John sent them to see Him, probably hoping that they might be convinced that He was the true Messiah and begin to feel more generous and trusting towards Him.

They found Jesus curing and healing all kinds of sickness and disease. They asked Him, 'Are you the one whom John said was to come, or shall we expect someone else?'

Jesus replied, 'Go back to John and tell him

about the things you have seen and heard; how the blind have received their sight, the deaf have had their hearing restored, the lame walk again and the dead have been brought back to life; and the good news of the Gospel has been preached to the poor.' (Gospel is really 'Godspell' which means 'good news'.)

John's disciples could not deny this, and they went back to John feeling reassured. When they had gone, Jesus spoke to the crowd about John: 'What did you expect to see when you went out

to the desert?' He asked them. 'A reed bent to the wind? A man in fine clothes? A prophet? Yes, you saw more than a prophet; for John is the one whom the scriptures foretold would be the messenger to go before Me to prepare the way. Truly there has not been a greater man than John the Baptist. Yet he who is least in the Kingdom of Heaven is greater than John.' (Jesus meant that the meanest and lowest Christian is greater in privilege than the greatest men in the whole world when seen through the eyes of God.)

Salome

Some time after this, Herod had a birthday, and he gave a great party for all the government officials, army commanders and leading people in Galilee. It was a most splendid affair.

During the party, Herodias's daughter, Salome, came in and danced before the guests, and everyone was delighted with her. King Herod was so pleased that he said to her, 'What would you like? You can ask for anything you wish, and I promise you shall have it—even if it is as much as half my kingdom.'

Salome did not know what to ask for, so she went and consulted her mother. 'What shall I say?' she asked her.

'Ask for the head of John the Baptist,' replied Herodias wickedly, for she had not forgotten her grudge against John.

Back went Salome to Herod and said, 'I want the head of John the Baptist given to me on a dish immediately.'

Herod was very sad when he heard this, for he did not want John killed, but as he had given a solemn promise in front of so many people, he felt he must not break his word. So he sent a soldier of the guard with orders to bring him John the Baptist's head at once.

The guard went and beheaded John, brought his head and gave it to Salome; and Salome gave it to her mother.

Herod's conscience continued to trouble him about this, and no wonder. Some time later he heard about the work of Jesus and the wonderful things He was doing. Some people thought Jesus was the prophet Elijah, but King Herod, greatly alarmed, said, 'It is John the Baptist, whose head I had cut off. He has come back to life.' King Herod felt greatly troubled.

The Story of the Good Samaritan

One day when Jesus was teaching, a lawyer came up to Him, hoping to trap Him with a clever question. 'What shall I do to gain eternal life?' he asked Jesus.

Jesus replied, 'What do the scriptures tell you? How do you interpret them?'

The lawyer replied, 'Love God with all your heart, with all your soul, with all your mind and with all your strength; and love your neighbour as you love yourself.'

'Quite right,' said Jesus. 'Do that and you will live.'

The lawyer, somewhat taken aback, tried to save face by asking another question. Perhaps his conscience pricked him and he wanted to justify his own lack of love.

'But who *is* my neighbour?' he asked, looking puzzled.

Instead of answering directly, Jesus told him a story as He often did when He was teaching. A story is a very good way of explaining a point, because people remember stories far more easily than they remember plain facts and they can repeat the stories to other people.

Jesus's stories had a deeper meaning than most and are called parables, 'earthly stories with a heavenly meaning'. This is the story He told to the lawyer.

Once there was a man who was going on a journey from Jerusalem to Jericho, a distance of about 27 km (17 miles). The way lay along a rocky, lonely and dangerous road infested by murderous brigands.

Suddenly a gang of robbers sprang out from behind some rocks and attacked the man. They tore off his clothes and beat him up, and then left him half dead, lying on the road in the blazing sun. His wounds were very painful, and flies bothered him and he was very thirsty, but there was no one anywhere near to come to his aid. His plight was terrible.

A while later it happened that a priest was travelling along the same road. When the wounded man heard footsteps, he opened his eyes, and when he saw that the figure was a priest, he felt a little happier. Surely here was someone who would help?

The priest saw the man, but he did not stop; he just hurried by on the other side. Perhaps he told himself he hadn't time to stop, as he was on important business for the temple, perhaps he was afraid robbers might attack him too if he stopped so he kept on going.

Sadly, the wounded man heard the footsteps die away in the distance.

Shortly afterwards, there were more footsteps, and the wounded man's hopes rose again when he saw that a Levite was coming that way. A Levite was a helper in the temple, and he might well be expected to be the sort of man who would help someone in distress.

But no, the Levite looked at the wounded man, and then he too hurried by on the other side of the road.

Once more the man heard the footsteps die away and the road became quiet and lonely again. The wounded man felt desperate.

Before long, the man heard more footsteps of a different kind. This time a donkey was coming

down the road with a man on his back. The wounded man was very disappointed to see that the rider was a Samaritan.

The Jews and the Samaritans had been enemies for a very long time. The Jews of Judah in the south hated the Samaritans who lived in Samaria in the north, for the Samaritans were a mixed race and were thought to be not wholly loyal to Israel's God. So the pure-blooded Jews scorned them.

The wounded man felt pretty sure he could not expect any help from a Samaritan, but, to his great surprise, the donkey stopped and the rider dismounted. He came over to the wounded man and looked kindly at him. He felt sorry and wondered what he could do to help. His own safety did not seem to worry him.

Then he went back to his donkey and brought over some oil and some wine which he had with him. These he put on the man's wounds, to act as antiseptic and ointment, and bandaged him up. He probably had to tear up some of his own

clothes in order to make strips for bandages as it is unlikely that he carried any with him.

Next he lifted up the wounded man gently and put him on his own donkey. Then, with the Samaritan walking at the side and holding the wounded man, they slowly made their way until they came to an inn.

The Samaritan asked the innkeeper for a room, and led the man to it and took care of him there. He put him to bed, bathed his wounds with water and bandaged them up afresh, and gave the man some food and drink. Then he made him comfortable and left him to sleep.

The following day the Samaritan had to continue his journey, but before he went, he wondered what else he could do for the wounded man who would have to remain resting at the inn for quite some time until he was well enough to return to his family.

He took out two coins and gave them to the innkeeper. 'Look after him,' he told the innkeeper, 'and if it should cost you any more than this, I will pay you the extra amount when I come back this way again.'

Having finished his story, Jesus turned to the lawyer and asked, 'Which of the three passers-by do you think acted like a neighbour to the man attacked by the robbers?'

'The one who showed pity and acted kindly to him,' replied the lawyer.

'Then go and do the same,' said Jesus.

The Story of the Prodigal Son

There was once a man who had two sons to whom he would leave all that he owned when he died.

One day the younger son went to his father and said, 'Father, give me my share of the property *now*.'

He wanted to go off and enjoy himself and did not want to wait until his father had died. His father loved him and did not want him to go away, but he also knew that the youth was old enough to go out into the world if he wished to do so. So he gave him his share of the property as the lad had asked.

The youth sold it and, with the money, he set off for a far country. Once there, he made lots of friends, because people were eager to know him when they found that he had a great deal of money to spend. He gave presents and parties and generally had what he thought was a good time. He did not look for work because he did not think it important when he had so much money. Instead he just went on wasting his time and his wealth doing silly and foolish things and having what he thought was a jolly good time.

The day came when he realized with a shock that all his money was spent. The people whom he had thought were friends did not want to know him now that he was poor, for they were not true friends and had only wanted him for what they could get out of him.

So there he was, without money, without friends, all alone in a foreign country. Worse still, a famine arose in the country and there was scarcely any food to be had. So, on top of everything, now he was hungry too.

He decided he would have to look for work, but it was difficult to find any as he had never learnt any skill or trade.

At last someone gave him a job looking after pigs, and he went out into the fields and fed the animals. He was so hungry himself, because no one gave him anything to eat, that he would gladly have eaten the pigs' food which was made up of scraps of all sorts of things that only pigs would find delicious.

One day it dawned upon him just how foolish he had been. He began to think about his father and his home, and how kindly he had been treated there. Even his father's servants were well fed and better off than he was, he thought, and yet he, the son of the house, was perishing with hunger in a foreign land.

He decided to swallow any pride he had left and go back home. He would tell his father how truly sorry he was and how ashamed he felt at what he had done. It would not be easy to own up in this way, and perhaps his father would refuse to have him back, but he felt he must try. It was his only hope of saving himself.

Meanwhile, at home, his father had never forgotten the younger son. He still loved him, and although he did not like the way he had behaved, he longed for his return. From time to time he would go out and look to see if there was any sign of the youth in the distance and after a while would return sadly to the house.

As he was watching one day, he saw a figure coming along far off on the road; and while he was still a great way away, he recognized his son! How

delighted the father was! He could hardly believe his eyes.

Wearily the youth trudged towards him, getting ready to say how sorry he was. But the father did not wait for his son to arrive; he ran out to meet him, and threw his arms around him and kissed him.

'Father,' began the son, 'I have sinned against God and against you. I'm not worth being called a son, and I don't deserve to be forgiven. Let me be one of your servants.'

But his father did not seem to be listening. He was calling his servants: 'Hurry up, bring the best robe and put it on him; put a ring on his finger and shoes on his feet. Then go and kill the prize calf and let us have a feast. For here is my son, whom we thought dead, but he is alive; he was lost but now is found!'

And so the joyful party began. There was feasting and dancing and music, because everyone rejoiced that the younger son had come home again safely.

As all this was taking place, the other son, the older one, was out working in the fields, and he did not know what had happened as he had seen no one all day.

On his way back, as he drew near the house, he heard the sounds of music and dancing and wondered what was going on. It was most odd!

He called one of the servants over and asked 'What's happening?'

'Your brother has come home and your father is giving a party because he is so glad to have him back safe and sound,' answered the servant and he rushed off to join in the feast.

Instead of rejoicing, as the others had done, the elder brother was angry and jealous, and refused to go into the house. His father came out and begged him to come in, but the son replied, 'All these years I have worked for you like a slave, and have always obeyed your orders. Yet you have never given me so much as a goat to have a party with my friends. But this wastrel son of yours comes back, having spent all your money in silly and foolish ways, and you give him a grand feast! It isn't fair!'

This mean and jealous attitude of his elder son spoilt the father's joy, and he said to him, 'My son, you are always with me, and everything I have is yours. It was right for us to celebrate and make merry when your brother came back home. For he was lost and is found!'

The father in the story represents God, and in telling the story, Jesus was showing how forgiving God is when anyone is truly sorry for the wrong things he or she has done.

The Stories of the Lost Sheep and the Lost Coin

Jesus told two other stories which show how ready God is to forgive and how happy He is when a sinner repents and goes back to Him.

The occasion arose when a group of tax-collectors and other people with a bad reputation had gathered together to listen to Jesus. The Pharisees, a group who were dedicated to keeping the law in every exact detail, and other teachers of the law started to grumble because Jesus was being friendly to such social outcasts. 'This man Jesus welcomes these outcasts and even goes so far as to eat with them,' they muttered.

Jesus knew what was in their minds, and saw that they were not interpreting the law with enough kindliness. So He told these stories:

'Suppose there was a shepherd who had a hundred sheep,' he began. 'One day he was counting them into the fold and he found that he had lost one, and that he only had ninety-nine.

'What would he do? Does he decide that one sheep is neither here nor there, and not worth bothering about? After all, he still has ninety-nine.

'No; he leaves the ninety-nine sheep safely in the pasture, and goes out and searches for the one that is lost; and he goes on looking, however long it takes, until he finds it.

'Then he is very happy, and he picks up the lost sheep, puts it on his shoulders, and carries it back home. He calls together his friends and neighbours and says to them, "Rejoice with me, for I have found my sheep which was lost!"'

'In the same way,' said Jesus, 'there is more joy in heaven when one person who has sinned repents and comes back to God's ways, than over ninety-nine righteous people who do not need to repent.'

The Lost Coin
The second story was about a woman who lost one of her precious coins.

In those days a woman often wore the coins which made up her dowry in a headdress or necklace. Because they were so important to her, she would consider it disastrous if she lost one and would take a light and peer into all the dark corners of the house, and sweep through it thoroughly until she found the lost coin.

When she did so, she would call together her friends and neighbours to rejoice with her that the lost coin was found.

The Good Shepherd
'I am the good Shepherd,' said Jesus. 'The good Shepherd lays down his life for the sheep.

'A hired man, who is not the shepherd, does not care for the sheep in the same way. He sees a wolf coming and, instead of staying to protect the sheep, he runs away, and so the wolf gets them.

'As God the Father knows Me and I know Him, so I know My sheep and they know Me.

'There are some sheep who belong to Me who are not in the fold, and I must bring them in too. So there will be one flock and one Shepherd.'

The Story of the Sower

Telling parables was one way for Jesus to sort out His listeners. He could tell which of them had come simply for the story and which really wanted to understand the point He was trying to teach.

One of the things which many people, including the disciples, found hard to understand was the nature of the Kingdom of God, about which Jesus talked a lot. So He told them several stories or parables to help them. One of the best-known of these is about a sower.

Jesus was down by the Sea of Galilee when He told this story, and the crowd was so great that He

found it better to get into a boat and push it out a little way. From there He could teach the crowd more easily, than if they were all jostling round Him.

It is quite likely that as He told this particular story, He could see a man sowing seed in one of the fields which sloped down towards the sea. This would make the story more real to His listeners.

One day a man went out to sow. As he scattered his seed in handfuls from his basket, some of it fell on the pathway, which was hard and well trodden by horses, mules and humans. There was little soil in which it might take root, and it was not long before the birds flew down and ate up the seed.

Some of the seed fell on rocky ground, for there were stones sticking up out of the land here and there. The soil was only very shallow, so although the seed started to grow, it could not take root. When the sun came out, the little plants were scorched and quickly withered away because they could not get enough food from the little amount of soil.

Some other seed fell among thornbushes, and though the plants began to grow, the thorns soon choked them and they died.

But some seed fell on the good rich soil, and these plants grew well; they produced lots of corn some 100 grains each, some sixty and some thirty.

The disciples were rather puzzled at this story and they asked Jesus to tell them what it meant. So Jesus explained that the seed is the word of God, and the sower is Jesus Himself.

The various types of soil represent the hearts and minds of people.

The seed which fell on the pathway can be compared to someone who hears the word of God and does not try hard enough to understand it. The birds are like the Devil who comes and takes away the message from their hearts. These people are so busy thinking of other things that it is easy for the Devil to snatch away God's word from them.

The seed which fell on rocky ground, can be compared to people who listen gladly to God's word, but they do not let it sink deeply enough into their hearts. They believe only for a while. Then, when they are faced with a time of testing, they easily fall away.

The seed which fell among thornbushes stands for those who hear, but let the worries and pleasures and riches of the world crowd in and choke the word of God, so that it never grows into anything lasting. These people fail because they try to serve God and the world, and it is not possible to do both.

The seed falling on good ground stands for those who hear the word and let it grow strong in their hearts.

The Parables of the Kingdom of Heaven

Jesus was very careful to explain that His Kingdom was not to be thought of like an earthly kingdom, with boundaries marking its territory. 'My Kingdom,' He said, 'is not of this world.'

His Kingdom was the reign of love and peace for everyone, and could be enjoyed here on earth as well as in the future. But the Kingdom would only come fully when everyone obeyed God's rule. People did not have to build or establish it themselves; all they had to do was to seek it and enter it by obeying God and living according to His laws.

The Parable of the Weeds

One day a man sowed good seed in his field. During the night, while everyone was asleep, a spiteful enemy came and sowed weeds, or tares, among the good seed. These weeds looked very much like wheat and it was not until the ears began to form that the weeds were noticed. The man's servants said to him, 'Sir, did you not sow good seed in this field? Where then have all these weeds come from?'

'An enemy has done it,' replied the man.

'Shall we go and pull up the weeds then?' asked the servants.

'No,' answered the man, 'because in gathering the weeds you might pull up some of the good wheat with them. Let them both grow together until the final harvest, and then I will tell the reapers to gather the weeds first and burn them, and then to gather in the wheat and put it in my barn.'

When the disciples asked Jesus to explain this parable, He said that the field represented the world, the man was Himself, and the enemy was the Devil. The good seed stood for true Christians, and the weeds were the people who belonged to the Devil. It is not for ordinary people to try and distinguish between true and false Christians; that must be left until the end of time (the harvest) when God would sort out the mixture of good and bad.

The Parable of the Mustard Seed

The Kingdom of Heaven, said Jesus, is also like a grain of mustard seed, one of the tiniest of all seeds, but which in hot countries grows to a great size. Here it can develop into a great tree which puts out branches so that birds can come and make their nests in its shade.

In this way each single follower of Christ can sow the Kingdom of God in the place where he lives, and who can say how much it will expand in time?

So the Kingdom of God, which began in an obscure province of Palestine with twelve Galilean disciples, who had neither great wealth nor education, rapidly grew into a worldwide Church.

The Parable of the Leaven

Here, Christ said, the Kingdom of Heaven is like leaven, or yeast, which a woman mixes into flour to make bread; there it bubbles and swells until the whole batch of dough rises.

So God can transform people from within.

The Parable of the Hidden Treasure

Again, Jesus said, the Kingdom is like great treasure hidden in a field. A man comes along and stumbles on it and is so overjoyed that he goes and sells all that he has in order to buy the field.

Selling everything one has is like giving up every sin or self-indulgence which hinders people from living a life wholly for God.

The Parable of the Pearl of Great Price

The Kingdom of Heaven is like a man who is searching for pearls. One day he finds one of supreme value. The cost is high, but he gladly sells everything that he possesses in order to buy that one pearl.

The Parable of the Drag-net

A drag-net is a long net used near the shore, with its bottom end weighted to brush along the sea bed, while the upper edge floats on the surface supported by corks. It catches all the fish in its wide sweep.

Jesus said the Kingdom of Heaven is like a drag-net which fishermen cast into the sea and which gathers in all kinds of fish. Then men bring it ashore and sort the good from the bad. The good they put in barrels and the bad they throw away. So the Church gathers in all kinds of people, good and bad, and of every nation, kingdom and language. The net must be spread wide to include all sorts of people, and at the end of time the sorting will be done by God. Meanwhile it is not for anyone else to decide that a certain person or race is not to be allowed in. Everyone is equal in the eyes of God.

The Story of the Talents

One day a certain man had to leave his home and set out on a long journey. Before he left, he called together his servants and put them in charge of his property while he was away.

He did not leave them all with an equal amount of responsibility, for he knew each man and what he was capable of doing, and so he gave them each a different amount, according to his ability. To one man he gave five talents, to another two talents, and to another one. (A talent was a measure in reckoning money, not a single coin, but a sum of high value. Nowadays we use the word 'talent' to mean a special gift or aptitude; we talk of a gifted or talented person, who can do something very well.)

Having so disposed of his wealth, the man then left.

The servant who had been given the five talents went away and traded with them. He put what had been entrusted to him to good use, and before long found that he had made a profit of another five talents.

The servant who had been given two talents also went and traded with them, and soon he, too, had made another two talents.

But the servant who had received the one talent was not nearly so enterprising. He did not bother to use his abilities to increase his talent in any way. He simply went off and dug a hole in the ground and buried his master's money. There it was of no use to anyone, not even to himself.

A long time passed, and one day the master returned home. One of the first things he did was to call his servants together and settle up accounts with them.

The servant who had received the five talents came and handed the money to his master and said, 'Sir, you gave me five talents, but here are another five which I have earned with them.'

'Well done,' said the master. 'You have been a good and faithful servant. As you have done so well in looking after a relatively small amount, I will now put you in charge of much greater amounts. Come and share my joy and happiness!'

Then the servant who had received the two talents handed the money back to his master and said, 'Sir, you gave me two talents, but I have earned these other two with them.'

'Well done,' said the master, 'you have been a good and faithful servant. As you have done so well in looking after a small amount, I will now put you in charge of greater amounts. Come and share my joy and happiness!'

Then it was the turn of the servant who had received the one talent. He came forward, full of excuses, and said churlishly, 'Sir, I knew you to be a hard man, reaping harvests where you did not sow them and gathering crops where you did not scatter seed. So I was afraid and went and buried your money in the ground. Here is the one talent which you gave me. Now I hand you back what is yours.'

So this servant made his master out to be as churlish as he himself was. He did not believe that his master would accept a small amount of work done sincerely for him. He thought that as he had only been given a small amount, it could not possibly matter what he did with it. How wrong he was! He had not learnt that even the smallest talent could be put to good use.

Naturally, the master was very displeased with him.

'You wicked and lazy servant!' he said. 'You thought, did you, that I reaped harvests where I did not sow, and gathered crops where I had not scattered seed? Why did you not then take my money and invest it? At least I would have got it back together with any interest it may have earned.'

The servant had not thought of that.

'Take the money away from him,' went on the master, 'and give it to the man who has ten talents. For to everyone who has something, more will be given, and so he will have more than enough. But the person who has little will have even the little he has taken away from him. As for this useless servant, he shall be cast into outer darkness, where he will weep and grind his teeth.'

The master in the story is like Jesus, and the servants are His followers. His going off on a long journey can be likened to Jesus's Ascension, when He returned to Heaven. He entrusted His followers with the task of increasing His kingdom on earth by using the different abilities (or talents) which God had given them.

Each person has been given some talent and has an ability to do something; he or she may be a teacher or a preacher, a musician or a writer, or have great wealth which can be used to help less fortunate people. Someone may be possessed of a kind heart and be able to do all manner of good and helpful things to aid others, or be observant and have the gift of noticing where things want doing, whereas many other people would miss them.

No matter how small it may be, everyone has been given some 'talent' and is good at something. It is no good saying, like the man with the one talent, that we have only been given a little and that therefore it is not worth bothering about.

The story also tells us that if we do not use the ability, talent or gift that we have, we shall soon lose it altogether.

Jesus was pointing out that if we use any talent or gift properly, then we shall find that it will develop and increase.

The Sermon on the Mount

The Sermon on the Mount is a collection of Jesus's teachings, which may not all have been given at one time. Most of Jesus's teaching was done in the open air, and we can imagine Him seated on a hillside with the crowds in their colourful robes gathered all about Him. They listened eagerly to what He was saying, for He spoke with great authority.

All that He said was really putting into words the way He already lived. The power by which He lived His life was the same power by which His followers must also live—namely, the power of prayer.

He showed that men ought not to live merely by a rigid set of rules, but rather by looking at life from God's point of view and by considering other people before themselves.

The Beatitudes

'Beatitude' means 'blessedness' or 'true happiness'.

Whereas people think that they must be rich or powerful in order to be happy, Jesus said that the truly happy person needs neither of these things.

He taught that the truly happy people are those who know they are spiritually poor and learn to rely on God; they are also those who are humble and who live as God wishes; those who are merciful and forgiving; those who are pure in heart, and those who are peacemakers.

The Work of His Disciples in the World

Jesus's followers are those who put 'seasoning' (salt) into life, and also those who light up the way for others. The things such people do and say help others to know something of what God is like. 'You are the salt of the earth', said Jesus, and also 'You are the light of the world.'

Teaching about the Law

Jesus said that He had not come to do away with the old law (the law which God had given Moses on Mount Sinai), but that He had come to fill it out, to extend it, and to show that it dealt not only with deeds, but with the thoughts which give rise to the deeds.

Not only is murder wrong, for example, but the kind of angry thought which could lead to murder is also wrong in itself.

Although the old law said 'an eye for an eye and a tooth for a tooth', Jesus said it is wrong to take vengeance on someone who has wronged you. That only makes a bad situation worse. It is far better to deal kindly with the person.

Jesus told people, 'Love your enemies and pray for those who terrorize you.' It used to be said that you should love your friends and hate your enemies. But there is nothing extraordinary in loving one's friends—anyone can do that—one must also deal kindly with those who are not one's friends.

As in the story of the Good Samaritan love, here, is not a matter of feelings, it is a matter of behaviour.

Warnings about Showing Off

Whatever your deeds may look like to people outside, it is what is in your heart that really matters, said Jesus. So do not make a big show about giving to the needy, so that everyone knows what you are doing. When you give help, do it in such a way that not even your closest friend will know of it.

Teaching about Prayer

Similarly, do not pray so that everyone will see you, but pray somewhere privately. Do not use long, meaningless words, but pray simply. Jesus then gave us a 'pattern prayer' like this:

'Our Father who art in heaven,
Hallowed be Thy Name,
Thy kingdom come,
Thy will be done, on earth as it is in heaven.
Give us this day our daily bread;
And forgive us our debts, as we also have
*   forgiven our debtors;*
And lead us not into temptation, but deliver us
*   from evil.*

Teaching about Riches and Possessions

You can choose whether money and material things or God and spiritual things are your main aim in life, said Jesus.

Do not store up riches on earth, He advised, where moths and rust can get at them and thieves can break in and steal them. Put God first in your life, and He who knows all your needs will supply them. You will then have no need to worry.

You cannot put both God and material things first in your life. You must choose one; but where your heart is, that is where your riches really are.

Judging Others

Do not be critical of others when there is so much that can be criticized in your own life. Jesus said, humorously, that it is like a man who wanted to take a tiny speck out of his brother's eye, but did not notice that there was something the size of a great log in his own eye!

Warning about People who Mislead

Beware of false prophets who look like the real thing but are not so. You can tell what sort any tree is by the fruit it bears. So you can tell what people are really like by the things that they do and they cannot deceive you.

Having the Right Base for Your Life

'Anyone who hears My words and lives by them,' said Jesus, 'is like a man who builds his house on a rock—a firm foundation. The rains may pour down in torrents, and the winds may blow a terrible hurricane, and the floods may swell, but the house will not fall, because it is standing firm on a rock.

'Anyone who hears My words and does not live by them is like a foolish man who builds his house on sand. Then, when the rains come in torrents, and the winds blow in a hurricane, and the floods swell, that house will crash down in ruins, because it was only built on sand which slips away.'

He meant that if you live by His standards, whatever storms and troubles come in life, they will be unable to defeat you.

Jesus Blesses the Children

One day Jesus and His disciples were going to Capernaum, and on the way the disciples were arguing among themselves as to who was the greatest and most important of them.

When they got indoors, Jesus questioned them about this. 'What were you all arguing about on the way here?' He asked. But the disciples would not answer, because they were all feeling somewhat ashamed of themselves. However, Jesus knew, without needing any answer from them, and He sat down and called them all to Him.

'If you want to be first and really important,' He said, 'you must put yourself last. You must be ready to be the servant of everyone else. Those are the people who are truly great.'

Now there was a little child listening to all this—perhaps he was the child who lived in the house—and Jesus put His arm round him, and said, 'The greatest in the Kingdom of Heaven is one who is as humble as this little child. Anyone who welcomes a child is welcoming Me. For he who is least among you is the greatest.'

Jesus was trying to explain to the disciples that God's Kingdom has very different standards from the world. Riches and power do not make anyone great in God's eyes. Being loving, generous, humble and forgiving are far more important, and people with these qualities are the ones who are truly great. Such people may seem as unimportant as a child to the world, but in God's Kingdom they are the ones who are the greatest.

Jesus loved children and as He went about He noticed them playing. Like children today, they liked to pretend they were grown-up, and sometimes they would play at weddings or funerals and fall out over their games.

On one occasion some people brought a number of children to Jesus, knowing how He loved them. They wanted Him to put His hands on them and bless them.

When the disciples saw this, they rebuked the people and tried to send the children away, for they did not want Jesus to be troubled by them. No doubt they thought that children were not important enough to claim His attention.

Jesus, however, thought very differently. He was never troubled by people coming to Him, no matter how young—or how old—they might be. He would never turn anyone away.

He did not like the way the disciples were dealing with the children, and He called them back to Him. Then He said, 'Let the children come to Me, and do not try to stop them, for the Kingdom of God belongs to such children as these. I tell you that whoever does not receive the Kingdom of God in the same spirit as a child, will never enter into it.'

He did not mean that people should be childish and never to grow up in their ideas. He meant that they should receive God's Kingdom in a child-like spirit—that is, one of humble, loving trust. This can apply to anyone of any age.

Then Jesus took the children in His arms and put His hands on each of them and blessed them.

Jesus Calms a Storm and Walks on the Water

On the evening of the day when Jesus had been telling the story of the sower to a crowd of people, He said to the disciples, 'Let us cross to the other side of the lake.'

So they left the crowd, and got into the little boat in which Jesus had been sitting to teach, and they began to row across.

The lake was the Sea of Galilee, which lies low about 183 m (600 ft) below sea-level. All around there are hills, with deep ravines and gorges, and these act as funnels, drawing down the winds from the mountains. From time to time, these winds lash the waters into a great fury, making it dangerous for small boats.

Suddenly, as Jesus and the disciples were crossing, one of these great strong winds blew up, tossing the little boat about and swooshing in lots of water, putting them all in great danger of sinking or overturning.

The disciples were panic-stricken, even though some of them were experienced sailors. They turned to Jesus and found Him in the back of the boat—fast asleep, for He was tired after being with the crowds all day.

It seemed as though the little boat would be completely swamped by the raging waves, and the terrified disciples rushed to wake Jesus up. 'Master! Master! We are going to perish!' they cried. 'Don't you care?'

Calmly Jesus got up and said to the wind, 'Be quiet!' and to the waves He said, 'Peace, be still.'

And there was at once a great calm.

'Why were you so frightened?' asked Jesus of the disciples. 'Haven't you any faith?'

The disciples looked at one another in awe and wonder and said, 'What sort of man is this—that even the winds and the sea obey Him?'

Jesus Walks on the Water

Another time, by Galilee, Jesus asked the disciples to get into a boat and row across to Bethsaida at the other side of the lake. Meanwhile, He sent the crowd of people home and went up on the hillside by Himself to pray.

By evening time, the disciples in their little boat were far out on the lake, and were being tossed about somewhat, for it was a windy night and the sea was choppy.

Sometime between 3 am and 6 am, when they had been rowing for about 5 or 6 km (3 miles), the disciples looked out and saw a figure walking towards them on the water. They were terrified and screamed with fear. 'It's a ghost!' they cried, their voices trembling.

Then the familiar and beloved voice of Jesus said, 'Do not be afraid. It is I.'

Now Peter, confident and enthusiastic as always, spoke up and said, 'Lord, if it is really You, tell me to come to You on the water.'

'Come,' said Jesus.

So Peter got out of the boat and began to walk on the water towards Jesus. But his faith did not last for long, and when he saw what a strong wind there was, he grew afraid—and as soon as he stopped trusting Jesus, he began to sink. 'Lord! Save me!' he cried out.

Jesus reached out and grabbed hold of his hand and said, 'What little faith you have! Why did you doubt?'

Then they both climbed into the boat, and the wind died down, the raging waves grew calm and the storm faded away.

The disciples turned to Jesus in awe saying, 'Truly, You are the Son of God.'

The Feeding of the Five Thousand

Crowds followed Jesus everywhere, for they saw His miracles and heard His teaching, and they wanted to see and hear more. He was becoming quite famous.

One day, near the time for the Passover Festival, when many Galileans came to Jerusalem, a huge crowd followed Jesus up a hillside. Jesus had been hoping to take His disciples away for a short rest, and they had gone to this quiet place by boat. The crowds, however, had followed round the lake, on foot, and many were already on the hillside when Jesus arrived.

Among them was a young boy whose mother had given him a picnic meal to take out with him. Perhaps he had told her that he was going to see and hear Jesus, the great teacher, and she knew he would probably be away all day. But there were few other people in the crowd, if any, who had thought to bring food with them, even to give to their children.

Jesus sat down on the top of a hill, and looked round at the hundreds of people gathered about Him. He felt sorry for them, for He knew they must be getting hungry and they were all a long way from home.

'It's getting late,' said the disciples. 'Send them all away so that they can go into the towns and villages and buy themselves something to eat.'

Jesus knew He could feed the multitude, but He wanted to test the disciples; so He turned to Philip and said, 'Where can we buy enough bread out here in the open to feed this great crowd?'

Philip said, 'Even if they each had only a little, it would take at least 200 silver coins.'

No one had that sort of money on them, for one silver coin was an average man's wage for a day's work, and 200 such coins would be equal to more than six months' wages.

Then another disciple, Andrew, who was Simon Peter's brother, noticed the boy with the picnic meal. 'There is a lad here,' said Andrew, 'who has brought with him five loaves of barley bread and two small fish—but they won't be anything like enough for all these people.' Andrew and the other disciples began to look worried.

There seemed to be no one else with any food at all.

'Make them all sit down,' said Jesus.

So they all sat down in groups on the green grass; there were about 100 people in some groups and about fifty in others, and in their beautifully coloured robes, in the sunshine, they looked rather like flower beds in a garden in the summertime.

Then Jesus took the five loaves which the boy had offered, gave thanks to God, and broke the loaves and gave them to the disciples to distribute among the people. Then He did the same with the fish.

There were 5,000 men in the crowd, not counting women and children, and the disciples went to each little group, giving food to everyone in it, men, women and children.

The wonderful thing was that no matter how much they gave out, the supply they carried was never finished. Everyone ate and soon they had all had as much as they wanted and felt satisfied and contented.

Jesus did not believe in wasting any of God's good gifts, so He said to the disciples, 'Now gather up all the pieces that remain, so that there shall be no waste.'

Each of the disciples took a large basket and went round collecting up all the scraps they could find; and each filled his basket. This meant that, after 5,000 and more people had been fed, there were still twelve baskets of food remaining from what had been one boy's picnic lunch of five small loaves and two little fish.

The people were all astonished, for they had seen the miracle with their own eyes. They said to one another, 'Surely this is the great prophet who was to come into the world.'

The boy who had given up his picnic must have had a wonderful story to tell his parents when he got back home!

Jesus the Healer

Jesus soon became well known for His works of healing and people came to Him from far and near to be cured of their illnesses.

Healing a Leper

One day, after Jesus had been teaching in Galilee, there came to Him a man who was suffering from a terrible skin disease called leprosy. Today it is possible to cure this disease, but in Jesus's day there was no hope at all. A leper had to keep right away from other people because the law regarded him as unclean. No one, knowing him to be a leper, dare approach him, but if anyone accidentally did come near him, the leper had to cry out 'Unclean!' and people would back hastily away in case they caught the disease.

Thus lepers, as well as being ill, led a very lonely life, entirely cut off from human company, except for other lepers.

But Jesus did not shun them, for He never shunned anyone in trouble. When this leper came and asked to be healed, Jesus stretched out His hand and touched him. The leper said, 'If you will, you can make me clean.'

'I will,' said Jesus. 'Be clean,' and immediately the disease went from the man.

Jesus instructed him not to spread the news of how he had been healed, because He did not want people to come and proclaim Him as the Messiah yet; but told the man to go to a priest to be examined, and to make an offering to prove that he was cured. This was as the law of Israel commanded.

However the man was naturally so excited that he told everyone he met, and the result was that Jesus could not go into the towns for a while and had to stay in the desert.

Jesus Heals Ten Lepers

One day, when Jesus was on the way to Jerusalem, He was entering a village when He was met by ten men who were lepers. They stood a distance away from Him and called, 'Jesus, Master! Have mercy on us!'

No doubt they had heard stories of this wonderful healer and thought that if anyone could heal them, He could.

Jesus saw them, went over to them, and said, 'Go and be examined by the priests.'

Obediently, the ten set off, and on the way they looked at one another and saw that all signs of their leprosy had vanished. Their skins were completely cured. They were delighted!

One of them, who was a Samaritan, turned back and went and threw himself at Jesus's feet and thanked Him.

'Were there not ten men healed?' said Jesus. 'Where are the other nine? Was this man, a foreigner, the only one to come back and give praise and thanks to God?'

Then He said to the leper, 'Get up and go on your way. Your faith has made you whole.'

By this He meant that not only had the leper's faith in Jesus healed his body, it had also healed his soul, because he had given thanks and praise to God to whom the glory was due.

The Centurion's Servant

In Capernaum there lived a centurion. The Roman army was divided into 'centuries', each of a hundred men, and each commanded by a centurion. The Romans worshipped many gods, but as this centurion had gone about among the Jews, he had heard about Jesus and he had faith in Him.

For this reason, when his servant became very ill, the first person the centurion thought of was Jesus. However, he thought, perhaps Jesus would not be likely to come to a Roman soldier's house, and so he sent some Jewish elders to ask Jesus's help.

'Please come,' said the elders to Jesus, 'for this man really deserves your help. Although he is a Roman, he is kind to our people and has even built us a synagogue.'

Jesus went with them, and when they came near to the centurion's house, another group of his Jewish friends came out to Jesus, with a message from the centurion. 'Please don't trouble yourself,' they said, 'for the centurion says he does not deserve to have you in his house, nor does he feel worthy to come to you in person. He says that if you just say the word, his servant will be healed. For he says, "I also am a man under authority, with soldiers under me. I order one to go and he goes, or to come and he comes, and if I tell my slave to do something, he does it."'

The centurion believed that, just as he had power over his men to command that something be done, so Jesus had power from God to speak a word, even at a distance, and his servant would be healed.

Jesus was amazed when He heard this message. 'I tell you,' he said to those around Him, 'I have not found such great faith anywhere else, not even in a Jew.'

When the centurion's messengers returned to the house, they found that the servant was well again.

Blind Bartimaeus

Jesus often made blind men see again, and one day, outside Jericho, there sat a blind man by the roadside. His name was Bartimaeus.

Most blind people have a keen sense of hearing, and Bartimaeus would be able to recognize the familiar sounds of people and animals passing by. He had also heard about the great healer, Jesus of Nazareth, and perhaps he thought about Him a great deal.

One day he heard the noise of a great crowd of people coming along the road, such a noise as he had never heard before. He could tell, from the scraps of conversation he heard, that Jesus was with them. He could not see Jesus, of course, but he wondered if Jesus could see him. He decided to call out and attract His attention. 'Jesus, son of David, have mercy on me!' he cried.

People in the crowd scolded him. 'Be quiet!' they said.

But Bartimaeus cried out all the more loudly, 'Son of David, have mercy on me!' Calling Him 'son of David' showed that Bartimaeus had given some thought as to who Jesus really was.

Jesus stopped and said to the people, 'Call him.'

So they called to him and said, 'Take heart; get up, for Jesus is calling you.'

Bartimaeus threw off his cloak, sprang up and made his way to Jesus.

'What do you want me to do?' Jesus asked.

'Lord, that I might receive my sight,' answered Bartimaeus.

'Go your way,' said Jesus, 'your faith has made you whole.'

And at once Bartimaeus was able to see, and he followed Jesus along the road.

A Blind Man at Bethsaida

Another time, at Bethsaida, some people brought a blind man to Jesus to be healed. Jesus led the man outside the village, touched his eyes with saliva, and placed His hands upon him. Then He asked, 'Can you see anything?'

The man was not used to seeing anything and at first his vision probably seemed blurred. 'Yes,' he said. 'I can see people, but they look like trees walking.'

Then Jesus put His hands on the man's eyes, and now the man saw everything quite clearly.

'Don't go into the village,' said Jesus, for He knew that news of His amazing powers could have

started a rising against the Roman occupiers. He did not want that, and it was important that His miracles should be understood along with His teaching about the Kingdom of God which He had come to bring. Only in this way would people see the full meaning of His mission.

The Man with the Withered Hand

One Sabbath day, when Jesus went to the synagogue, He saw there a man who had a withered, or paralysed, hand. (There is a book—not the Bible—which tells us that this man was a mason, who used to earn his living by using his hands; now he could no longer do so, he had to beg, and he felt this to be a disgrace.)

Some of Jesus's enemies were there too, and they hoped that, if Jesus healed the man, they might be able to accuse Him of breaking the strict Sabbath laws. 'Is it legal to heal on the Sabbath?' they asked.

Jesus replied, 'If you had a sheep and it fell into a pit on the Sabbath, would you or would you not

pull it out? Of how much more value is a man than a sheep? Yes, it is right to do good on the Sabbath.'

His accusers did not reply, for they must have known in their hearts that He was right.

Jesus looked at them, feeling both angry and sorry because they were so stubborn and rigid in their outlook.

He turned to the man and said, 'Stretch out your hand.' The man did so, and found it was mended and whole like the other.

Jesus's accusers then left the synagogue and began to plot how they might bring Him down and destroy Him.

The Woman with the Bent Back

Another Sabbath day, Jesus was teaching in the synagogue and there was a crippled woman present. Her back was bent over so that she could not straighten up, and she had been ill for eighteen years.

She did not ask Jesus to cure her, as others had done, but when He saw her, He called her to Him and, placing His hands upon her, said, 'You are free from your illness.'

At once she straightened her back and stood up and praised God.

Again Jesus was accused, this time by the ruler of the synagogue, of healing on the Sabbath day. This man regarded healing as work, and the law said no work should be done on the Sabbath.

Jesus pointed out how hypocritical this was, for the man would surely feed and water his animals on the Sabbath. Why then should this woman not be healed? His enemies were put to shame, but the ordinary people rejoiced at the wonderful things Jesus did.

The Man with Dropsy

Yet another Sabbath day, Jesus was dining in the house of one of the rulers of the Pharisees, when a man who was suffering from dropsy was brought before Him. (Dropsy is a disease which causes the body to swell.)

Jesus asked the lawyers and Pharisees who were there a testing question: 'Is it lawful to heal on the Sabbath or not?' But they were silent and would not answer.

So Jesus took the man and healed him.

The Nobleman's Son

At Capernaum there lived a nobleman, one of the officials of Herod Antipas, whose son was very ill. He was a rich and important official, but no amount of money had been able to make his son well.

When the man heard that Jesus had come from Judea to Galilee, he set out to look for Him, hoping that He would cure his son.

When eventually he found Jesus, he beseeched Him, 'Please come and heal my son, for he is at the point of death.'

Jesus said, rather sadly, to him, 'Unless you see signs and wonders, you will not believe.' Jesus did not want people to believe in Him just because they saw His miracles. He wanted them to follow His teaching, live by it, and believe in Him for His own sake.

But the nobleman had faith in Jesus and he said, 'Sir, come down before my son dies.'

'Go your way,' said Jesus. 'Your son will live.'

The nobleman believed Him and he set off for home. When he was part of the way there, he saw his servants coming out to meet him. What could it mean? But as he drew nearer, he saw that they looked happy, and he knew the news was good:

'Your son is much better,' they told him. 'He is going to live.'

'What time was it when he started to recover?' asked the nobleman.

'At one o'clock yesterday afternoon the fever left him,' they replied.

The nobleman recalled that this was the very hour when Jesus had told him, 'Your son will live.'

After that, not only he, but all his household, believed in Jesus.

The Man at the Pool

Near the Sheep Gate in Jerusalem, there was a pool with five porches or porticoes; it was called the Pool of Bethesda. This pool, with its five porticoes has since been discovered by archaeologists, down below the level of present-day Jerusalem.

A large number of sick people used to lie in the porches waiting for the waters to become stirred up or 'troubled'. This happened from time to time, perhaps caused by the bubbling up of an underground stream, but the people believed that the first to go into the water when it was bubbling would be cured of his or her illness.

When Jesus went there, He saw, among the crowds of sick people, one man who had been ill for thirty-eight years. He was lying on a mat, and seemed to be the sort of person who had lost all 'drive'.

'Do you really want to get well?' asked Jesus, stopping beside him.

'Sir,' replied the man, 'I have no one to help me into the pool when the water is troubled, and while I am struggling to get in on my own, someone else gets there first, and I lose my chance.'

Obviously the man needed somebody to give him encouragement.

'Get up, pick up your mat, and walk!' said Jesus to him. Immediately the man found he could stand, and he picked up his mat and started to walk.

As this was the Sabbath, it wasn't long before some of the Jews told him he was breaking the law by carrying his mat on the Sabbath day—the law was so rigid that even this was regarded as work, and work was forbidden on the Sabbath. 'But the man who healed me told me to pick it up and walk,' said the man. When he was asked 'Who was that?' he did not know.

Some time afterwards Jesus found the same man in the temple and warned him, 'Now that you are well, you must stop sinning, lest something worse happens to you.'

The man then knew that it was Jesus who had healed him, and when he told the Jews this, they began to persecute Jesus because He performed miracles on the Sabbath.

The Deaf and Dumb Man
One day the people brought to Jesus a man who was deaf and who had great difficulty in speaking.

Most likely, this was because of his deafness. We all learn to speak by repeating the sounds we hear, and if this man had never heard the sounds of speech, he would find it very hard to imitate them.

The people who brought him begged Jesus to heal him.

In His kind and considerate way, Jesus took the man away from the crowd where he would be able to concentrate more easily, for deaf people who can hear slightly find more than one voice at a time to be very distracting.

Because the man could not hear, Jesus used sign language. He put His fingers in the man's ears and touched his tongue. Then He looked up to heaven and sighed.

He said to the man, '*Ephphatha*', which means, 'Be opened'.

Immediately the man's ears were opened and his speech was restored, and he began to speak plainly without any trouble.

'How wonderful Jesus is!' said the crowd. 'He even makes the deaf people hear and the dumb people speak.'

The Man with the Evil Spirit
One day, Jesus saw in the synagogue at Capernaum a man possessed by an evil spirit. In other words, he was insane.

'What have You to do with us, Jesus of Nazareth?' screamed the man. 'Have You come to destroy us? I know You. You are God's Holy One.'

'Be quiet, and come out of the man!' ordered Jesus, and the evil came out of him and he fell to the floor unharmed.

Reports of what Jesus had done spread to every part of the region.

Jairus's Daughter
Near the Sea of Galilee there lived a rich man named Jairus who was an official of the local synagogue. He had a daughter who was twelve, and she was ill—so ill that it seemed she would not recover.

When Jairus saw Jesus with a large crowd around Him, he ran towards Him and begged, 'My

daughter is very ill. Please come and lay Your hands on her and make her well.'

So Jesus set off towards Jairus's house, and a great number of people went too, crowding and jostling Him on all sides.

In this crowd was a woman who had had an illness which caused severe bleeding for twelve years. She had spent all her money on doctors and medicines, but instead of getting better, she grew worse. She had heard about Jesus, and she thought to herself, 'If I can only just touch the hem of His robes, I shall be made well.'

So she pushed her way through the crowd and touched His cloak, and she knew she had been made well right at that moment.

Now there was nothing magic about Jesus's clothes, but He could tell the difference between the jostling of the crowd and someone reaching out to Him in real need. 'Who touched Me?' He asked.

The disciples were amazed at this question, and they said, 'Look how hard the crowd is pressing around You, and yet You ask, "Who touched Me?"'

But Jesus knew that someone had touched Him deliberately, and He looked to see who it was. The poor woman, who had hoped not to be noticed,

now came forward and fell at Jesus's feet, trembling, and poured out the whole story.

'Don't be afraid,' said Jesus gently, 'your faith has made you well. Go home in peace.'

While He was saying this, some messengers came from Jairus's house and said, 'Don't trouble the Master any more, for your daughter has just died.'

Jesus ignored this and said to Jairus, 'Don't be afraid, just believe, and your daughter will be made well.' And He pressed on.

When they reached Jairus's house, there was a terrible noise going on. Everyone was crying and mourning for the child. 'Why do you make this noise?' asked Jesus. 'The child is not dead, she is asleep.'

But they laughed at Him, for they knew, or thought they knew, that she was really and truly dead.

Then Jesus put them all outside and took with Him only the child's parents and Peter, James and John, and He went into the little girl's room. He took her by the hand and said, 'Get up, little girl.' And her life returned and she started to walk around.

'Give her something to eat,' said Jesus, as He returned her to her overjoyed parents.

The Healing of the Paralysed Man

One day Jesus was teaching in a house in Capernaum, where crowds of people had gone to listen to Him, because news spread quickly when Jesus was about.

This time the house was so full of people that it was impossible even to get through the door, and a great number of people were gathered outside too.

A number of Pharisees and teachers of the law were also there. They had come from Jerusalem and from every town in Galilee and Judea, and some of them had come hoping to oppose Jesus in whatever He said.

But there was one man who could not go to see Jesus, for he was unable to walk. He had an illness which left him paralysed, and all he could do was lie on his bed all day and listen to the people going by outside. (Some versions of the Bible refer to this illness as being 'sick of the palsy'.)

This man was unhappy for another reason, and that was because, in the past, he had led a very sinful life and now he bitterly regretted it. His very illness may have been the result of his past sins—for some sins do result in physical illness—so that, as well as being helpless, the man was also ashamed of himself.

However, he did have four good friends who used to come and visit him and bring him all the news. When they came and told him that Jesus was back in town, how the paralysed man wished that he could see Him! But he could not go to Jesus, and it did not seem very likely that Jesus would call at his house.

When the four friends heard how much the man wanted to see Jesus, they had an idea. Why not take their friend to Him? But how?

They soon solved this problem by deciding to take a corner of the bed each and carry him there themselves. The bed was a flat mat, probably of straw or rushes, which was placed on the floor, and could be rolled up and put aside when not in use.

So the friends set off, through the streets of Capernaum, carrying their friend carefully to the house where Jesus was teaching.

But a great disappointment met them when they got there, for the crowd was so great that they could not get through to take him to Jesus.

However, they were undaunted, for they were the type of men who believe that difficulties are there to be overcome.

They saw that the house had an outside staircase leading to a flat roof. This roof would be used for sleeping on in the warm climate of the country, and also for spreading out flax, or clothing to dry in the sun. It could also be used as extra accommodation if the house became too full.

Why not take the man up the outside staircase and make a hole in the roof and let him in that way? These flat roofs were made of a layer of clay spread over reeds supported on branches which were carried on beams. It would not, therefore, be very difficult to make a hole in the roof which could fairly easily be repaired afterwards.

So the four friends carried the man gently up the stairs and put him down while they set to work to make a hole above the place where Jesus was teaching. Then, using ropes tied to each corner of the mat, they carefully let their friend down, right at Jesus's feet.

Jesus looked at the man on the bed, and then up

at the four anxious faces peering down through the hole in the roof. They did not need to ask Him anything; He knew why they had come, and He knew how great their faith was in Him. But, even so, perhaps they were surprised at what happened next.

Jesus looked down at the paralysed man and said, 'My son, your sins are forgiven you.'

The crowd listening were very surprised too, but to the sick man, it was like a great weight being lifted from his mind. Even if Jesus did not cure him of his paralysis, much of which he knew he deserved, then at least he would now feel happier in his mind.

The teachers of the law and the Pharisees who were listening were anything but happy. They began muttering angrily to themselves saying, 'Who is this who dares to forgive sins? No one can forgive sins but God. This is blasphemy.' ('Blasphemy' means words spoken against the honour of God.)

Jesus knew what they were thinking, and He turned to them and said, 'Why are you thinking such evil things? Which is easier to say to this man, "Your sins are forgiven you," or "Rise, take up your bed and walk."? I will prove to you that the Son of Man has power on earth to forgive sins.' By 'Son of Man' Jesus meant Himself.

Then He turned to the paralysed man and said, 'I say to you, get up, pick up your bed, and go home.'

At once the man found that he had new strength, and he stood up, rolled up the bed on which he had been lying and, praising God, set off for home—to the great astonishment of everyone who was there and who saw the miracle.

The man himself could not have felt happier—his illness was cured and his sins were forgiven, and he was able to make a completely fresh start in life. No doubt his four friends hurried down to rejoice with him.

The crowd went home, full of awe, and they too praised God saying, 'What marvellous things we have seen!'

The Anointing of Jesus

One day Jesus was invited to a meal at the house of one of the religious leaders—a Pharisee named Simon.

Simon does not seem to have loved Jesus very much, even though he invited Him to dinner; he did not attend to the little courtesies which were normal when one invited a guest to a meal. The roads of Palestine were hot and dusty, and it was usual for someone—a servant—to wash the feet of the guests before the meal began—or for water to be provided so that a guest might wash himself and be comfortable.

The host also normally greeted guests with a kiss and sometimes the guest's head was anointed with ointments or perfumes. But Simon the Pharisee had omitted all these polite customs, and perhaps had only invited Jesus out of curiosity, not because he felt particularly friendly towards Him. Perhaps he wanted to have a closer look at this famous teacher whom everyone was talking about, and who was said to perform miracles.

During this meal at Simon's house, a woman whom everyone knew had led a very sinful life, entered the house. There was nothing strange in this, because banquets were often public functions; the dining room may have opened on to the street and have been screened only by curtains, so that entrance was quite easy and people could walk in unannounced.

This woman had heard that Jesus was dining at the house of Simon the Pharisee, and so she had come specially, bringing with her a precious alabaster box full of perfume. (Alabaster is a stone which looks something like marble.)

Jesus was sitting facing inwards towards the table, and the woman moved forward, crying. She was thinking of her past life. As His back was to her, Jesus did not see her approach.

She knelt at Jesus's feet and her tears fell on them, and she wiped them dry with her long hair. This was a very generous act, for it caused the greatest shame in those days for a woman to be seen with her hair loose and untidy. Usually women tied their hair back and covered their heads.

Then this woman kissed Jesus's feet and poured the perfume on to them.

Simon watched all this with growing surprise, and felt that Jesus could not possibly know the woman's history. He thought to himself, 'If this man Jesus was really the prophet He says He is, He would know all about this bad woman and would refuse to have anything to do with her. He would tell her to go away.'

Jesus knew what Simon was thinking, and He looked at him and said, 'Simon, I have something to say to you.'

'Yes,' said Simon, 'tell me what it is.' Despite his shock at what had happened, Simon was interested.

Jesus began to tell Simon one of His parables:

'Once there were two men, and both of them owed money to a money-lender. One owed as much as 500 silver coins, and the other owed him fifty. Neither of them had sufficient money to pay back his debt, but when the money-lender found out, he forgave them both and cancelled their debts. Which man do you think loved him more?'

'I suppose the one to whom he forgave more,' answered Simon.

'That is right,' said Jesus. Then He turned to the woman and, still speaking to Simon, said, 'Do you see this woman, Simon? I came as a guest to your house, yet you did not give Me any water for My feet, but she has washed My feet with her tears and dried them with the hairs of her head. You did not greet Me with a kiss, but she has not ceased to kiss My feet since I came. You provided no oil for My head, but she has poured perfume on My feet. She has shown her great love by her actions and so proves that her many sins in the past have been forgiven. But those who have been forgiven little only love little.'

Jesus meant 'It is plain through the little love that you have shown that you have not been brought to repentance through Me.'

Then Jesus turned to the woman again and said, 'Your sins are forgiven.'

Some of the people sitting around began muttering to themselves, 'Who is this man who can even forgive sins?'

But Jesus was still concerned with the woman, and He said to her, 'Your faith has saved you; go in peace.'

The Woman at Bethany

On another occasion, nearer to the end of His ministry, Jesus was in Bethany, in the house of a man who had once been a leper.

Here a woman came to Him with a jar of very expensive perfume and poured it on His head. The disciples were there and some of them felt angry, especially Judas Iscariot. They said, 'What a dreadful waste! Why couldn't this perfume have been sold for 300 silver coins and the money given to the poor? Surely it is wrong to be so extravagant when so many are hungry and in need!'

Jesus did not agree. 'Leave her alone,' He said. 'It is a fine and loving thing that she has done for Me. You always have the poor with you and you can help them at any time, but you will not always have Me. She has done what she could to prepare My body ahead for the time of My burial. Wherever the Gospel is preached in the whole world, this action of hers will be told to remind people of her.'

The Transfiguration

One day, as Jesus and His disciples were nearing the town of Caesarea Philippi, He asked them, 'Who do people say that I am?'

They answered, 'Some say that You are John the Baptist, others say You are Elijah or Jeremiah, or some other prophet.'

'But what about you?' asked Jesus. 'Who do you think I am?'

The group's natural spokesman, Simon Peter, said firmly, 'You are the Messiah, the Son of the Living God.'

'Well done,' said Jesus. 'You are a rock, Peter, and on this foundation rock I will build My church.' Jesus saw in Peter the man he would eventually become, as firm in his belief as a rock.

Some days later, Jesus gave the three leading disciples a special glimpse of His glory to help and encourage them further.

They had all been working hard with Him, teaching and helping people, and learning new things about Him. Just beyond Caesarea Philippi is a high mountain peak, Mount Hermon, which rises some 2,740 m (9,000 ft) above sea level, and it is believed that this is the mountain on to which Jesus took the three disciples, Peter, James and John.

It would be cooler on the mountain, and the disciples would be glad of a rest, and to be alone with Jesus for a while.

Jesus walked a little way beyond them and began to pray. Suddenly the disciples saw the brightest light they had ever seen, and it came from Jesus Himself. His whole appearance changed; His face shone like the sun and His clothing became white and glistening.

As they got used to the brilliant light, the disciples saw that Jesus was no longer alone, but that there were two other figures with Him. One was Moses, the great law-giver, and the other was Elijah, the great prophet, and they were talking with Jesus. Peter, James and John were so frightened that they did not know what to say.

Then as Moses and Elijah were about to leave Jesus, Peter found his voice and spoke up, 'Master, it is good to be here,' he said; 'let us make three shelters, one for You, one for Moses, and one for Elijah.'

Peter wanted to hold on to the moment, for it was good to be in such glorious surroundings. He thought that if he made shelters for them, like the Tabernacle-tent of the old days in which God was present, then perhaps Moses and Elijah would stay. But he did not really know what he was saying.

As he spoke, a shining cloud appeared and covered them, and the disciples were filled with awe. From out of the cloud came a voice saying, 'This is My own Son; listen to Him.'

Then Jesus came and touched them and said, 'Get up, don't be afraid.' They looked up and the cloud had gone, and Jesus alone stood there.

Peter, James and John had seen the glory of God burst through. Perhaps God had let them see this holy thing in order to turn their thoughts right away from Jesus as an earthly king. Or it may have been to give them some extra help and encouragement to sustain them through the terrible time of Jesus's crucifixion which was soon to come.

As they came down the mountain, Jesus asked them not to speak of what they had seen until after He Himself had risen from the dead. They obeyed, but discussed among themselves what 'rising from the dead' could mean.

This wonderful experience on the mountain is called the Transfiguration.

Jesus Cures a Sick Child

When Jesus and Peter, James and John returned from Mount Hermon, they found the other disciples in the midst of a buzzing crowd of people.

When Jesus asked what was happening a man stepped forward.

'I have a son who is possessed by a devil which makes him speechless and throws him down on the ground where he struggles and grinds his teeth. He has been like this since he was a child. Your disciples are unable to help him.'

Jesus asked to see the boy who was brought before Him and was at once taken ill with a fit.

The father begged Jesus to help his son who frequently harmed himself during one of these attacks.

Jesus commanded the illness to leave the boy and never to return. At once the child gave a loud cry and fell down and lay quite still as if he was dead. Then Jesus took his hand and the boy got to his feet, completely cured, and was returned to the arms of his father.

The description given in the Bible sounds like the illness we call epilepsy. In earlier times people were much less well educated than they are today and thought that people who suffered from epilepsy were possessed by devils. Gradually, as doctors and scientists have learned more about what causes this illness, modern medicines have been developed so that nowadays people with epilepsy lead normal lives.

Zacchaeus

In Jericho there lived a chief tax-collector whose name was Zacchaeus. Because of his job no one liked him, and he had become something of a social outcast. Like the other tax-collectors, he made himself a rich living by demanding more money than was actually due to pay the Roman taxes and keeping what was left over for himself.

Zacchaeus, however, must have had some troublings of conscience, for one day, when he heard that Jesus was going to pass through Jericho, he felt he must have a look at Him.

When he knew that Jesus was near he ran out to see; but there were crowds of people on the road who had all come to see Jesus, and Zacchaeus was only a very small figure. Try as he would, he could not find a gap in the crowd through which it might be possible to see the great teacher, nor was he tall enough to see over the people's heads.

Then he had an idea. He noticed a sycomore tree nearby. This was a tree with leaves like a mulberry and fruit like a fig. It grew to some 10 to 12 m (36 ft) high and had a short trunk and wide spreading branches.

Zacchaeus decided that he would climb this tree, and then he would be able to see Jesus and yet not be seen himself. So he ran on ahead of the crowd, and climbed up into the branches.

Along came Jesus, and Zacchaeus peered through the branches with much interest. To his great surprise, when Jesus reached the tree, he paused and looked up into its branches and said, 'Come down, Zacchaeus, because I am coming to your house today.'

Zacchaeus was amazed, almost too amazed to do anything. After all, there were many priests' houses in Jericho; surely Jesus would be much more likely to go to one of them. To come to the house of a tax-collector was unthinkable. Why, Zacchaeus did not even know how Jesus knew who he was!

Surprised and delighted, Zacchaeus hurried down and greeted Jesus with great joy.

There were murmurings and grumblings in the crowd. 'This man has gone to be the guest of a tax-collector, a sinner,' they said.

Meanwhile at Zacchaeus's house, Jesus was doubtless given a meal, after which He and Zacchaeus had a talk.

Zacchaeus was greatly impressed by Jesus, and he began to realize just how badly he had been living in the past. He knew that he could not go on living as he had been doing, and that now he was face to face with Jesus he must make a choice.

He had hardly ever given any money away to charity before, but now, he decided, was the time to make amends. He must also examine his past dealings and pay back those he had robbed.

So Zacchaeus stood up and said, 'Listen, Lord, I will give half of my goods to the poor, and where I have cheated anyone of money in the past, I will now repay him four times as much.'

Jesus was pleased. 'This shows you to be a true son of Abraham,' He said. 'Salvation has come not only to you, but to your family and household today.'

The crowd, the self-righteous people outside, had been critical of Jesus's action in going to the house of a sinner like Zacchaeus. 'But,' said Jesus, 'I, the Son of Man, came to seek and to save those who are lost.'

Mary, Martha and Lazarus

Among Jesus's many friends was a family of two sisters and a brother. They were named Martha, Mary and Lazarus, and they lived in the village of Bethany which was less than 3 km (1½ miles) from Jerusalem.

One day, when Jesus went to visit them, Mary came and sat beside Him to listen to His teaching. Martha, on the other hand, bustled about getting the best possible meal she could for their visitor, for she was a very hospitable sort of person and liked to make people feel at home.

When she saw that Mary was not helping her, she went to Jesus and said, 'Lord, don't You care that Mary has left me to do all the work myself? Tell her to come and help me. I am terribly busy getting everything ready.'

But Jesus gently reproved her and said, 'Martha, Martha, you are worried over doing so much, but only one thing is needed. Mary has chosen rightly, and it won't be taken away from her.'

Jesus felt that Martha would have honoured Him more by listening to Him, rather than by preparing an elaborate dinner. He would have been just as content with a simple meal and a quiet talk with Martha too.

One day Martha and Mary's brother Lazarus became very ill. His sisters sent a message to Jesus to tell Him how ill His friend was for they felt sure Jesus would help.

When Jesus received the message, He did not go to Bethany for two days. By then He knew that Lazarus had died, but He also knew that He could bring him back to life. He told the disciples that Lazarus was already dead, and added, 'For your sakes, I am glad we were not there.' He meant that the disciples' faith would be strengthened when they reached Bethany and saw what Jesus was going to do.

So they set off, and by the time they got to Bethany, Lazarus had already been dead for four days. Bethany was near to Jerusalem and so many people had come out to see Martha and Mary and to console and comfort them on their brother's death. These visits to comfort mourners were always paid with great ceremony for a week after a death.

When Martha heard that Jesus was on the way, she went out and met Him before He reached Bethany. Meanwhile Mary sat in the house the very picture of grief.

'If You had been here,' said Martha to Jesus, 'Lazarus would not have died. But, even now, I know that God will give You whatever You ask Him.'

Martha had great faith, yet she hardly dared say in words that she hoped Jesus might bring her brother back to life.

'Your brother will return to life again,' said Jesus.

Then Jesus said, 'I am the resurrection and the life; whoever believes in me will live, even if he has died, and those who live and believe in me will never die. Do you believe this, Martha?'

Pious Jews believed in a future resurrection and Jesus was saying that Lazarus was a believer and that therefore he was about to be raised from the dead. To Christians, death is not really death, because it does not break the living union between the soul and God.

Martha gave a wonderful answer to Jesus's

question. 'Yes, Lord,' she said, 'I believe that You are the Messiah, the Son of God, who was to come to the world.'

Then Martha went back into the house and said quietly to Mary, 'The teacher is here,' and Mary got up and hurried out to meet Jesus. The people who were in the house trying to comfort her, followed when they saw her go out. They thought Mary was going to visit the grave to weep there for her dead brother.

For three days the mourners used to visit the grave, believing that the soul was still about and might re-enter the body; on the fourth day it was thought the soul had departed and the mourners went home again.

But Mary did not go to the grave; instead she went straight to Jesus. When she saw Him, she fell at His feet and said, as Martha had done, 'Lord, if You had been here, my brother wouldn't have died.'

Jesus saw that she was weeping, and that many others were weeping too, and His heart was touched. He felt a great sorrow and sympathy for them. 'Where is Lazarus buried?' He asked, very kindly.

'Come and see,' they answered.

Then Jesus Himself wept, showing how deeply He felt and how much He understood Martha and Mary's sorrow.

'See how much He loved Lazarus,' said the people; but a few of them wondered why Jesus had not kept Lazarus from dying if He cared so much about him.

Much moved, Jesus went to the tomb, which was a cave in a hillside with a big stone at its entrance. 'Remove the stone,' He ordered. Everyone looked a little startled.

Martha, losing her faith for a moment, thought that Jesus wanted to take a last look at His friend, and she tried to prevent Him, fearing that by now there would be a bad smell, as Lazarus had been dead for four days. But Jesus said to her, 'Did I not say to you that if you believed, you would see God's glory?'

So they took the stone away, and Jesus looked upwards and prayed. He thanked God for the miracle, as if it had been already performed, and He offered the miracle as a proof of His divine mission so that the people standing by might believe in Him. Then He called out in a loud voice, 'Lazarus, come out!'

And Lazarus walked out, still with the grave-clothes wrapped around him.

'Unloose him,' said Jesus, 'and let him go.'

The Entry into Jerusalem

It was Passover time, a busy time in the city, when thousands of Jews were going up to the temple in Jerusalem to keep the festival, the great feast which commemorated the nation's deliverance from Egypt.

Jesus and His disciples were on their way to Jerusalem too, but the disciples could sense that this time their journey had a much more serious feel to it. Although they did not realize it at the time, this was the start of Jesus's last week of life on earth.

Jesus was very set and determined and walked on a little ahead of them. The people following were afraid, for they knew that the rulers wanted to seize Jesus, and by going into Jerusalem they felt that He was heading for certain capture.

Jesus took His twelve disciples aside and said to them, 'We are going to Jerusalem where the chief priests and rulers will condemn the Son of Man to death, and hand Him over to the Gentiles (non-Jews) who will mock, whip and crucify Him. But after three days He will rise again.'

He was talking about Himself and what was to happen, but the disciples did not understand.

As they drew near to the city, they came to Bethphage, which was about 3 km (1½ miles) outside Jerusalem, and near to the Mount of Olives. Here Jesus gave the disciples some special instructions. 'Go into the village over there,' He said, 'and you will find a colt (a young donkey) tied up, on which no one has ever ridden. Untie it and bring it to me. If anyone asks what you are doing, you are to say, "The Master needs it and will return it at once." Then the man will allow you to bring it to me.'

The disciples went and found the colt just as Jesus had said, and as they were untying it, the owners asked what they were doing. The disciples replied as Jesus had told them, and the owners said no more.

When the disciples brought the animal to Jesus, some of them threw their cloaks over it, and Jesus mounted to ride the rest of the way into Jerusalem.

Now the people who had been present when Jesus had brought Lazarus to life again had told many people about what had happened. So when they heard that Jesus was coming to Jerusalem, a great crowd went out to meet Him.

The Pharisees were most put out at this, and they said to one another in frustration, 'You see, we can do nothing; the whole world is following Him.'

The great crowd wanted to honour and praise Jesus as their king. Many knew that it was customary to put down a carpet for a king to walk on, and so they spread their brightly coloured cloaks in the path of Jesus to make a carpet for Him, as a gesture of respect. Other people climbed palm trees along the route, and cut down branches to wave or to spread along the road.

'Hosanna!' they cried, 'Praise to the Son of David! Blessed is He who comes in the name of the Lord! Praise God!'

There were crowds in front and crowds behind, so that the whole city was thrown into an uproar. Among the thousands who had gone up to Jerusalem for the Passover were some from far away places who had never heard anything about Jesus. So they asked, 'Who is He?'

'It is the prophet Jesus, from Nazareth in Galilee,' answered the people.

Some of the Pharisees in the crowd went up to Jesus and said, 'Command Your followers to be quiet.'

But Jesus answered, 'Even if they were quiet, the stones themselves would cry out instead.'

As He came closer to Jerusalem, Jesus wept and said to the city, 'If only you knew what is needed for peace! Yet you cannot see it. Your enemies will destroy you, because you have not recognized that God came to save you.'

That day was the first Palm Sunday.

Cleansing the Temple

The next day Jesus went into the temple. Now the temple was, in a special sense, the place of God's presence, although since the coming of Jesus, people have understood that God is everywhere and is not confined to a special place.

In the outer court of the temple, the Court of the Gentiles, there were a number of money-changers working when Jesus went there.

Jews who came from other countries were not allowed to use their own foreign coins to pay the temple taxes, nor could they buy animals for sacrifice with anything but Jewish money. This meant that they had to go to the money-changers before they could play their part in the festival.

Now the money-changers fixed a very dishonest rate of exchange and charged very high sums, even to the poorest people who could only afford the cheapest sacrifice, which was two pigeons.

Jesus was rightly very angry when He saw all the cheating and robbing that was going on within the temple area. He overturned the money-changers' tables and the stalls of those who were selling pigeons, and He drove all those who were doing such business out of the temple. 'My house is a house of prayer,' He cried, 'but you have made it a den of thieves!'

Then blind and crippled people came to Him to be healed and He healed them in the temple. The chief priests and lawyers were angry at the wonderful things He did—while, on the other hand, they had turned a blind eye to the dishonesty of the money-changers.

Some children came in and shouted praises to Jesus, the praises which they had heard others shouting along the road to Jerusalem. 'Do you hear them? Listen to what they are saying,' said the chief priests and lawyers to Jesus.

'Yes,' answered Jesus. 'Haven't you read in the scriptures, "Out of the mouths of babies and children shall come perfect praise"?' And He left them and went with the disciples to Bethany to lodge for the night.

The Last Supper

During the week which began with the first Palm Sunday came the Passover festival which was celebrated all over Israel.

Jesus and His disciples, who were now in Jerusalem, were also to celebrate the festival, and the disciples asked Jesus, 'Where would you like us to go to get the Passover meal ready, for we must make the arrangements?'

Jesus replied by giving special instructions to two of the disciples: 'Go into the city,' He said, 'and a man carrying a pitcher of water will meet you. Follow him into the house which he enters, and ask the householder where the room is where I am to eat the Passover with my disciples. He will show you an upper room and it is there that you are to prepare the Passover. The rest of us will join you there.'

The two disciples went and found everything as Jesus had said.

In the evening of that day, which was Thursday, Jesus and His disciples assembled in the upper room. They did not know it then, but this was to be no ordinary Passover meal; Jesus was about to transform it into the Lord's Supper—a meal which has been continued in the Church all over the world ever since.

When the supper had been served, Jesus rose from the table, took off His outer garment, and tied a towel round His waist. Then He poured water into a basin and did the job which was normally performed by a slave—He began to wash the disciples' feet.

Not long before, the disciples had been arguing as to who was the greatest, and it seems that not one of them had wanted to do the menial act of feet-washing at the supper for fear of being thought less important than the others. So when Jesus saw that none of them offered to do this courteous act, He rose and willingly did it Himself for the whole company.

When He came to Simon Peter, that disciple protested, 'You shall never wash my feet, Lord. It is not right.'

'If I don't,' said Jesus, 'you have no part with me.'

Jesus meant this symbolically—that unless He washed Peter's sins from him, then he had no link with Jesus.

Then Peter, perhaps beginning to understand, said, 'Lord, not only my feet, but also my hands and my head.'

When Jesus had washed all the disciples' feet, He returned to His place at the table and sat down facing them all.

Then He said, 'You call me teacher and Lord, and you are right to do so, for that is what I am. But if I, your Lord and teacher, have washed your feet, so ought you to follow my example and wash one another's feet.'

Again He was teaching them that the truly great people are those who do not put themselves first, but who serve others and do not think only of their own needs.

As they were eating, Jesus said something startling. 'I tell you truly,' He said, 'that one of you will betray me.'

The disciples were puzzled and looked at one another in alarm, each thinking, 'Surely He cannot mean me.' Peter motioned to the disciple who was sitting next to Jesus (most likely John) to ask Him whom He meant. The disciple asked Him quietly and Jesus replied, 'It is the one to whom I give a piece of bread which I have dipped in the sauce of this dish.'

Then He took a piece of bread, dipped it, and gave it to Judas Iscariot. It was Jesus's last appeal to Judas, but Judas rejected it.

'Do quickly what you are about to do,' said Jesus to Judas, and again the disciples did not understand what Jesus meant, for they did not know that Judas was going to betray their master. Some of them thought that, since Judas was in charge of the money, Jesus was telling him to go out and buy what they needed for the festival, or

perhaps that he should give some of their money to the poor.

But Judas, after he had accepted the bread from Jesus, got up and went out into the night through the dark streets of the city.

During the meal, Jesus did something wonderful. He took a piece of bread, said a prayer of thanks, broke the bread and gave it to His disciples saying, 'Take and eat; this is My body which is given for you.'

Then He took a cup of wine, gave thanks to God, and handed it to them saying, 'This is My blood which is poured out for many for the forgiveness of sins. Do this in memory of Me.'

After Judas had left, Jesus spoke again to the disciples and tried to help them to understand why His death had to happen. 'I shall not be with you for very much longer,' He said, 'and you cannot come where I am going. Now I give you a new commandment, that you love one another. If you act in this way, then everyone will know that you are my disciples.'

'Why can't I follow You now?' asked Peter. 'I am ready to die for You.'

'Are you?' said Jesus sadly. 'I tell you that before the cock crows, you will have said three times that you did not know Me.'

'I'll never say that,' said Peter stoutly, 'even if I have to die with You.'

And the other disciples said the same, protesting their loyalty to Jesus.

Jesus told them much else about what was to happen. He would be returning to His Father and preparing the way for others to come to Him too. His return to God would bring them new power through the Holy Spirit; and the Holy Spirit would be with them all the time all over the world wherever they went, not limited to one particular place, as Jesus in human form had been.

Ever since that night Christians have held the service of the Lord's Supper or Holy Communion in memory of that last meal which Jesus ate with his disciples. This service is held on both weekdays and Sundays throughout the year.

The Garden of Gethsemane

Now Judas was the treasurer of the little band of Jesus's disciples and therefore had charge of the money. He had not always been honest and had at times helped himself from the money bag. Yet for nearly three years he had been among the group of Jesus's closest followers, listening to Him, watching His wonderful deeds, and learning from Him. It was sad that he did not live up to Jesus's hopes for him when He first called him to be a disciple.

Some time before the Last Supper, Judas had gone to the chief priests and had asked, 'How much will you give me if I betray Jesus to you?'

'Thirty silver coins,' they said.

From that time Judas kept on the lookout for an opportunity to betray his master. The chief priests and elders wanted Jesus arrested secretly, for they feared that if they took Him openly, there would be a riot among the people.

When the Passover meal, that Last Supper, ended, Jesus and the disciples sang a hymn and went to the Garden of Gethsemane, which was near the foot of the slopes of the Mount of Olives. It was a quiet garden, away from the noise and bustle of Jerusalem.

Here Jesus said to eight of the disciples, 'Sit here while I go over there and pray.' Then He took Peter, James and John on a little further. To these three He said, 'Wait here and keep watch with Me; for the sorrow in My heart is very great.'

He Himself went a short distance further and threw Himself face down on the ground and prayed to God, 'Father, if it is possible, take this cup of suffering away from me; nevertheless, let not what I wish happen here, but what You wish.' And God sent Him the strength to go through with what was to happen.

Then He got up and went back to the three disciples, and found that they had fallen asleep, for they were tired and worn out by grief and worry. Jesus said to Peter, 'Weren't you able to keep watch with me for even one hour? Watch and pray that you do not fall into temptation. The spirit is willing, but the flesh is weak.'

Jesus went back and prayed, and again when He returned, He found the disciples had fallen asleep, for they could not keep their eyes open. He went away and prayed a third time, and found the disciples sleeping once more when He came back to them. 'Are you still sleeping and resting?' He said. 'Look, the time has come for the Son of Man to be given over into the hands of wicked men. Rise up! Let us be going, for the man who is to betray Me is here.'

While Jesus was still speaking, a crowd of soldiers and other people, including some temple guards, came into the garden. The chief priests and elders had sent them, and they were all armed with swords and clubs and carried lanterns.

Among them was Judas. He had given them a signal, saying, 'The man I kiss is the one you are after. Go up and seize Him and lead Him away safely.'

Judas went up to Jesus and said, 'Hail, master!' and kissed Him.

'Do you betray the Son of Man with a kiss, Judas?' asked Jesus. Then He stepped forward and asked the soldiers, 'Whom do you seek?'

'Jesus of Nazareth,' they answered.

'I am He,' replied Jesus, and as He said this, they all moved back.

Then Simon Peter, who had a sword with him, drew it and struck one of the high priest's servants. His name was Malchus, and the blow cut off his right ear.

'Enough of that!' said Jesus to Peter, and He touched Malchus's ear and healed it. 'Put your sword away. Do you think I will not drink the cup of suffering which My Father has given Me? Do not harm them.'

Jesus then turned to the soldiers and chief priests and said, 'Did you have to come out to fetch Me with swords and clubs as though I were a robber? I was with you in the temple day after day, and yet you did not arrest Me there. This is the hour you act, when the power of darkness rules.'

And the disciples all deserted their master and ran away.

Then the soldiers and the temple guards took hold of Jesus, bound Him and took Him to the house of Annas who was the father-in-law of Caiaphas, the High Priest that year, and a very influential man. He questioned Jesus about His disciples and His teaching and all the things He had done which had angered the high priests.

While this was going on, Simon Peter had been troubled in his conscience about forsaking Jesus, and he had secretly followed Him. He went into the courtyard of the High Priest's house, and the girl who kept the door said to him, 'Aren't you one of that man's disciples?'

'No,' said Peter, 'I am not. I don't even know Him.'

It was a cold night and so the servants and guards had made a charcoal fire and were standing by it and trying to get warm. Peter went over and stood with them.

Meanwhile Jesus was still being questioned, and Annas was trying to trap Him into saying that He had started a secret society. 'I have always spoken openly,' said Jesus to Annas. 'I taught in the synagogues and in the temple, where the Jews meet together. I said nothing secretly. Why don't you ask those who heard Me? They know what I said.'

At this, one of the guards standing by struck Jesus with his hand. 'How dare You speak so?' he said.

Jesus replied, 'If I have said anything wrong, tell Me, but if I have not, why do you hit Me?'

Then Annas sent Him, still bound, to Caiaphas.

Peter was still standing in the courtyard warming himself, and one of those present said, 'Aren't you one of that man's disciples? After all, your speech gives you away as a Galilean.'

'I am not,' said Peter again.

Then one of the servants of the High Priest spoke up. (He was a relative of the man whose ear Peter had cut off.) 'Did I not see you in the garden with Him?' he asked.

Again Peter answered, 'No', and immediately the sound of a cock crowing was heard. And Peter remembered how Jesus had said to him, 'Before the cock crows, you will deny Me three times.' Then he went away and wept bitterly.

The Trials and Crucifixion

Jesus was taken that night to the house of Caiaphas, the High Priest, where all the lawyers and elders had gathered together. They did their best to find some false evidence against Jesus so that they could have Him put to death; but they were unable to find any, even though many of the 'witnesses' did not tell the truth at all, but made things up and twisted the facts of real events.

Jesus kept silent, and it was not until Caiaphas asked, 'Are You the Messiah, the Son of God?' that Jesus replied, 'You have said so. I tell you all that you will see the Son of Man sitting at the right hand of God and coming on the clouds of heaven.'

'Blasphemy!' shrieked the High Priest in furious anger. 'We don't need any more witnesses. You have just heard what He said. What do you think of that?'

'He is guilty and must die,' they replied full of rage and revenge.

Early the next morning the chief priests and elders completed their plans to have Jesus put to death. They bound Him in chains and handed Him over to Pilate, the Roman governor who was Caesar's representative in those parts.

When Pilate saw Jesus before him, he asked, 'Are You the King of the Jews?'

'So you have said,' replied Jesus, but when the chief priests and elders made further accusations against Him, He did not answer, but stood in silence before them.

'Do You hear all these things of which they are accusing You?' asked Pilate.

But when Jesus, with quiet dignity, still refused to answer, Pilate was amazed. 'I find no reason to condemn this man,' he said.

'His teaching is starting a riot,' the accusers urged. 'It began in Galilee and now He has come here.'

When Pilate heard that Jesus was a Galilean, and from the region ruled by Herod, he saw a way out of his difficulty. Herod was in Jerusalem at the time, for the Passover, and so Pilate sent Jesus to him.

Now Herod had been wanting to see Jesus for some time; he had heard about His miracles and hoped to see Him perform one. So he asked Jesus many questions, but still Jesus refused to answer and Herod grew angry. He was not accustomed to such defiance.

Then the chief priests and lawyers made all sorts of accusations against Him, and the soldiers mocked Him. Contemptuously, they put a fine robe on Him and returned Him to Pilate again for his judgment.

At every Passover time it was the custom for the governor to set free one prisoner—whichever one the crowds asked for, and at that time a notorious bandit named Barabbas was being held who was sure to be put to death for his crimes.

When the crowd gathered together, Pilate saw an opportunity to free Jesus. 'Which prisoner shall I set free?' he asked the assembly, 'Jesus or Barabbas?'

'Barabbas!' shouted the crowd, for the chief priests and elders had been about among the people persuading them to ask for Barabbas although they knew what a bad man he was.

'What shall I do with Jesus then?' asked Pilate.

'Crucify Him,' they cried.

'But what crime has He committed?' asked

Pilate, and for answer they shouted all the more, 'Crucify Him!'

While all this was going on, Pilate's wife sent him a message saying, 'Have nothing to do with this just man; I suffered much in a dream last night because of Him.'

She may have realized that Jesus was no ordinary religious teacher, and that her husband would be doing a great wrong if he allowed such an obviously innocent man to be killed. But Pilate saw there was little use in continuing to hope that Jesus might be freed, and as a sign that he was having nothing to do with it, he took a bowl of water and washed his hands in front of them all. 'I am not responsible for this man's death,' he said. 'It is your doing.'

So Barabbas was freed and Jesus was whipped and handed over to be crucified. Pilate's soldiers mocked Him, stripped off His clothes and put a purple robe on Him. Then they made a crown of thorns and put it on His head, and placed a reed in His hand. 'Hail, King of the Jews!' they shouted, and struck Him and spat on Him. It was brutal behaviour.

Once more Pilate tried to reason with the crowd; he took Jesus out to them, hoping perhaps that they would take pity on Him. 'Look at Him,' said Pilate, in desperation, 'I cannot find any reason to condemn Him.'

But still the crowds shouted, 'Crucify Him! Crucify Him!'

'Take Him yourselves and crucify Him,' said Pilate.

'Our law says He ought to die because He claimed to be the Son of God', shouted someone, and everyone else roared in agreement.

This made Pilate afraid and he took Jesus aside and questioned Him again, but still Jesus would not reply. 'You know that I have the power to set You free or to have You crucified?' said Pilate, and this time Jesus did reply. He said, 'You only have power over Me because it was given to you by God Himself.'

Then the crowd shouted to Pilate, 'If you set this man free, you're no friend of Caesar's.' That was enough for Pilate. He greatly feared the emperor and so he handed Jesus over to the crowd to be crucified.

The Crucifixion

Crucifixion was a most horrible form of death. The victim was nailed to a cross and left hanging there to die in agony. He also had to carry his own cross to the site.

As Jesus was being led to the hill of Calvary, outside the city wall, He fainted under the weight of His cross, and a man named Simon from Cyrene was forced by the soldiers to carry it for Him to the place of execution.

Jesus was hung between two thieves who were also crucified. Above His head Pilate had had a notice placed reading, 'Jesus of Nazareth, King of the Jews.'

Jesus was on the cross for six hours, and during that time He spoke seven times.

First He prayed for the people and the soldiers saying, 'Father, forgive them for they do not know what they are doing.'

Then He spoke to one of the thieves who was repenting of his past, saying, 'Truly I say to you, today you will be with Me in paradise.'

Then He placed His mother Mary in the care of His disciple John: 'Woman, behold your son! Behold your mother!'

Next, in great agony, He repeated some words from a psalm, 'My God, My God, why hast Thou forsaken Me?'

Then He said, 'I thirst', and a sponge soaked in cheap wine was passed up to Him, after which He said, 'It is finished.'

Finally, He prayed, 'Father, into Thy hands I commit My spirit,' and then He died.

For the last three hours that Jesus was on the cross, the sun ceased to shine and there was darkness over all the land; also the curtain which hung in the temple was torn in two.

When Jesus had died, one of the soldiers plunged his spear into His side to make certain He was dead. The people who had gathered there went back home, many feeling very sad, especially those who had known Jesus personally and who were still loyal to him.

Among those who remained loyal to Jesus were two important men who wished to see that He had a proper burial. One man was named Joseph and came from Arimathea in Judea; although he was a member of the council, he had not agreed with their decision over Jesus. The other was a man named Nicodemus, who had come to Jesus one night to talk about the Kingdom of God and to learn more about Jesus's way of life.

Joseph went to Pilate and asked if he could have Jesus's body. Pilate agreed, and with Nicodemus, Joseph took the body to a tomb cut in a rock in his own garden, which he had prepared for himself. Nicodemus brought costly spices with which to anoint the body, as was the custom, and they wrapped it in linen and laid it in the tomb. Then they placed a large heavy stone over the entrance.

Mary Magdalene, one of Jesus's followers, and another woman called Mary were watching and they saw where the body of Jesus was lain and went to tell the disciples.

So ended the first Good Friday.

The next day some of the Pharisees and chief priests went to Pilate and said, 'We remember that this man Jesus said He would rise again in three days. Will you give orders that the tomb is guarded until the third day, so that His disciples don't steal the body and tell people He has risen? They could cause a great deal of trouble.'

'Take a guard and make the tomb as secure as possible,' said Pilate.

So they went and put a seal over the stone entrance and left it guarded by Roman soldiers, both by day and by night.

The First Easter Day

The day after Jesus's crucifixion was the seventh day of the week, the Jewish Sabbath (Saturday) when work was forbidden. The following day was the first day of the week (Sunday).

Very early on the morning of that day, before it was properly light, Mary Magdalene and the women who had been loyal to Jesus to the end, went to the tomb taking some sweet-smelling spices for His body.

On the way they remembered the huge stone which had been rolled across the entrance to the tomb and realized that they would probably be unable to move it. 'Who will roll away the stone for us?' they wondered.

As they got nearer, however, they saw to their surprise that the stone had already been moved. St Matthew's Gospel tells us that there had been a violent earthquake, and that an angel had come down and rolled the stone away; the guards had trembled with fear and had 'become like dead men'.

The women crept up to the tomb and looked inside—the body of Jesus had gone! Where He had been lying stood two angels in shining white, who spoke to the women who were frightened and bowed their faces to the ground. 'Don't be afraid,' said the angels. 'Why are you looking for the living among the dead? Jesus is not here. He has risen. You remember that He told you when He was in Galilee that He would be crucified but would rise again on the third day. Go and tell His disciples, and Peter, that He is going before you into Galilee, and there you will see Him.'

Trembling with fear and astonishment, the women ran back to Jerusalem to tell the disciples what had happened. But the disciples didn't believe them and thought that they were talking nonsense.

However, Peter and John decided after a while that they had better go and see for themselves, and so they both ran off to the tomb. Now John was younger than Peter, and so he could run faster and he got there first. He stooped down and looked inside the tomb. Certainly Jesus's body was not there, but the grave-clothes were there, with the cloth which had been around Jesus's head lying separately. Obviously no one would have hurriedly taken off the grave-clothes in order to take Jesus's body away. It was as though the body had simply miraculously passed through them.

Then up came Peter, and he went straight into the tomb. John followed him—and they saw and believed, but still did not understand just what had happened. Feeling very puzzled, they returned to their homes.

Mary Magdalene had gone back to the tomb, and stood outside it weeping. She too looked inside, perhaps wondering if her eyes had deceived her the first time she had looked.

This time there were two angels sitting where the body of Jesus had been—one at the head and the other at the feet. They asked her, 'Why are you weeping?'

Mary replied, 'Because they have taken away my Lord, and I do not know where they have put Him.'

As she said this, she turned and saw someone standing there. It was still not properly light and her eyes were blurred with tears, and so she could not see clearly who it was. 'Woman, why are you weeping? Who is it that you are looking for?' the figure asked.

Thinking that it was probably the gardener who was speaking to her, Mary said, 'Sir, if you have taken Him, tell me where you have laid Him, and I will take Him away.'

Then He said, 'Mary!', and Mary knew it was Jesus! No one else said 'Mary' just like that!

'Teacher!' she said to Him.

'Don't touch Me,' said Jesus, 'for I have not yet gone back to My Father; but go and tell My brothers that I am returning to My Father and their Father, to My God and their God.'

Joyfully Mary went to the disciples to tell them the exciting news. She had seen Jesus! And she told them all that He had said.

Meanwhile the soldiers who had been set to guard Jesus's tomb were terrified and completely baffled at what had happened. They decided that the best thing to do was to go and tell the chief priests just what had occurred—so far as they were able.

The chief priests and elders met, no doubt extremely worried, and decided that they had better try and cover up as best they could. So they gave the soldiers some money and said, 'You must say that Jesus's disciples came in the night and stole His body while you were asleep. If it gets to the governor's ears, we will tell him it wasn't your fault. Don't worry.'

No group of people could have been more miserable and dispirited than the disciples had been when Jesus had died. With their leader gone, they felt that all He had stood for, and all that they had worked for, was now lost. They were without hope, very sad and very afraid.

Peter especially was completely wretched, remembering how he had denied his Lord. How marvellous then to hear that special message which the angels had given to the women! 'Tell His disciples, *and Peter*, that He is going before you into Galilee.'

The Bible does not tell us what happened when Peter met Jesus again. No doubt this was something which Peter would want to keep to himself for ever. But we do know that Jesus did appear to Peter.

Since the wonderful event of Jesus's resurrection, upon which the Christian religion places its firm foundation, Christians have changed their main day of worship from the seventh day of the week (Saturday) to the first day (Sunday), as a reminder that the resurrection happened on a Sunday, the first day of the week.

The First Easter Night

Later on, towards the evening of that wonderful first Easter day, two of Jesus's followers were walking from Jerusalem to the little village of Emmaus, a distance of about 11 km (7 miles).

They did not know that Jesus had risen from the dead, though they had been hearing some strange rumours, and they talked together about the recent and terrible happenings in Jerusalem. How sad that Jesus, their friend and leader, had been put to death! It was the end of their hopes.

As they talked, Jesus Himself came up and walked along with them, but they did not recognize Him. Perhaps His appearance had changed somewhat at His resurrection, or He may have prevented their knowing Him. Certainly they would not be expecting to see Him.

'What are you talking about? What makes you look so unhappy? asked Jesus.

They stood still, looking very sad. Then one of them, named Cleopas, said, 'You must be the only visitor to Jerusalem who does not know about all the things that have been happening there during the past few days.'

'What things?' asked Jesus.

'About Jesus of Nazareth, who was a wonderful prophet, mighty in deed and word,' they answered. 'The chief priests and rulers of the people had Him condemned to death, and He was crucified three days ago. We had hoped that He was the one, promised in the scriptures, who was going to set Israel free.

'But then there was a very surprising report. Some women went to His tomb this morning and could not find His body. They came back and said that they had seen angels who had told them that Jesus was alive. Then some others went to the tomb and found it as the women had said. But they did not see Jesus.'

'O foolish men, slow to believe all that the prophets foretold,' said Jesus. 'Ought not the Messiah to have suffered these things and to have entered into His glory?'

Then, beginning with the laws of Moses and the writings of the prophets, Jesus explained to them what had been said about Himself in the scriptures. Cleopas and his companion must have found it hard to understand.

By this time, they were approaching the village of Emmaus, and it seemed as though Jesus intended to go on further. But, as it was getting dark, the two followers held Him back and said, 'Stay with us, for it is almost dark and the day has nearly gone.'

Jesus accepted their kind invitation and went in to stay and have a meal with them. As they began to eat, Jesus took some bread and blessed it, and then broke it in pieces and gave it to them.

Suddenly they realized who He was! Perhaps it was the words He spoke as He blessed the bread which seemed familiar to them, or they may have looked closely at His hands as He broke it and seen the marks of the nails. Whatever it was, they knew now, without doubt, that this was Jesus. Then when they looked again, He had gone!

They turned to one another and said, 'We should have known! Didn't it seem like fire burning in us while He was talking to us on the road?'

Although it was late, they got up at once and

hurried all the long way back to Jerusalem to tell the disciples the stupendous news.

They found them gathered together, behind locked doors because they feared the Jewish authorities, but were somewhat surprised when the disciples greeted them with the news, 'The Lord is risen and has appeared to Simon!'

Then, while Cleopas and his companion were telling the disciples their story about what had happened at Emmaus, Jesus Himself suddenly appeared among them. They were all terrified and thought they were seeing a ghost.

'Peace be with you,' said Jesus. 'Why are you so frightened and full of doubts? Look at My hands and My feet. Touch Me, and you will know that it is I, for a spirit does not have flesh and bones as you can see I have.' And He showed them His hands and His feet.

Still the disciples found it hard to believe, although they were full of happiness.

'Have you anything here to eat?' asked Jesus, and they gave Him a piece of cooked fish, which He ate as further proof that He was not a spirit.

Now one of the eleven disciples, Thomas, was not present on this occasion, and when they met him later the other disciples burst out with the news, 'We have seen the Lord!'

Thomas just couldn't believe it and he said, 'Unless I see the marks of the nails in His hands, and put my finger in them, and place my hand in the wound in His side, I will not believe it.' Thomas, like many others, would only be satisfied with the evidence of his senses.

Eight days later, the disciples were together, again behind locked doors, and this time Thomas was present. Once more Jesus came and stood among them. 'Thomas,' He said, 'Put your finger here and see My hands, put your hand in My side, and do not doubt any more, but believe.'

Thomas knew then it was truly Jesus and he said, 'My Lord and my God!'

'You believe because you have seen,' said Jesus, 'but happy are the people who believe without seeing Me.'

Breakfast on the Shore

Some time after this, seven of the disciples were by the Sea of Galilee. The seven were Simon Peter, James and John, Thomas, Nathanael, and two others. Simon Peter said, 'I'm going fishing.'

'We'll come too,' said the others, and they all set out in a boat.

Although the disciples worked hard all night, they did not catch any fish. Usually it was easier to catch fish at night, because they could not see the nets, but the fishermen had no success on this night.

As dawn broke and the sun began to rise, they noticed someone standing by the water's edge. 'Young men,' He called, 'have you caught any fish?'

'Not one,' they answered.

'Let your net down over the right side of the boat, and then you will catch some,' advised the man.

So, despite their unsuccessful and tiring night, they threw the net out as instructed, and to their amazement found that they could not pull it back in because they had caught so many fish.

John then realized who the man on the shore was. 'It is the Lord!' he gasped.

As soon as Peter heard that, he wrapped his coat around him, jumped out of the boat and waded ashore, for they were only about 100 m (109 yd) from the land. The other disciples followed in the boat, dragging the net, heavy with the catch.

As they got nearer, they saw that Jesus had prepared a charcoal fire and had some fish and bread ready for them. 'Bring some of those fish you've just caught,' He said.

Peter went to help drag in the net and, when they counted, they found that they had caught 153 large fish; yet, much to their surprise and relief, the net was not broken, despite the great weight it held.

'Come and eat,' said Jesus, and He gave them the bread and fish.

When they had eaten, Jesus said to Simon Peter, 'Simon, do you love me more than these others?'

Peter had earlier boasted of his great love and loyalty for Jesus, but now, after his denials, he was more humble. 'Lord, You know that I love You,' he replied.

'Take care of My lambs,' said Jesus, meaning His followers.

Then a second time Jesus asked Peter if he loved Him. 'Yes, Lord, You know that I do,' said Peter.

'Take care of My sheep,' said Jesus.

A third time Jesus asked the same question, and Peter said, 'Lord, You know everything. You know I love You.'

'Take care of My sheep,' said Jesus again.

This would not be an easy task, but Peter was to stick to it and help many 'sheep' to come to love and work for Jesus, the Good Shepherd.

Peter was sad that Jesus had asked him three times if he loved Him, but as he had once denied Jesus three times, perhaps this was Jesus's way of cancelling out these three denials with the three statements that Peter really did love Him. It was also a way of restoring Peter to his old position as leader, and of giving him the task of caring for people.

The Ascension and First Whitsunday

For forty days after Jesus had risen from the dead on the first Easter Sunday, He was seen by many of His friends at various times. There could be no doubt that He was alive again and had risen from the dead, just as He had said He would.

Sometimes He was with them, sometimes He was not. He could appear among them even if they were in a room with all the doors and windows firmly closed, for His body was different since His resurrection.

When He came in the midst of them like that He always knew what had been happening just beforehand. Gradually they began to realize that whether they could see Him or not, whether they could hear Him or not, He was always with them and this gave them great comfort.

During this time—sometimes referred to as the 'Great Forty Days'—the disciples listened hard to what He told them, learning no doubt that they would be expected to carry on His work. For He knew that the time was coming when He would have to leave them in bodily form, and they would not actually see and hear Him on earth any more as they had until now.

He charged the disciples: 'Go into all the world and make people My disciples, baptizing them in the name of the Father, and of the Son, and of the Holy Spirit, and teaching them to obey My commands. And I will be with you always, even until the end of the world.'

Now on the fortieth day after the resurrection, He had led them out as far as Bethany and on to a hill. He had given them special orders that they were not to leave Jerusalem until they received the gift of the Holy Spirit which would strengthen them for their great work and give them the courage they would need.

'Are You now going to restore Israel to be a great nation again?' asked the disciples. They hoped He would make the Jewish nation independent of Rome, which was what the Jews had always thought the Messiah would do. They still had not learned that God's Kingdom is not of this world. After all, if He who had been killed and had then risen from the dead were to show Himself to all the people in Jerusalem and to the chief priests and elders and to Pilate and King Herod, surely then they would have to accept that He was truly the Messiah, the Son of God, King of the Jews.

'It is not for anyone to know that,' said Jesus, 'for times and seasons belong to God's authority alone.'

Meanwhile the disciples had to set about the task of winning the world for God—a seemingly impossible job for such a small band of men, but Jesus knew that with God all things are possible, and He said, 'When the Holy Spirit comes to you, you will be filled with power and will be My witnesses in Jerusalem, in all Judea and Samaria, and to the ends of the earth.'

After He had said this, He blessed them, and then a cloud covered Him and took Him up out of their sight.

As the disciples stood gazing at the sky, two angels appeared beside them and said, 'You men of Galilee, why are you standing gazing up into heaven? This same Jesus, who was taken from you into heaven, will come back in the same way that you have seen Him depart from you into heaven.'

Although the disciples would see Jesus no more, they felt happy and returned to Jerusalem with great joy. They were happy because He had blessed them, and full of joy that He would always be with them, even though they could not see Him any longer as they had done before.

Now they could look forward to the coming of God's Holy Spirit which would give them power and strength for the great work which was ahead.

The day on which Jesus ascended (went back up) to heaven is called Ascension Day, and it is celebrated by the Church each year on the fortieth day after Easter (always on a Thursday).

'Ascension' means 'going up'. When we say that Jesus 'ascended to heaven', we do not necessarily mean that heaven is a place above the sky. 'Up' in this sense means 'better, different', rather as you might say you were 'going up' in school, even though your new classroom may be on a lower floor than your previous one.

The First Whitsunday

After Jesus's ascension into heaven, the disciples went back to Jerusalem. They were still afraid of the Jewish authorities who had killed Jesus, so they stayed indoors where they felt safer. Each day after the ascension they wondered if the gift of the Holy Spirit would come that day and they watched and waited.

A week went by, then eight days, nine days, and, at last, on the tenth day something strange and wonderful happened.

Now the tenth day happened to be the feast of Pentecost. Pentecost means 'fifty', and this feast always came fifty days after the Passover. Pentecost marked the end of the barley harvest, when the Jews presented freshly baked loaves of new, fine, leavened flour in the temple. It was a day of rejoicing and gratitude for the gifts of the earth—rather like a harvest festival. Many people from many countries came to Jerusalem to take part in the feast of Pentecost. It was always a very happy and busy time in the city.

Jesus's band of inner disciples now numbered

twelve again, for a new man named Matthias had been chosen to replace Judas Iscariot who had killed himself after his evil deed of betrayal on that night in the Garden of Gethsemane.

This band of twelve are known as the twelve apostles—the word 'apostle' means 'one who is sent' (to preach and teach). The word 'disciple' means 'learner'—and all those who followed Jesus, believed in Him and wanted to obey His teachings were considered as disciples, including the apostles.

On this day of Pentecost, the apostles and probably some other disciples were all gathered together in one place.

Suddenly there was a loud noise, like a rushing mighty wind, and it filled the whole house where they were sitting. They looked at one another in astonishment and saw a glowing light split up into what looked like flames of fire hovering above each of their heads. This was the outward sign that the promised gift of God's Holy Spirit had now come to them.

The mighty wind was a symbol of the power and energy of the Holy Spirit, and the flames of fire were a symbol of the fiery zeal with which the disciples would now be able to proclaim the Gospel.

The effect on them was tremendous. No longer were they weak, cowering, frightened people; instead they felt strong and brave and were filled with a great strength. They found, too, that they could do things which they had been unable to do before. When they spoke to the crowds a little later, they discovered that people who did not speak their language could still understand what they said.

The disciples felt filled with such courage and strength that they immediately left the house and went among the crowds of people outside. These included not only those who lived in Jerusalem, but also countless visitors who had come to Jerusalem for the feast of Pentecost. There were Parthians, Medes and Elamites, representing countries from beyond the influence of the Roman Empire; there were people from Mesopotamia, from Judea, from Cappadocia, Asia Minor, Pamphylia, Egypt and Libya, Crete and Arabia. Yet they could all understand what the disciples were telling them about the wonderful and mighty works of God.

Normally the Galilean speech of the disciples would not have been easy to follow. Now everyone in the crowd heard his own language being spoken. They were amazed and puzzled.

'What does it mean?' the crowds asked one another. 'They are drunk with wine,' said others mockingly.

Then Peter, standing up with the other eleven apostles, began to speak courageously to the crowd in a loud voice. It was the first ever Christian sermon. 'These people are not drunk with wine,' he began; 'but what you see and hear is what the prophet Joel said would happen. He said that God would send His Spirit to all.' (Peter was quoting from the prophet Joel whose book forms part of the Old Testament.)

'Listen to these words, men of Israel,' went on Peter, 'Jesus of Nazareth was sent by God—a fact proved by all the wonders and miracles which God worked through Him. Yet by the hands of sinful and lawless men He was crucified. But God raised Him from the dead, and set Him free from the power of death. Moreover, He has ascended to the right hand of God, and has sent His Holy Spirit as He promised. What you now see and hear is that gift of the Holy Spirit which is poured out upon us. It is certain that this Jesus, whom you crucified, is the One whom God has sent to be our Lord and Messiah.'

When the people heard this brave message, many of them were upset and very troubled. They said to the apostles, 'What shall we do then?'

Peter replied, 'You must start afresh. Give up your sins and be baptized in the name of Jesus Christ. Your sins will then be forgiven, and you will receive the gift of the Holy Spirit.'

Many of the crowd believed Peter's powerful words and they came to be baptized. About 3,000 people were added to the group of believers on that day. They learnt from the apostles and shared fellowship meals and prayer.

Because of their firm faith, the apostles were able to perform many miracles and wonders, and more and more believers were added to their number. Baptism was followed by a new sense of community, which resulted in a practical sharing of their belongings with one another. The richer ones among them sold their property and possessions and gave the money to those who were in need. Every day they went to the temple, and had meals together in their homes.

Such was the way in which the Christian Church began on the first Whitsunday. (Whitsun got its name because it was originally a day for baptisms when those to be baptized dressed in white. It therefore came to be called White-Sunday or Whitsunday.)

Peter and John and the Lame Man

One day Peter and John went to the temple at three o'clock in the afternoon, which was one of the set hours for prayer. The temple was a beautiful building, and one of its doors (or gates) was so lovely that it was called the Beautiful Gate. It is thought that this gate was of Corinthian brass and that it was adorned in a costly manner, with much richer and thicker plates of gold and silver than the others.

In front of this gate was a man who had been lame all his life and was unable to walk. Friends carried him there each day and left him to beg for money, for there would always be plenty of people coming and going at this spot.

When the lame man saw Peter and John approaching, he held out his hands asking for money. He may have thought they looked kindly, or he might even have known that they had been friends of Jesus.

Peter and John stopped. 'Look at us,' said Peter. So the lame man looked, hopefully, expecting that they would now give him something.

But Peter and John had no money, and the lame man was very surprised at what Peter said next. 'I haven't any money, but what I do have I will give you,' said Peter. 'In the name of Jesus Christ of Nazareth, get up and walk!'

He took hold of the man's right hand and helped him up. At once the man felt strength come into his feet and ankles, and he stood up and found that he could move around.

Walking and jumping for joy, he went with Peter and John into the temple and praised God.

The people standing around were absolutely amazed. 'Isn't this the beggar who sat asking for alms at the Beautiful Gate?' they asked one another. As the man held on to Peter and John, the astonished people ran up to them. Peter saw the crowd and spoke to them.

'Men of Israel,' he said, 'why are you so surprised and why do you keep staring at us? Do you think it was through our own power that we made this man walk? No, it was through faith in the name of Jesus that this man was made well, and was given perfect health—the same Jesus you rejected in Pilate's presence, even when Pilate wanted to set Him free. He was holy and good, but you asked Pilate to set free a murderer, Barabbas, instead, and killed Jesus; but God raised Him from the dead.

'I know that what you and your leaders did was due to ignorance, but now you must repent and turn to God, so that He can forgive your sins. For God sent Jesus to you Jews first, to bless you in turning away from your wickedness.'

Peter and John were still speaking when some priests, the captain of the temple guard, and some Sadducees arrived. They were annoyed with Peter and John, because the two apostles were telling people that Jesus had risen from the dead, and the Sadducees, in particular, did not believe in resurrection. They arrested Peter and John, and put them in prison until the next day, for it was by now getting late.

Even so, many of the people outside believed what Peter and John had been telling them, and the number of believers grew to be about 5,000 strong.

The next day a full and important meeting of the Sanhedrin (the Jewish Council) was summoned. They commanded Peter and John to appear before them. 'By what power did you make the lame man walk?' they demanded of the two apostles.

Peter, inspired by the Holy Spirit, began to address them: 'Leaders of the people and elders,' he began, 'we are being examined today because of a good deed which we did to a cripple, and you want to know how we healed him. It was through the power of Jesus Christ of Nazareth, whom you crucified and whom God raised from the dead. He is the stone which was rejected by the builders and yet has become the most important corner-stone of all. You can only be saved through Him, for in all the world there is no one else who can save us from our sins.'

The members of the Council were astounded when they heard this speech, for they saw that Peter and John were only untrained ordinary men, but they knew too that they had been with Jesus.

However, seeing the cripple standing up straight and able to walk, they found it difficult to condemn them. The puzzled Council members then sent Peter and John outside while they held a private conference.

'What shall we do with these men?' they asked one another. 'We certainly cannot deny that the lame man has been healed. All Jerusalem can see that. Yet we don't want their teaching to spread further among the people. We'd better warn them.'

So they called Peter and John in again and said, 'You must not speak or teach any more in the name of Jesus.'

But Peter and John would have none of that. They felt far too strongly to let anyone stop them teaching about Jesus. They replied, 'You must judge whether it is right to listen to God or to listen to you, but we cannot help speaking of what we have seen and heard.'

The Council warned them even more threateningly and then let them go. They knew they dare not punish them, because of all the people who were praising God for what had happened.

Peter and John returned to their friends and told them what had occurred. The believers gathered together and prayed to God to help them to be bold. When they had finished praying, the place where they were meeting began to shake, and they were all filled with the Holy Spirit and went out to preach God's message fearlessly.

Peter and Cornelius

Up to now, the disciples had been preaching the Gospel only to Jews, converts and Samaritans who observed the law of Moses. But God did not want the news to remain limited. So, using Peter and a Roman centurion named Cornelius, He showed clearly that the Gospel was for all men—Jews and Gentiles alike.

Cornelius was a Roman centurion living in Caesarea. He was a good man whose whole family worshipped God; he often prayed and gave generously to the poor.

About three o'clock one afternoon he had a vision in which he clearly saw an angel come to him and say, 'Cornelius!' Staring at the angel in terror, Cornelius said, 'What is it, Lord?'

The angel replied, 'The Lord has heard your prayers and seen your good deeds. Now, send some men to Joppa for a man named Simon Peter; he is lodging with a leather-worker named Simon, whose house is by the sea.'

Cornelius obeyed, and sent two servants and a soldier to Joppa, having explained to them what had happened.

The next day, as they were still on their way and just approaching Joppa, which was some 50 km (34 miles) from Caesarea, Peter went up on to the flat roof of Simon's house to pray. It was about noon.

He was feeling hungry and had asked for something to eat. While the food was being prepared, Peter too had a vision. He saw the heavens opened and something like a large sheet lowered by its four corners to the earth. In the sheet were all kinds of animals, reptiles and wild birds. Then a voice said, 'Rise, Peter, kill and eat.'

'Certainly not,' replied Peter, 'for I have never eaten anything common or unclean.' (The Jews had strict laws about food, dividing it into things that were 'clean' and could be eaten, and those that were 'unclean' and could not. They were, for instance, generally allowed to eat animals which chewed the cud and had cloven hooves. Gentiles, on the other hand, ate food which the Jews considered unclean, like pork and shellfish.)

The voice came to Peter a second time saying, 'What God has cleansed you must not call common or unclean.'

This happened three times and then the sheet was taken back into heaven.

Peter's vision showed that Jews and Gentiles were to eat together on terms of equality. It reminded Peter that he was not to despise the Gentiles, nor anything which God had created. Jesus had once said that what goes into a man's heart defiles him much more than that which goes into his stomach—but Peter had not understood what He meant.

While Peter was still puzzling over what all this could mean, the three men sent by Cornelius arrived. They stood at the gate and asked, 'Have you a guest here named Simon Peter?'

Peter was still on the roof wondering about the vision when the Holy Spirit said to him, 'There are three men here looking for you. Go down and accompany them, for I have sent them.'

So Peter went down and said, 'I am the man you are seeking. Why have you come?'

'The centurion Cornelius sent us,' they replied. 'He is a good, God-fearing man, highly respected by the Jews. An angel told him to send for you.'

Peter invited the men in and they stayed for the night. The next day the four of them set off back to Caesarea, and some of the believers in Joppa also went with them. When they arrived, Cornelius met them, and he fell down at Peter's feet and worshipped him. 'Get up,' said Peter, 'I am only a man.'

They went into the house where many of Cornelius's relations and close friends had gathered.

Peter said to them, 'You know that it is unlawful for a Jew to visit or associate with Gentiles. But God has shown me that I should not despise any man. So when I was sent for, I came without objection. Now, why did you send for me?'

Cornelius explained about his vision and ended, 'Now that you have come, we are all gathered here in God's sight to hear everything that He has commanded you to say.'

Peter replied, 'I now know that God treats everyone alike. Anyone who worships Him and does what is right is accepted by Him, whether he be Jew or Gentile.'

Then he went on to tell them about Jesus, and how with God's Holy Spirit, He had gone about healing people and doing good. The disciples had been witnesses of all this. Then Jesus had been put to death, but had risen again on the third day, and had appeared to many of His friends and had commanded them to preach the Gospel to people everywhere.

Peter ended by saying, 'Everyone who believes in Him receives forgiveness of sins through the power of His Name.'

While he was speaking to Cornelius's family and friends, the Holy Spirit came down upon them. The believers who had come with Peter from Joppa were surprised that the Holy Spirit should come to Gentiles, for they heard them praising God's greatness and speaking in strange tongues.

'These people have received the Holy Spirit, just as we did,' said Peter. 'What is to stop them from being baptized?'

He ordered that they should be baptized in the name of Jesus Christ. Then they asked him to stay with them for some days.

Later, when Peter went up to Jerusalem, he was criticized for going to the Gentiles and eating with them.

He explained about his vision and how the Holy Spirit had come to those at Caesarea. 'If God gave them the same gift as He gave to us,' he said, 'who was I to withstand God?'

The critics were silenced, but said, 'Then God has also given the Gentiles the opportunity to repent and to live.'

Peter in Prison

The new Church was not left in peace for very long, for there were always people ready to try and stamp out the rule of God. This time it was Herod, the king who had started a wave of persecution against the Christians. (He was Herod Agrippa I, grandson of Herod the Great.) He had seized James (the brother of John and one of Jesus's inner band of three) and had had him put to death with a sword. Then, when he saw how pleased the Jews were with what he had done, he arrested Peter too and put him in prison as well. As it was Passover time, he planned to put him on trial after the festival.

Peter was tied with two chains, and four squads, each of four soldiers, were set to take turns in

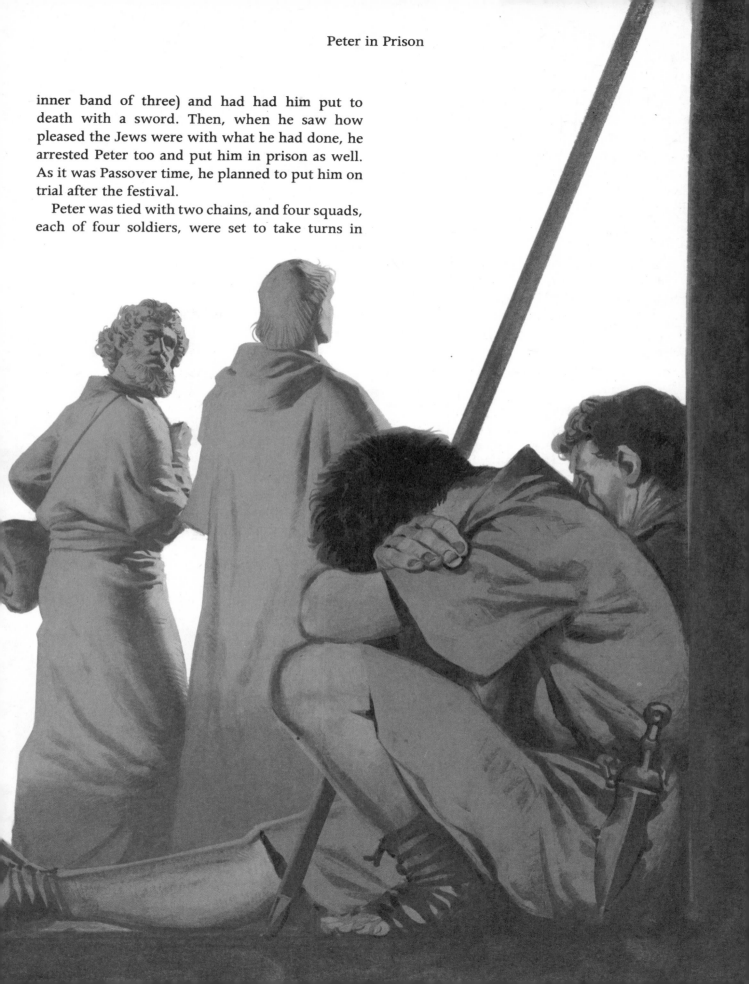

guarding him. Peter must have thought that his own days were numbered just as those of James had been.

Outside, however, the disciples were praying for him, and Peter knew that the Holy Spirit would be with him, even in prison and that God would never desert him.

Time dragged slowly by, until it came to the last night before Peter was due to go on trial. Tomorrow Herod would almost certainly have him killed.

Suddenly Peter started. Someone was shaking him by the shoulder and he heard a voice saying, 'Get up quickly!' It was an angel, who had appeared in his cell.

The chains fell from Peter's hands, and the angel said, 'Dress yourself and put on your sandals, wrap your cloak around you and follow me as quickly as possible.'

Peter could hardly believe this was happening; he thought he was dreaming and that, when he awoke, the chains would be there just as firmly as they had been before. But he followed the angel, past the first guard post, then the second, until they came to the great iron gate which led from the prison into the city. Now, surely he would wake up, but, no, the iron gate swung open of its own accord, and out they went into the dark and silent street.

Then the angel disappeared, and Peter realized that it wasn't a dream after all. The wonderful event was true!

No doubt he wondered what would happen when his escape was discovered; soldiers would be sent out to search the city until he was found. He decided he had better take refuge in a friend's house, and he went to the home of Mary, the mother of one of Peter's friends named John Mark. A company of his friends had gathered there to pray for Peter, and doubtless they had been praying very late that night, because they knew that on the morrow Peter would be brought to trial before King Herod.

Peter knocked at the door—not too loudly, for fear there were any enemies about. The friends inside were nervous, wondering whether some more of Herod's soldiers had come to arrest them and drag them off to prison too.

A servant-girl named Rhoda came to the door. She knew better than to open it straightaway, for it may well have been an enemy outside. When she recognized Peter's voice, she was absolutely delighted—so much so that she forgot to open the door and ran back instead to tell the others about it. 'It's Peter!' she cried.

'No! You're crazy!' they said, and refused to believe her.

'But it is Peter,' insisted Rhoda.

'It must be his angel,' they answered.

All this time Peter continued to knock on the door, until at last one of his friends went to open it. They were all overjoyed and amazed when they found that it really was Peter.

Peter put up his hand to motion them to be quiet, and then he explained to them how the angel had come and how he had been able to walk out of the prison. The friends knew that God had indeed answered their prayers.

Peter said that the friends should tell the other believers about the wonderful happenings of that night, but that he must leave them and go somewhere else for safety. Herod's soldiers would almost certainly think of looking for him in the houses of his friends; and, if discovered, that would mean danger for them too.

Peter knew that wherever he went, God would be with him, and that his friends would be praying to ask God to guide him through any difficulties which he might meet.

The next morning, when it was discovered that Peter was missing, there was tremendous confusion among the guards. Herod gave orders for a search party to go out, but they did not find Peter. How he had managed to escape was a complete mystery to them.

Herod, however, was very angry about the whole affair. He had the guards questioned, and when they could give no satisfactory answer, he ordered them to be put to death in a fit of rage and wickedness.

Stephen the Martyr

The Christian Church continued spreading, so much so that the apostles found that there was more work than the twelve of them could do. As well as the preaching and teaching, and the important need for prayer, there was the work of sharing and helping the needy.

It was some complaints from the Greek-speaking Jews which really brought matters to a head; they said that their widows were being neglected.

So the twelve apostles summoned a meeting of the disciples and said, 'It is not right for us to leave off preaching God's word in order to deal with money and food-sharing. We propose that you choose seven men from among you to be put in charge of the sharing; then we twelve can give our full time to prayer and preaching.'

The meeting set about choosing seven new helpers. They were named Philip, Prochorus, Nicanor, Timon, Parmenas, Nicolaus and Stephen.

One of them, Stephen, performed great miracles and wonders, but there were some religious leaders who were very much against Stephen and they argued with him; although they could not deny that he spoke with great wisdom. So, secretly, they produced some men to say that they had heard Stephen speak blasphemous words against God and against Moses. This was completely untrue, but, in this way, they managed to stir up the people. Stephen was arrested and brought before the Council.

There they brought in some false witnesses to tell lies about him and to exaggerate and twist what he had said. 'This man,' they lied, 'is always speaking against the temple and the Law. We've heard him say that Jesus of Nazareth will destroy this place and change the customs of Moses.'

The men sitting in the Council looked at Stephen, expecting a denial, but there was neither anger nor fear in his expression. Instead his face looked like that of an angel. The High Priest asked, 'Is it true?'

Stephen made a long speech in reply. First he told them the history of the Jews, beginning with Abraham and Moses and reminded them how God had delivered the Jews out of the bondage of Egypt; and how the Israelites had turned away from God and had worshipped a golden calf instead. He spoke of David and of Solomon and ended by saying that Israel of old had rejected the prophets, and now they had betrayed and murdered the Messiah Himself.

'You are deaf to God's message, just as your ancestors were. You are the ones who received God's law, yet you are the ones who disobey it.'

When the Council heard these things, they were furious, but Stephen gazed towards heaven and said, 'I see heaven opened and the Son of Man at the right hand of God.'

The Council shouted angrily, covering their ears with their hands at what they considered to be blasphemy. They rushed on Stephen and dragged him out of the city to stone him, leaving their cloaks in the charge of a young man named Saul.

As they were stoning Stephen, he prayed, 'Lord Jesus, receive my spirit.' He knelt down and prayed for his tormentors, crying out, 'Lord, do not hold this sin against them.' Then he died.

Saul, who was in charge of the cloaks, approved of his murder, yet he was to become a very important figure in the life of the Church in the days to come.

The Road to Damascus

The young man named Saul, who had been in charge of the cloaks of those who had stoned Stephen, was born in the city of Tarsus in the south of Asia Minor. He had had a good education, being a clever boy, and had studied in Jerusalem under a famous teacher called Gamaliel.

He grew up to be a firm upholder of the law and a hater of the teaching of Jesus of Nazareth. He resolved to do all in his power to stamp out this new religion and, in raging fury, he sought out Jesus's followers and persecuted them whenever he found them. Not only did he have many of them shut up in prison, but he readily voted against them when they were ordered to be put to death.

One day he was on his way to Damascus, the capital city of Syria, to seek out and arrest the believers there. He had been given letters of introduction to the synagogues in Damascus, so that if he found any of the followers of Jesus there, he could bring them back, bound, to Jerusalem.

Full of threats and hate, he journeyed to Damascus in the company of a group of other men. Suddenly, as they were approaching the city, a brilliant blinding light, brighter than the sun, stopped them in their tracks.

Saul fell to the ground and, as he did so, he heard a voice saying, 'Saul! Saul! Why are you persecuting Me?'

'Who are You, Lord?' asked Saul.

'I am Jesus whom you are persecuting,' came the reply. 'Get up and go into the city, and there you will be told what to do.'

The men who were travelling with Saul were astonished, for they could hear the voice but could not see anyone speaking. They themselves were speechless.

Saul got up from the ground and found that when he opened his eyes he could not see anything. He was blind.

His companions took him by the hand and led

him into Damascus, where for three days he was unable to see and did not eat or drink anything.

Now in Damascus there was a disciple named Ananias, and he had a vision in which the Lord spoke to him. 'Ananias!'

'Here I am, Lord,' replied Ananias.

'Get up and go to the house of a man named Judas in Straight Street, and there ask for a man called Saul from Tarsus. He is praying and in a vision he has seen a man named Ananias come and place his hands on him so that his sight may be restored.'

Ananias was troubled when he heard this and he said, 'But Lord, I have heard about this man and of all the terrible things he has done to Your followers in Jerusalem; and here he has authority from the chief priests to arrest and bind any believers he can find.'

Ananias could not believe that God would want this man; but God knew how Saul would change. 'Go,' He said, 'for he is the man I have chosen to make My name known to the Gentiles and the kings and people of Israel. He will suffer much for the sake of My name.'

So Ananias went to the house in Straight Street where Saul was staying. Obedient to God's will, he placed his hands on him and said, 'Brother Saul, the Lord Jesus, who appeared to you on the road as you were coming, has sent me so that your sight may be restored and that you might be filled with the Holy Spirit.'

Immediately it seemed as though scales fell from Saul's eyes and he found that he could see again.

'Why wait any longer?' said Ananias. 'Be baptized and wash away your sins and call on the name of Jesus.'

Saul got up and he was baptized, and from that time became an unswerving follower of Jesus.

This was a great turning-point in the history of the early Church; from being a violent enemy of the way of Christ, Saul turned about completely and became one of the Church's most ardent leaders. He soon became known as Paul, which was his Roman name and is the name by which he is more familiarly known.

He stayed a few days in Damascus and went into the synagogue and began to preach that Jesus was the Son of God. The disciples in Damascus were amazed. Here was the man who had come to arrest and imprison them actually preaching that they must believe and follow Jesus.

The Jews were furious when they found that this energetic hater of Jesus had now gone over to Jesus's way of life, so they had a meeting and made plans to kill him.

They watched the city gates all day and all night in order to catch Paul if he were to go out of the city. His life was certainly in danger, just as the lives of the believers had been when the old Saul had been persecuting them.

However, Paul's friends discovered the plot and determined to find a way for him to escape. One night, under cover of darkness, they put him in a big basket and lowered him over the city wall. Thus he was able to return safely to Jerusalem.

As soon as he returned to Jerusalem, Paul tried to join the disciples there. Somewhat naturally, they were all afraid of him and could not believe that he had now become one of Jesus's disciples. They suspected he might be using his new life as a trick to arrest them.

One of them, however, a man named Barnabas, believed Paul and he brought him to the apostles and told them how he had been converted on the road to Damascus, and how at Damascus he had preached boldly in the name of Jesus.

Now Paul went all over Jerusalem preaching in Jesus's name, but there were still some Greek-speaking Jews who were against him and wanted to kill him; and when the believers found out about this, they sent Paul back to Tarsus for a while for his own safety.

Paul's First Missionary Journey

Some time later Barnabas went to Tarsus to look for Paul. When he found him, he brought him to Antioch in Syria, and for a year the two men met believers and taught many people. It was at Antioch that the believers were first called 'Christians'.

The group was worshipping one day in Antioch, when they felt that the Holy Spirit was urging them to send Paul and Barnabas to take the message of God's good news to other lands. So they fasted and prayed with them and sent them off on their way to carry Jesus's message.

They set off from Seleucia, which was on the coast, about 26 km (16 miles) from Antioch, and sailed across the sea to the island of Cyprus. There they preached at Salamis and at Paphos, which was the seat of government. The governor of the island, Sergius Paulus, summoned them before him because he wanted to hear why they had come and what they had to say.

At the court there was a false prophet, a sorcerer named Elymas. He was a friend of the governor's and tried to stop the governor from hearing about the true faith. But Paul looked hard at Elymas and said, 'You are a son of the Devil, and the enemy of everything that is good. By your evil tricks you keep trying to distort the truth of God. Now you will be blinded and unable to see anything at all for a time.'

Immediately the false prophet felt mist and darkness come upon his eyes and had to get people to lead him about by the hand. Thus his evil ways were overcome, and the governor became a believer and was astonished at the wonderful teaching about God.

When Paul and his companions left Cyprus they sailed to the mainland where they went to Perga and thence to Antioch in Pisidia (not the same town as Antioch in Syria from which they had started their journey).

Here, at Antioch in Pisidia, they were invited to speak to the people and to give them a message of encouragement. So Paul told them about the great nation of Israel, about how God brought them out of bondage in Egypt, and about Samuel, David and John the Baptist.

Then, addressing both Jews and the Gentiles who worshipped God, he said that it was to all that the message of salvation had been sent, through Jesus's death and resurrection.

The people invited Paul and Barnabas to come back the next Sabbath and tell them more. They did so, and nearly everyone in the town came to hear them. Some Jews, however, were jealous—perhaps because the message was addressed to the Gentiles as well as to themselves, and they contradicted Paul and insulted him and called him a liar.

'The message came to you Jews first,' said Paul and Barnabas even more boldly, 'but you rejected it and so we turned to the Gentiles. For God has set us to be light to the Gentiles and to bring salvation to the whole world.'

The Gentiles were pleased to hear this, but the Jews started a persecution against Paul and Barnabas and drove them out of the district. Undaunted, Paul and Barnabas shook the dust off their feet, and travelled on to Iconium, where their reception was much the same. A great many Jews and Gentiles became believers, but some, both

Jews and Gentiles, were against the apostles and decided to stone them out of the city. When Paul and Barnabas learnt about it, they fled southwards to the cities of Lystra and Derbe.

In Lystra there was a crippled man who had never walked in his life. He sat there, listening intently to Paul's words, and Paul could see that he had great faith. So he said to the man in a loud voice, 'Stand up on your feet!' And the man leapt up and started to walk around, quite overjoyed at the change which had come over him.

When the crowds saw this, they were amazed, and said in their own Lycaonian language, 'The gods have become like men and have come down to us.' They called Barnabas Zeus and Paul Hermes because he was the chief speaker. The priest of Zeus brought bulls and garlands and wanted to offer sacrifice with the people. Paul and Barnabas were not at all pleased at this, and they ran out into the crowd shouting, 'Why are you doing this? We aren't gods—we are humans like you! We have come to bring you good news. You should turn away from idols and worship the real, living God who made heaven and earth and sea, and all that is in them. He sends the rain and the crops to grow at the right time, and so gives you food and happiness.'

Even with these words, Paul and Barnabas were hard put to it to stop the crowds from offering a sacrifice to them.

Then some Jews from Antioch in Pisidia and from Iconium arrived and stirred up the people; they stoned Paul and dragged him out of the city, thinking that he was dead, but the believers came and gathered round him, to protect and help him, and he recovered.

The next day he and Barnabas travelled some 40 km (25 miles) to Derbe. There they made many disciples, and then they started on their return journey home. They went through Lystra, Iconium and Antioch in Pisidia, and were not afraid to go back to places where there were enemies of the faith. They strengthened the Christians and encouraged them to remain true to God, no matter what trials and tribulations might come. Paul himself certainly set a fine example in this no matter what danger he faced.

In each church they appointed elders to look after the new Christians and to continue God's work, and finally they sailed back to Syria and arrived in Antioch in Syria from whence they had started.

Paul's Second Missionary Journey

After a while, Paul and Barnabas felt they must travel again and visit the groups of Christians in Europe and find out how the churches which they had started were getting on.

This time there was a difference of opinion between them and they went separately—Barnabas taking with him a believer called John Mark, while Paul took another disciple named Silas, a leading member of the Church in Jerusalem.

Paul and Silas went overland, travelling through Derbe and Lystra again, and at Lystra a Christian named Timothy joined them. The churches were strengthened in the faith and grew in numbers daily.

The apostles went on to the port of Troas, which was near the site of the old city of Troy. At Troas Paul had a vision, during the night, of a man from Macedonia standing and beseeching him, 'Come over to Macedonia and help us!'

Macedonia was the northern part of Greece, so this meant another sea-crossing; but, as Paul and Silas felt that God wanted them to go, they set off to carry the Gospel.

Eventually they arrived at the inland city of Philippi, which was a Roman colony, and there they spent several days.

On the Sabbath, Paul and Silas went down to the riverside where they found a group of women gathered. (Where there were not enough Jews to build a synagogue, they would meet in open-air places for prayer.) Among this group was a wealthy woman named Lydia who was a dealer in purple cloth. She was already a worshipper of God, but she listened to Paul, and then she and her household were baptized. She also invited Paul and Silas to come and stay at her house.

One day, as Paul and Silas were going to the place of prayer, they were met by a slave-girl who was possessed by an evil spirit, through which she told the future. This spirit was using her to encourage people to find out about the future instead of trusting God. She followed Paul and Silas, crying, 'These men are servants of the Most High God, and they tell you how you can be saved.'

Although what she said was true, Paul did not like it, because he felt it came from the evil spirit. So he turned to the girl and said, 'In the name of Jesus Christ, I order you to come out of her!'

The spirit left her and she was free. Her masters, who owned her, were furious when they discovered that the girl could no longer earn money for them by supposedly telling the future, so they dragged Paul and Silas into the market-place and reported them to the magistrates. 'These men are Jews and are disturbing our city,' they said, 'and are teaching customs which we Roman citizens cannot accept.'

The crowd joined in the attack and the magistrates tore the apostles' garments off and ordered them to be beaten with rods. Then they threw them into prison and ordered the jailer to make them very secure. The jailer put them into an inner cell with their feet firmly fixed in the stocks.

Paul and Silas were quite prepared to suffer hardship for the sake of Jesus and they cheerfully made the best of a bad situation. About midnight they were praying and singing hymns and the other prisoners were listening to them. All of a sudden there was a great earthquake and the foundations of the prison were shaken; it made the doors fall open and the chains with which the prisoners were held were ripped away.

The jailer awoke and saw that the prison doors were open, and he was terrified that the prisoners had escaped and that the governor would think it was his fault. He drew his sword and was about to kill himself, rather than face the prison governor, when Paul's voice called out, 'Don't harm yourself! We are all here.'

The jailer called for a light and rushed, trembling, to Paul and Silas. 'What must I do to be saved?' he cried.

'Believe in the Lord Jesus,' they answered, and they explained to him and his family about Jesus.

Then the jailer took Paul and Silas and washed their wounds; and he and his family were baptized.

The next morning Paul and Silas were set free, after the officials had discovered they were in fact Roman citizens and had apologized to them.

Paul and Silas travelled westwards and came to Thessalonica, where, for three weeks, Paul preached in the synagogue. Many people were converted and joined them. Some Jews, however, were angry and set the city in an uproar, saying, 'These men who have caused trouble elsewhere have now come here; they are breaking the laws of the emperor by saying there is another king, whose name is Jesus.'

As soon as it was night, the believers sent Paul and Silas on to Berea. Here the people were more open-minded and listened seriously to the apostles. But the Jews in Thessalonica heard about it and they came over and stirred up the people. So the believers sent Paul to the coast, whence he was to go to Athens; Silas and Timothy stayed in Berea, with instructions to join Paul as soon as they could.

Athens was a great centre of learning and Paul was upset to find that the city was full of idols; he even saw an altar which was inscribed 'To the unknown god'.

He stood up in front of the city council and told them about the God whom they worshipped without knowing it, and about Jesus and the resurrection. Some of his hearers mocked him, but others wanted to hear more.

Leaving Athens, Paul went on to Corinth, where Silas and Timothy joined him. There he stayed with a Jew named Aquila, and his wife Priscilla. They were tent-makers, which was the trade that Paul had once learned.

When the Jews in Corinth refused to believe that Jesus was the Messiah, Paul angrily told them, 'From now on I will go to the Gentiles.'

But the leader of the synagogue was a believer, and many others also believed and were baptized. Paul stayed a year and a half in Corinth, strengthened by a vision he had in which God encouraged him. Then he returned to Antioch.

Paul's Third Missionary Journey

When Paul set out on his third great journey he followed a similar route to his previous one—from Antioch in Syria and through Galatia and Phrygia, where he strengthened and encouraged the believers.

He then went on to the great commercial centre of Ephesus. There he found about twelve disciples who had been baptized by John, but, they said, they had never heard of the Holy Spirit. So Paul laid his hands on them and the Holy Spirit came to them.

Paul continued to preach boldly about Jesus and to discuss the Kingdom of God, first in the synagogue and then the lecture hall for about two years, so that many people heard the word of the Lord, and it continued to spread and grow stronger.

Now Ephesus was also a centre for the worship of the goddess Diana (or Artemis), and silversmiths in the city often made models of the temple of the goddess to sell to the Ephesians and to people who came to the city on pilgrimages.

One of the silversmiths, named Demetrius, did a great deal of business selling these silver shrines, and when he saw that Paul was turning people away from the worship of such idols, he grew greatly alarmed. He called a meeting of the craftsmen and other workers and said to them, 'You know that we get our wealth from this work, and you also know that this man Paul is telling people that man-made gods are not gods at all. This is likely to bring our trade into disrepute, and the temple of the goddess will come to mean nothing, and she may even be deposed.'

The men were furious when they heard this and they began shouting, 'Great is Diana of the Ephesians!', and soon the whole city was in an uproar.

The mob seized two of Paul's companions and dragged them to the theatre—a huge place which could hold more than 20,000 people. Paul wanted to go too, but the disciples would not let him endanger himself.

Meanwhile there was great confusion in the assembly—with some people shouting one thing and some another, and many of them not even knowing why they had come and what the meeting was about.

Some of the Jews pushed a man named Alexander up to the front, and he tried to quieten the crowd; but when they recognized that he was a Jew, they began shouting again, 'Great is Diana of the Ephesians!', and they went on shouting for two hours.

At last, the town clerk, who was the leading civic official, managed to quieten the mob. He knew that he would have to answer to the Romans for this riotous meeting. 'Men of Ephesus,' he said, 'you all know that our city is the keeper of the temple of the great Diana. No one can contradict that, so you ought to calm down and do nothing rash. If Demetrius and his men have a complaint, they can take it to the courts; and if you want anything more, it can be settled by a legal assembly of the citizens. For what has happened today may mean that we shall be charged with rioting, and we shall not be able to give a good reason for it, for there is no excuse for all this commotion.'

With these wise words he dismissed the meeting; order was restored and more serious trouble averted.

After the uproar had stopped, Paul called together the believers and encouraged them. Then it was time for him to continue his travels.

A Greek doctor named Luke was travelling with him, as he had been for at least part of the time on Paul's previous journey. (Luke wrote the third Gospel in the Bible, and also the Book of Acts of the Apostles in which the adventures of Paul are told.)

Paul travelled on through Macedonia to Greece, and eventually came back to Troas. On Paul's last evening there, the believers gathered to celebrate the Lord's Supper in an upstairs room. Paul spoke to the company and went on talking until about midnight, as he was due to leave the next day.

Many lamps were burning and the room grew warm, and one young man named Eutychus sat in the window where there would doubtless be more air. As Paul went on talking, Eutychus grew very dozy and finally went to sleep and fell out of the window to the ground three storeys below on to the hard stone courtyard.

Everyone thought he must be dead and they rushed down to see. Paul bent over him and said, 'Don't be alarmed; he is alive,' and they were able to take Eutychus home safely, much to everyone's relief.

The next day Paul set off on his journey, hoping to reach Jerusalem in time for the day of Pentecost.

When Paul and his company reached Caesarea, they stayed for a while at the house of Philip, one of the seven who had been chosen as helpers at Jerusalem.

While they were there, a prophet named Agabus arrived. He did a strange thing. He took Paul's belt and bound up his own feet and hands. Then he said, 'The Holy Spirit says that the owner of this belt will be bound like this in Jerusalem and will be handed over to the Gentiles.'

Everyone was very upset when they heard this and they begged Paul not to go on to Jerusalem. Paul, however, was made of much sterner stuff, and he said to them, 'Why are you all crying like this? I am ready not only to be tied up and imprisoned, but even to die for the name of the Lord Jesus.'

Undaunted he went on to Jerusalem.

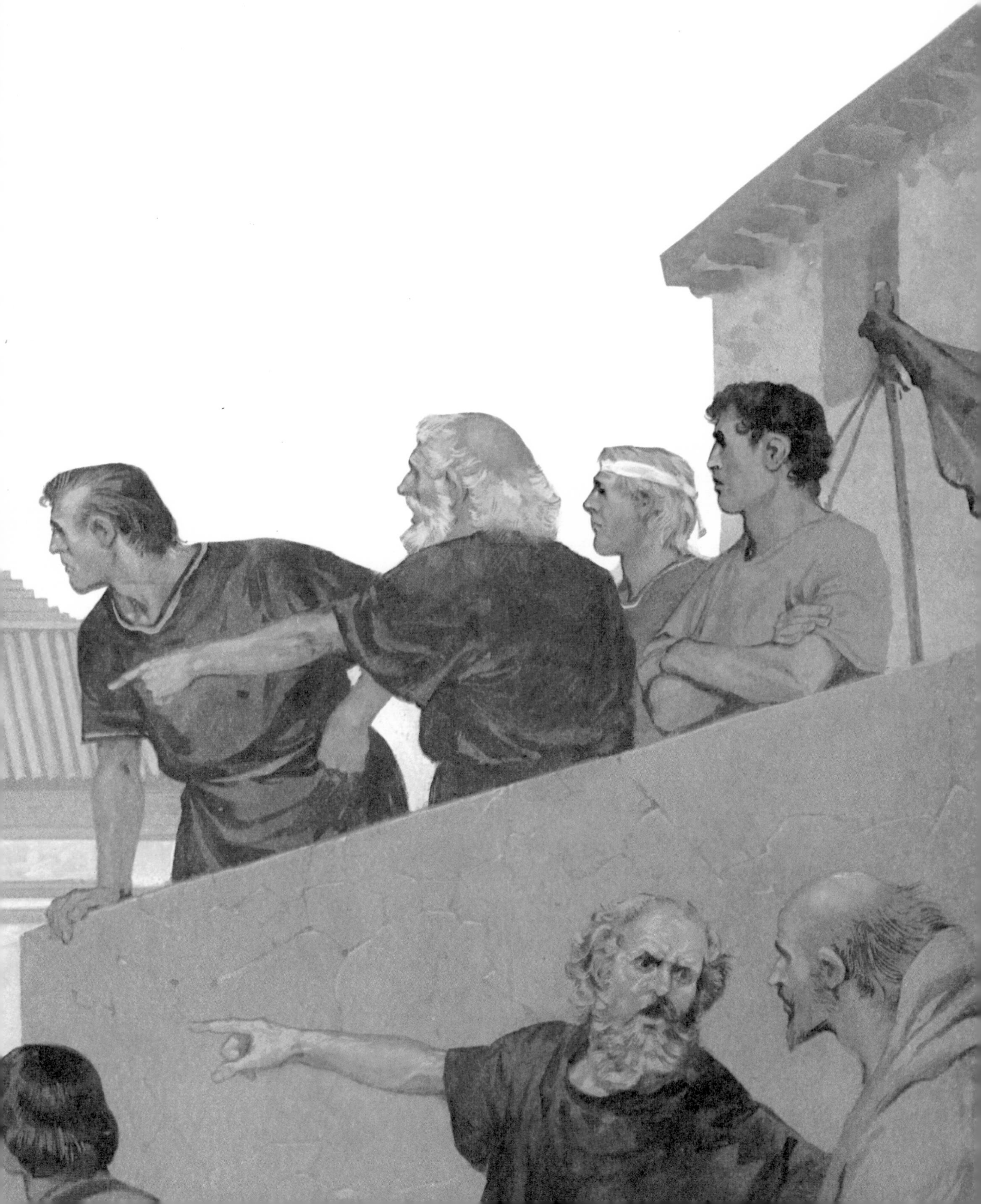

Paul Shipwrecked

Paul arrived safely in Jerusalem, where he greeted his friends and told them all that he had done. In their turn they told him that, while many thousands of Jews had become believers, there had been very confused accounts about what Paul had been teaching and it was thought that he had been encouraging people to forsake the law of Moses.

All this led some of the Jews to arrest Paul when he was in the temple one day, and this caused a great uproar during which they tried to kill him. The Roman soldiers heard the riot and came to Paul's rescue. He was allowed to speak to the crowd, and he told them how he himself was a Jew and how he had been converted to Christianity. Many did not believe him and shouted again for him to be killed. They screamed, waved their clothing and threw dust in the air, until the Roman commander had Paul taken into the fort for his own safety.

They had tied him up ready to be whipped when Paul told them that, by birth, he was a Roman citizen. At once they drew back and were frightened because they had treated a citizen of Rome in this way.

The commander wanted to find out just what the Jews were accusing Paul of, and he had him sent before the Council. But they could not agree whether he had done any wrong or not, and the soldiers had to go and get Paul away from them and take him to the fort.

The next morning more than forty Jews vowed that they would not eat or drink until Paul had been killed. They tried to get the Roman commander to bring back Paul to the Council on a false pretext, while they waited to kill him on the way. But the ambush failed, for Paul's nephew heard of it and told the Roman commander who ordered 200 soldiers, seventy horsemen and 200 spearmen to take Paul safely to Felix, the governor at Caesarea, in the middle of the night.

Felix heard the case and kept Paul in custody for two whole years. Then a new governor, Festus, was appointed. He, too, heard Paul's case and wanted to send him back to Jerusalem. Paul realized that Festus was just trying to please the Jews, and so he decided to appeal to Caesar in Rome. Festus conferred with his advisers and said, 'Very well; you have appealed to Caesar, so to Caesar you shall go.'

Some time later King Agrippa arrived in Caesarea, and he, too, listened to what Paul had to say. Both Agrippa and Festus agreed that Paul had not done anything to deserve imprisonment. 'He could have been set free if he hadn't already appealed to Caesar,' said Agrippa to Festus.

Paul was taken to a ship which was sailing for Asia, and Luke went with him. Paul and some other prisoners were handed over to a centurion named Julius; he was kind and allowed Paul to go to his friends and to be given what he needed for the journey. They sailed as far as Myra, and there they changed to a ship which was carrying wheat and was heading for Italy.

There was a strong wind and the going was rough, so that they only proceeded slowly. They kept as close to the coast as they could, and eventually arrived at a bay called Fair Havens which was on the southern coast of Crete.

Paul felt that they should stay there and warned them that there would be damage to the ship and cargo and also loss of life if they were to continue now. But the centurion paid more attention to the captain of the ship and to its owner than to Paul, and decided to go on, hoping to reach Phoenix, a harbour in Crete, which would be a better place to winter in. When the wind blew only gently they felt it was safe to sail, and so they set off, with a total of 276 people on board.

They had not been out at sea long when the wind blew up into a tremendous gale; the ship was blown right off course, and they had to lower the sail and let the wind carry them where it would. They fastened ropes around the hull to hold the ship's timbers together, and very much feared that they would be driven on to a sandbank.

The storm raged on, and the next day they decided they had better throw some of the ship's cargo overboard in order to lighten the load. The following day they threw out some of the ship's tackle, hoping that this would ease their problems. But the storm continued unabated and they did not see the sun or the stars for many days. Most of the men gave up all hope of ever being saved.

Paul said that they should have listened to his earlier warning and not left the harbour. 'But', he said, 'cheer up, for the God whom I worship told me last night that no life will be lost.'

Fourteen nights passed, and the sailors began to suspect that they were getting close to land. They took soundings and found that the water was 40 m (130 ft) deep; a little later they tried again and found it was now only 30 m (98 ft) deep. Fearing that they would be driven on to the rocks, they lowered the anchors and prayed for daylight.

Some of the sailors tried to escape from the ship, having lowered a boat into the sea while pretending they were laying out the anchors. But Paul told the centurion and the soldiers, 'Unless they all stay in the ship, you cannot be saved.'

Just before dawn, Paul urged them to eat some food, for they had not eaten for a fortnight. He himself took some bread, gave thanks to God for it, and ate it, and this encouraged everyone to follow his example and eat too, after which they felt much better. When they had all had enough, they threw the remaining wheat into the sea to lighten the ship.

When day came, they found that they were in a bay, and decided to try to run the ship aground there. They raised the sail, so that the wind could blow the ship forwards, and headed for the beach. But the front of the ship got stuck on a sandbank and could not move, and the back was dashed to pieces by the fury of the waves.

The soldiers wanted to kill the prisoners, to prevent them escaping by swimming to the shore, but the centurion forbade this because he particularly wanted Paul to be saved. Instead he ordered those who could swim to jump overboard and make for the shore, and the rest to follow holding on to planks of wood or pieces of the ship. In this way, they all reached the land and, as God had promised Paul, no lives were lost.

They soon discovered that they had landed on the island of Malta. It was cold and raining, but the natives were friendly and lit a fire for them. Paul helped by collecting bundles of sticks.

He was putting some of these on the fire, when a snake slithered out, driven by the heat, and fastened itself on to Paul's hand. When the natives saw it they thought that Paul must be a murderer who, having escaped the sea, was now to be justly punished by being killed by the bite of a poisonous snake. Paul shook the snake off and, to the surprise of the natives, suffered no harm at all. He did not drop down dead nor did he even swell up. So they changed their minds and decided that he must be a god.

The chief of the island was named Publius and he welcomed Paul and Luke and invited them to be his guests for three days.

Publius's father was ill with a fever, and Paul went into his room, prayed and placed his hands on the old man; and, through God's power, he was healed. News of this quickly got about and many other sick people on the island came to Paul and were healed.

After being on the island for three months, another ship was able to take the company on to Italy, and so they came to Rome. There the Christians came out to greet Paul and Luke.

Paul Shipwrecked

Paul was allowed to live in a proper house, but had a soldier to guard him. He was in Rome for two years and during that time many people came to see him. He spent long hours talking to them about the Kingdom of God and about Jesus. He also wrote letters to some of the young churches and to individuals to encourage them and to help them to live Christian lives. Some of these letters form part of the New Testament.

The Bible does not tell us about Paul's death, but from other sources, it is believed that he was put to death by the Emperor Nero about AD 67.

Philemon and the Runaway Slave

About one-third of the New Testament is taken up with letters (or epistles); they are real letters written by people in real situations. Most of them were written to the new young churches to help and encourage them, but a few were written to individual Christians.

Thirteen of the letters are under Paul's name, three were written by John, two by Peter, one by James, one by Jude, and there is one to the Hebrews but its author is not known.

Several of Paul's letters were written while he was a prisoner, in Rome and in other places, and one of these is addressed to somebody named Philemon.

Philemon was a prominent Christian and probably belonged to the church at Colossae. He had a slave whose name was Onesimus.

Now Onesimus had robbed his master and had then run away. By some means he had met and talked to Paul while he was a prisoner and Paul's words and manner had so impressed Onesimus that he had become a Christian.

Paul grew very fond of him and treated him like a son, and Onesimus (whose name means 'useful') had in his turn been very helpful to Paul. Paul would have liked to have kept Onesimus with him and to have had his help all the time; but he knew it would be wrong to do this, and that, although it might be hard for him, Onesimus must go back to his master.

To keep Onesimus would have meant forcing Philemon (Onesimus's legal owner) to do a good deed for Paul, for Onesimus's service to Paul was like a gift from Philemon who should rightly have had the slave's service. Paul would rather have had Philemon's help of his own free will.

So he decided that Onesimus must go back. Under the law of the time, Onesimus could expect very severe punishment from his master for running away. There were also dreadful penalties for those who harboured runaways. So for both these reasons. Onesimus was probably somewhat afraid to go back.

Paul, therefore, wrote this special letter to Philemon, for Onesimus to take with him, and in it he asked Philemon to take Onesimus back, no longer as a slave, but more as a beloved brother, because Onesimus had become a Christian.

Paul admitted that sending him back would be like being deprived of a part of himself.

'Receive him as you would receive me,' wrote Paul, 'and if he has wronged you in any way, or owes you any money, I will pay.'

In the past it seems that Philemon must have treated Onesimus kindly, so that now the slave had repented of his wrong-doing, Paul felt he would be even more dear to his master than he was to Paul himself. It would thus be impossible for Philemon to be bitter against the runaway or to punish him.

'I am sure you will do as I ask,' wrote Paul; 'in fact, I know that you will do even more.'

The fact that this letter has been preserved shows that almost certainly Philemon did as Paul asked and welcomed Onesimus back as a Christian brother.

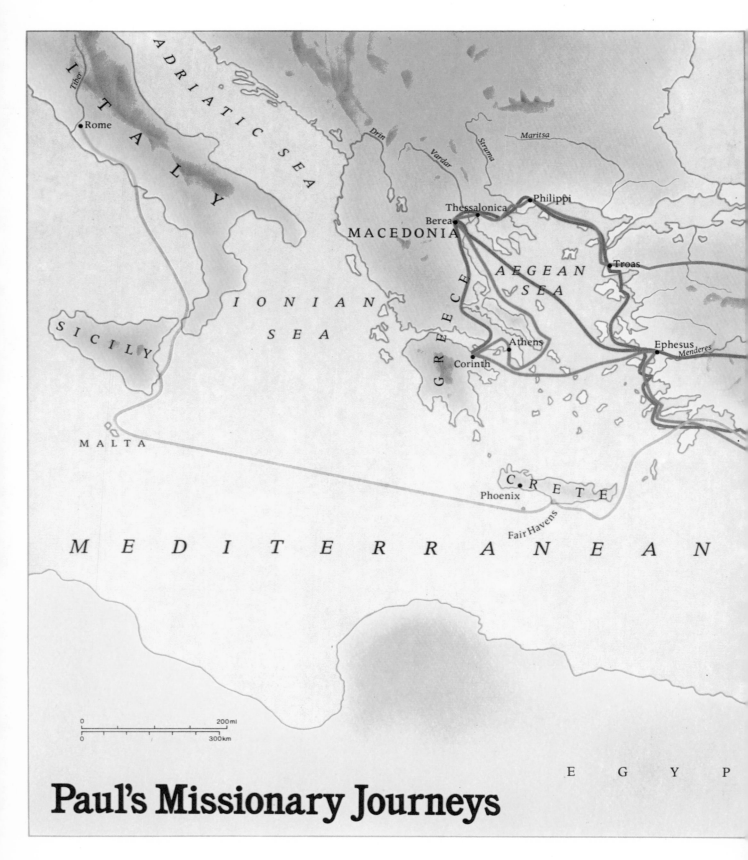

Paul's Missionary Journeys

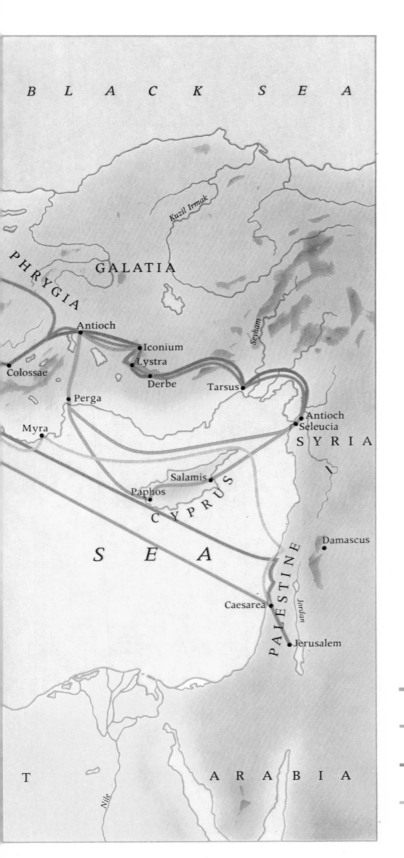

BLACK SEA

Kuzil Irmak

PHRYGIA

GALATIA

Seyham

Antioch
Iconium
Lystra
Colossae
Derbe
Tarsus
Perga
Antioch
Seleucia
Myra
SYRIA
Salamis
Paphos
CYPRUS
Damascus
SEA
Caesarea
Jordan
PALESTINE
Jerusalem

T
ARABIA
Nile

─────── *First*

─────── *Second*

─────── *Third*

─────── *Fourth (Paul shipwrecked)*

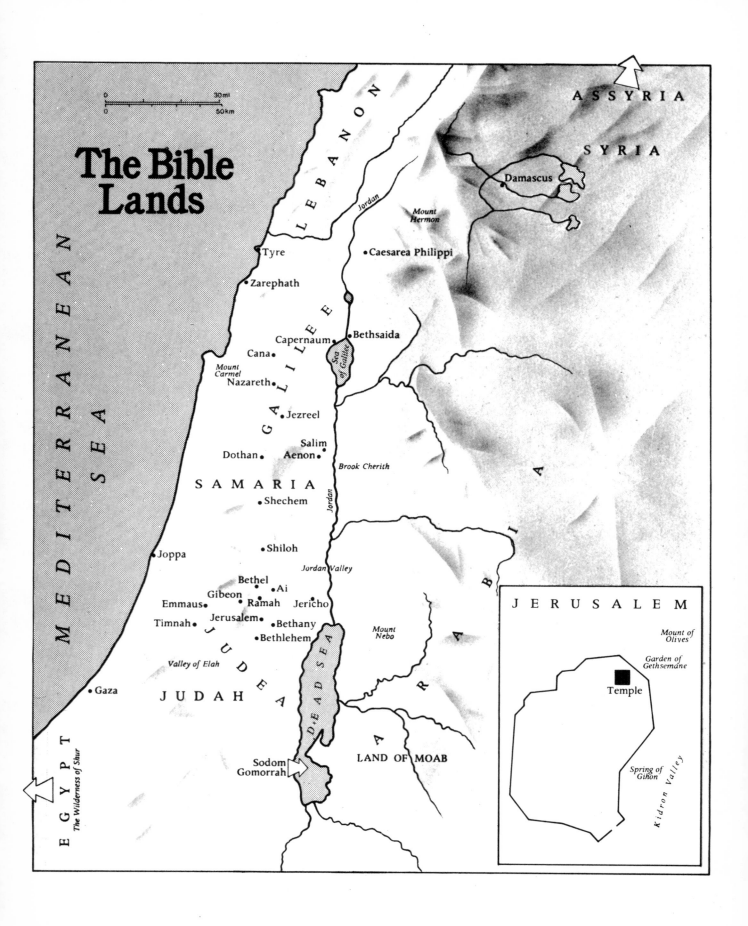

The Bible Lands

30mi
50km

ASSYRIA

SYRIA

Damascus

MEDITERRANEAN SEA

L E B A N O N

Jordan

Mount Hermon

Tyre

• Caesarea Philippi

• Zarephath

Capernaum • Bethsaida

Cana

Mount Carmel

Nazareth

G A L I L E E

Sea of Galilee

Jezreel

Salim
Aenon

Dothan

Brook Cherith

S A M A R I A

Shechem

Jordan

Joppa

Shiloh

Jordan Valley

Bethel
• Ai
Gibeon
Emmaus • Ramah Jericho
Timnah Jerusalem • Bethany

J U D E A

Mount Nebo

Bethlehem

Valley of Elah

D E A D   S E A

Gaza

J U D A H

A
R
A
B
I
A

Sodom
Gomorrah

LAND OF MOAB

E G Y P T
The Wilderness of Shur

J E R U S A L E M

Mount of Olives

Garden of Gethsemane

Temple

Spring of Gihon

Kidron Valley